though they are to be pitied, they are not the chief sufferers. The chief sufferer is the man who has a nagging conscience, who knows that he has been insincere, that he has played falsely his part, who has come to one of those moments which sooner or later do come in life, when he faces the insincerity of his past and feels unclean.

—"Six Ways of Dealing with Conscience,"
The Hope of the World, pp. 149-50.

Enlarging the Meaning of Life

LET US put it this way: one of the major factors in an effective life is a sense of the meaningfulness of existence. When anyone loses that, he is in a bad way. Men can bear up under extraordinary hardship if only they feel that life has significance. But when the sense of the meaningfulness of existence collapses, then comes the deluge. We are seeing that exhibited on a vast scale to-day. I suspect that the hardest thing to endure upon this planet is a sense of the absurdity of life, that it has no meaning.

A friend of mine visited not long ago one of the greatest of our modern physicists. My friend is a religious man and in the course of the conversation he asked the scientist if it was really true that he had no religious faith of any kind. The scientist answered, Yes, that was true; and then, rising from his chair and pacing the floor, he burst out, "But, oh, how I wish I had! It would be like finding a father and mother again."

That is a revealing outburst. That great scientist represents multitudes. To find the universe itself meaningful, with purpose running through it, requiring personality to explain it, so that the highest things in us are congruous with the deepest things in it—that is like finding a father and mother again. And until one finds that, life seems blowzy and meaningless. As Carlyle put it, "This

61

Harry Emerson Fosdick (1878–1969) was born in Buffalo, New York. He received his formal education from the Buffalo Public Schools, from Colgate University (A.B., 1900), Union Theological Seminary (B.S., 1904), and Columbia University (A.M., 1908). Ordained to the ministry of the Baptist Church in 1903, he served as pastor of the First Baptist Church, Montclair, N. J., 1904–1915, as associate minister of the First Presbyterian Church, New York, 1918–1925, as pastor of the Park Avenue Baptist Church (known as the Riverside Church after 1930) from 1926 to 1946. From 1908 to 1915 he was instructor in homiletics at Union Theological Seminary, and from 1915 to 1946, professor of practical theology. He has received numerous honorary degrees, among them the D.D. from Colgate University, 1914, from Yale University, 1923, Glasgow (Scotland) University, 1924, Harvard University, 1933. His more than twenty published books include several volumes of sermons (beginning in 1933, with *The Hope of the World*), and the popularly received devotional guides, *The Meaning of Prayer,* 1915, *The Meaning of Faith,* 1917, and *The Meaning of Service,* 1920. After his retirement in 1946, Dr. Fosdick was pastor emeritus of the Riverside Church and professor emeritus of Union Theological Seminary.

Harry Emerson Fosdick's Art of Preaching
AN ANTHOLOGY

Compiled and Edited by

LIONEL CROCKER
*Professor Emeritus
Department of Speech
Denison University
Granville, Ohio*

CHARLES C THOMAS · PUBLISHER
Springfield · Illinois · U.S.A.

Published and Distributed Throughout the World by
CHARLES C THOMAS • PUBLISHER
BANNERSTONE HOUSE
301-327 East Lawrence Avenue, Springfield, Illinois, U.S.A.
NATCHEZ PLANTATION HOUSE
735 North Atlantic Boulevard, Ford Lauderdale, Florida, U.S.A.

This book is protected by copyright. No part of it may be reproduced in any manner without written permission from the publisher.

© *1971, by* CHARLES C THOMAS • PUBLISHER
Library of Congress Catalog Card Number: 74-130922

With THOMAS BOOKS *careful attention is given to all details of manufacturing and design. It is the Publisher's desire to present books that are satisfactory as to their physical qualities and artistic possibilities and appropriate for their particular use.* THOMAS BOOKS *will be true to those laws of quality that assure a good name and good will.*

Printed in the United States of America

To
Eugene Exman

Preface

THIS IS A BOOK on communication. It is an attempt to state the rhetorical theory of the greatest preacher of the twentieth century. This anthology falls naturally into two parts:

Part I consists of statements on the art of preaching by Harry Emerson Fosdick.

Part II consists of studies in the preaching of Harry Emerson Fosdick by students of communication.

The compiler wishes to express his appreciation to all who assisted in the preparation of this book. Appropriate acknowledgment is given in the course of the book. My special thanks go to Eugene Exman and to Elinor Fosdick Downs, who gave permission to proceed with the project.

LIONEL CROCKER

Introduction

SEVERAL YEARS AGO the idea of an anthology such as this occurred to me. I wrote to my friend, Eugene Exman, the religious book editor of Harper & Brothers, publishers, and he gave encouragement to the project. However, Harry Emerson Fosdick refused to permit the publication of a collection of articles by him on the subject of preaching. In his autobiography he says: "I have often been asked to deliver lectures on the art of preaching with a view to their subsequent publication in a book, but I have always declined." So, the matter was dropped.

But when Dr. Fosdick died, I opened the question again with Mr. Exman. He suggested I write to his daughter, Dr. Elinor Fosdick Downs, for her permission. She saw no objection and gave the green light to the project. It is strange that Dr. Fosdick did not want to publish a book on this subject because he taught a course in homiletics for years at Union Theological Seminary.

Students of the history of rhetoric are impressed by the number of preachers who have added to the sum total of man's knowledge of the instruments of persuasion. For example, think of such preacher-rhetoricians as Hugh Blair, George Campbell, Richard Whately, and François Fénelon. More recent preachers who have contributed to our knowledge of rhetoric are such lecturers on the *Lyman Beecher Yale Lectures on Preaching* as Henry Ward Beecher, Robert W. Dale, Matthew Simpson, Phillips Brooks, and Charles Reynolds Brown. Lacking a series of lectures on the art of preaching by Dr. Fosdick, students of speech communication and homiletics set themselves the task of trying to deduce his rhetorical theory from his fugitive essays and sermons. A preacher who, year in and year out, drew congregations that had to present tickets for admission must have had a theory of communication worthy of formulation.

This anthology includes many of these studies on audience analysis, arrangement, invention, style, use of memory, and delivery.

In addition to these rhetorical studies there are valuable reflections on his preaching by his colleagues in the ministry.

And most valuable of all are the statements by Dr. Fosdick himself on his understanding of the problems of preaching. These are brought together for the first time.

On the worth of these studies by individuals interested in discovering the secrets of his pulpit success, we have the word of Dr. Fosdick himself. He wrote to Edmund Holt Linn, author of *Preaching as Counseling:* "I am stunned by the endless and meticulous labor expended on everything I ever did or said. You know much more about me than I know about myself. Again and again, I gasped as I read, recognizing in something you had dug up a long-forgotten incident or idea."

A word needs to be said about the unavoidable repetition in the anthology. I hope that such repetitions will not annoy the reader but that on the other hand, they will serve to emphasize what were the fundamental principles upon which Fosdick based his preaching.

The appeal of a volume such as this will be wide and varied. We all want to know how best to use our powers of persuasion. Not only church related personnel but students of public speaking will find help in mastering their own communication problems.

Contents

	Page
Preface	vii
Introduction	ix

PART ONE
Essays on Preaching
by Harry Emerson Fosdick

Chapter

1. LEARNING TO PREACH 5
2. WHAT IS THE MATTER WITH PREACHING? 27
3. HOW I PREPARE MY SERMONS 42
4. ANIMATED CONVERSATION 47
5. PERSONAL COUNSELING AND PREACHING 51
6. THE CHRISTIAN MINISTRY 58
7. TO THOSE INTERESTED IN THE PROFESSION OF THE MINISTRY 69

PART TWO
Essays on Harry Emerson Fosdick's Preaching

8. A YOUNG PREACHER LISTENS TO FOSDICK
    Samuel H. Miller 75
9. HOW DR. FOSDICK USES THE BIBLE IN PREACHING
    Eugene May 80

10. HARRY EMERSON FOSDICK AND REINHOLD NIEBUHR: A CONTRAST IN THE METHODS OF THE TEACHING PREACHER
     Erdman Harris 86
11. HARRY EMERSON FOSDICK: REALIST AND IDEALIST
     Edgar Dewitt Jones 100
12. HARRY EMERSON FOSDICK: TITAN OF THE PULPIT
     Edgar Dewitt Jones 108
13. HARRY EMERSON FOSDICK: A STUDY IN SOURCES OF EFFECTIVENESS
     Roy C. McCall 115
14. HARRY EMERSON FOSDICK: THE GROWTH OF A GREAT PREACHER
     Robert D. Clark 128
15. HARRY EMERSON FOSDICK AND THE TECHNIQUES OF ORGANIZATION
     Edmund H. Linn 186
16. STRUCTURAL ANALYSIS OF THE SERMONS OF DR. HARRY EMERSON FOSDICK
     Gilbert Stillman Macvaugh 210
17. HARRY EMERSON FOSDICK: THE METHODS OF A MASTER
     Charles F. Kemp 225
18. THE RHETORICAL THEORY OF HARRY EMERSON FOSDICK
     Lionel Crocker 228
19. HENRY WARD BEECHER AND HARRY EMERSON FOSDICK
     Lionel Crocker 236
20. PHILLIPS BROOKS AND HARRY EMERSON FOSDICK
     Lionel Crocker 246
21. A RHETORICAL ANALYSIS OF HARRY EMERSON FOSDICK'S SERMON, "THE POWER TO SEE IT THROUGH"
     Lionel Crocker 255

Appendix
   STUDIES IN THE PREACHING OF HARRY EMERSON FOSDICK 274
Index 277

Harry Emerson Fosdick's
Art of Preaching
AN ANTHOLOGY

PART ONE

Essays on Preaching
by
HARRY EMERSON FOSDICK

Chapter 1

Learning to Preach

HARRY EMERSON FOSDICK

I WAS TOSSED into my first parish over fifty years ago, like a boy thrown into deep water and told to swim when he does not know how. At the beginning I was an ignoramus about the effective preparation of a sermon. The seminary's courses in homiletics had been of slight use to me. We listened to lectures on preaching, full of good advice, I do not doubt, but lacking relevance to any actual experience of our own and soon forgotten because not implemented in practice. You cannot teach an art simply by talking about it. Years afterward, along with Henry Sloane Coffin and others, I played a small part in helping to make the teaching of homiletics at the seminary an affair of practical drill. We brought groups of students into the chapel, heard them preach, and then fell upon them with approval where they deserved it and with rigorous criticism of their faults. That kind of training would have saved me a protracted struggle in my first pastorate, but in those old days theologues had little or nothing of such discipline. What saved me was my earlier training in public speaking so that, however little I had to say, I could somehow manage to say it.

I recall vividly the tormented weeks I spent during the first year and more in Montclair, often distraught myself and fairly driving

---

Note: Reprinted with permission from Harry Emerson Fosdick: *The Living of These Days.* New York, Harper & Bros., 1956.

my wife to distraction, trying to prepare sermons that would be worth preaching. Probably my memory exaggerates the occasion when improvement began. One Sunday morning, quite unexpectedly, in the midst of my sermon, the idea I was dealing with caught fire. I had a flaming few minutes when I could feel the congregation's kindling response. I am sure that they were as much surprised as I was. I had never preached like that before, and I went home sure that preaching could mean that kind of moving and effective communication of truth.

Nevertheless, it was a struggle. Preaching for me has never been easy, and at the start it was often exceedingly painful. In later years I used to envy some of my students at the seminary who from the start seemed to know instinctively how to prepare a sermon and deliver it. Ralph Sockman, for example, in his first student sermon, exhibited such mature ability and skill that I told the class he acted as though he had had twenty years of experience behind him and I doubted whether even a homiletical professor could spoil him. My road as a preacher was very rough at the beginning, but little by little I saw more clearly what I verily believed and wanted most to say, and as clairvoyance into the needs of those to whom I spoke increased, I discovered, at least occasionally, the satisfaction of preaching so that something creative happened in the listener.

Because Montclair had been religiously well taken care of already, before the Baptist congregation was organized, denominational peculiarities were stressed in the new church as a justification for its founding, and at the heart of it were some reactionary sectarians. Dr. Lorimer, hearing rumors of cantankerous elements in the congregation to which I was going, said to me in our last conversation: "Young man, never you fear the face of mortal clay!" I needed that admonition. There were, however, saving factors in the situation. The church, having already had some unpleasant experiences in its eighteen years of existence, sincerely wanted to get on with me and were willing to put up with a good deal to do it. Moreover, on the fringes of the congregation were new people, waiting to be members if things went well. This new group was, on the whole, liberal in spirit, and the church, for every sort of reason, needed its support. So, while skating at times on thin ice, I got along. Even close communion had been the accepted custom before I arrived; no general invitation was extended to non-Baptist Christians to partake of the Lord's Supper. On that point, taking matters into my own hands, I extended an open invitation to all Christians to join in celebrating the first Lord's Supper at which I officiated. No one cared to start a fight about that with the new minister, but there was grumbling over my irregular assumption of authority.

The only crisis I had on matters of orthodoxy came after more than a year had passed. I had painfully felt my way at first, having plenty of inward troubles of my own, and my preaching, which was as much an endeavor to discover what I thought myself as it was to help anyone else, was, I suspect, not particularly disturbing. The issue between old and new theology, however, could not remain hidden, and at a meeting of the official board, when I was absent, two deacons complained about the liberal drift of my sermons. Having in hand at that time what amounted to two calls from other churches, one of them offering greater opportunity than was conceivable in Montclair, I invited those two deacons to a private conference. Not disposed to stay where I was not wanted, I told them, I put it up to them to say whether I should stay in liberty and peace or leave at once. They capitulated, and while they never agreed with me about theology, they stood by me, albeit with some pain, until the end.

The auditorium in which my pastorate began was the chapel of what was intended to be later a larger structure. As I recall the growing congregation that at last crowded us to the doors—it took less than three hundred to do it—I am reminded of the relative nature of all satisfactions. No preacher ever found more encouragement from vast assemblages of auditors than I found as I watched the growing numbers of those to whom my message was welcome in that little chapel. When the time came to venture on a building enterprise, the church was ready for a fresh start altogether. In 1911, seven years after my pastorate began, a new building on a new site was dedicated.

From then on my memories of the Montclair ministry are very satisfying, save for regret at my own shortcomings and mistakes. The people were overwhelmingly kind, and life-long friendships have their roots in those happy days. The church flourished and grew steadily in numbers. An associate membership was established so that Christians of all denominational backgrounds could become actively incorporated into the congregation, and while this compromise was far short of what was later done at Riverside Church, it was a start.

To be sure, I found preaching two sermons on Sunday difficult. I used to burn the logwood in the morning and the chips at night, and the first sometimes made a slow blaze and the latter a thin one. Still, my congregation was merciful and sustained me with a friendliness for which I am endlessly grateful. I have seen many a young minister so maltreated by his first parish, so twisted by criticism and disheartened by meanness and coldness, that irreparable damage was done him. I was fortunate.

One member of the church, Clayton Cooper, was a leader in the student work of the Y.M.C.A., and one June he invited me to share in the Northfield student conference. In those days John R. Mott, Robert E. Speer, and others like them stirred great audiences of students gathered at Northfield from the colleges of the east. I went there first as a teacher of a daily Bible class, and for many years, beginning at Northfield and going on to Silver Bay, New York, I shared in those student gatherings and in other similar conferences across the country.

I do not recall that I ever cherished any ambition to be an author. I wanted to teach and preach, but I remember no aspiration to write. One summer at Northfield, however, I delivered a message on Jesus' saying about going the second mile, and when my friends in the Association Press—especially Frederick Harris, to whose encouragement I owe a great debt—asked for the publication of it in expanded form, I tried my hand at writing it out. The result looked satisfactory to me until I showed it to my wife. She definitely thought otherwise. She fell upon it tooth and talon. Its loose sentences, redundancies, circumlocutions, and verbosities were a trouble to her. So I discovered that, along with other blessings, I had married my best literary critic. She insisted on conciseness, succinctness, directness, and simplicity. When we finished the manuscript, a brief booklet of fifty-two pages was the result, and under the title, *The Second Mile,* it is in circulation yet.

As a result of these student conferences, invitations to preach in college chapels began coming in. I still remember my amazement when the first invitation came from Harvard and my trepidation in accepting it. I was too immature to handle adequately that challenge. When the time came I spent a sleepless Saturday night, and the next day in Appleton Chapel, very ill at ease, I faced an audience which later I learned to love but which on that first occasion petrified me. It was several years before Harvard asked me back again!

College preaching in those days was an adventure. Compulsory chapel was the practice in many institutions, and the students, often resenting it, treated it with neither reverence nor attention unless the preacher made it impossible to do otherwise. The first time I preached at Princeton, I faced a sea of Sunday newspapers spread wide open when I began the sermon, and in the middle of the first sentence, a huge six-footer on the center aisle heaved himself up with extended arms in a mighty yawn. For five minutes it was a tussle to see whether they would sleep, or read their papers, or listen to this cub preacher they had never heard of. I hope I may be forgiven some reminiscent satisfaction in the fact that I won.

An itinerant ministry, speaking ever to new audiences, with only a chance to strike a glancing blow, has never been my first love. I have cherished more the opportunity of dealing steadily with a congregation on whom a sustained ministry might have cumulative effect. Life would have been much poorer, however, had it not been for enriching experiences with many varied audiences in this and other lands. Especially at the beginning it was an encouragement to see the doors open. And I am indebted also to college preaching for personal friendships with men like Andrew D. White and Jacob Gould Schurman, presidents of Cornell, President Lawrence Lowell of Harvard, President Woodrow Wilson of Princeton, and many others.

I do not see how a man can preach without writing. I always have thought with my pen in hand. My preaching naturally began to turn into books. Wanting to know what I really thought about immortality, I broke up my questions into as orderly an arrangement as I could manage and announced a series of Sunday evening sermons on the subject. Then I was in for it. I read everything pro and con that I could lay my hands on, and under the coercion of teaching others, taught myself everything I could learn from books and searched my own mind for what I honestly thought. Those Sunday evening sermons were a rough-and-ready product, but they at least surveyed the field, and whatever they did for others, they did much for me. Afterward, I wrote the book, *The Assurance of Immortality,* not really expecting that any publisher would accept it. To my surprise, it was welcomed.

The greatest single satisfaction I ever had from an accepted manuscript, however, had come before any of my books were written. I submitted to the *Atlantic Monthly* an article on "Heckling the Church," and it was given a warm greeting. Ellery Sedgwick's letter accepting the manuscript was a notable event in my life. His graciousness about the article, his apology—very humorous to me—because he had not the faintest idea who I was, and his friendly hopefulness about my work were an encouragement I have never forgotten.

The Manhood of the Master was written by request of the Association Press. The basic material in it was first presented in addresses at the church and then reworked into a book. Its gratifying reception is, I suppose, one of the major reasons why I have gone on writing books. It was even translated into Coptic in Egypt, although under unique conditions, so far as my experience goes. My name was not in any way associated with the Coptic version, and the anonymous manuscript was altered to suit the opinions of the translators, with omissions where they disagreed and additions where they thought some doctrine of the Coptic Church should be introduced. Moreover, so my friends in Egypt told me, this was done without the slightest conscious dishonesty, the procedure illustrating the free, anonymous way writings were handled in preprinting and precopyright days. The only way I have ever succeeded in fulfilling my childhood's desire to be a foreign missionary has been through my books. *The Manhood of the Master,* written forty years ago, has been many times translated on the mission fields, and recently I received from India a new rendition of it into Tamil. My greatest single source of satisfaction, so far as this early book of mine is concerned, is that during one of his imprisonments Mahatma Gandhi read it. A friend of his saw his copy, well underlined and annotated, and wrote me about it. Gandhi has been one of my heroes; he will remain an unforgettable character in man's spiritual history; I wish more than I can say that I could have had the privilege of meeting him. Imagining him in prison reading that book of mine about the Master, I have been both humbled and encouraged.

The Meaning of Prayer, which has been translated into at least seventeen foreign languages, sprang originally from my desire to clarify my own thinking. It started with a series of sermons, went on to a series of midweek discussions where I could get the questions, objections, and difficulties of the people, and then in an abandoned cottage on the Maine coast, near our summer home, I sat down daily for two months at a rickety kitchen table in a bare room and wrote the book. When I sent the manuscript to the publishers, I told them that a book on prayer could not expect a large sale and that I thought two thousand copies would be adequate. I guessed wrong that time. I never met Luther Gulick —uncle of the present well-known bearer of that name—without remembering the first time I saw him, more than forty years ago, in the office of our publishers, the Association Press. When Fred Harris introduced us, Gulick looked at me with my nonmonastic, nonascetic, "prosperous butcher-boy" appearance—as one newspaper reporter once described me—and said: "You certainly do not look like the author of *The Meaning of Prayer.*" And I looked at him—lean, spare and gaunt—and answered: "You certainly do not look like the author of *The Dynamic of Manhood.*"

Meanwhile, my struggle to discover how to preach went on with no little perplexity. The stereotyped routine into which old-fashioned expository preaching had fallen was impossible to me. First, elucidation of a Scriptural text, its historic occasion, its logical meaning in the context, its setting in the theology and ethic of the ancient writer; second, application to the auditors of the truth involved; third, exhortation to decide about the truth and act on it—such was the pattern in accordance with which every week multitudes of sermons were manufactured. That a vital preacher could use that model to good effect goes without saying, but there was something the matter with the model. To start with a passage from Moses, Jeremiah, Paul, or John and spend the first half of the sermon or more on its historic explanation and exposition, presupposed the assumption that the congregation came to church that morning primarily concerned about the meaning of those ancient texts. That certainly was not what my congregation in Montclair was bothered about.

It was easier, however, to be impatient with the prevailing stereotype than constructively to replace it with a better method. I spent some vexatious years, impatient and floundering. "Only the preacher," I petulantly wrote, "proceeds still upon the idea that folk come to church desperately anxious to discover what happened to the Jebusites."

One difficulty was that rebels against this prevailing pattern of expository preaching commonly became topical preachers. They searched contemporary life in general and the newspapers in particular for subjects. Instead of concentrating on textual analysis, they dealt with present-day themes about which everyone was thinking. I watched those topical preachers with a dubious mind. Week after week turning their pulpits into platforms and their sermons into lectures, they strained after new intriguing subjects, and one knew that in private they were straining even more strenuously after new intriguing ideas about them. Instead of launching out from a great text they started with their own opinions on some matter of current interest, often much farther away than a good Biblical text would be from the congregation's vital concerns and needs. Indeed, the fact that history had thought it worth while to preserve the text for centuries would cause a wise gambler to venture confidently on the text's superior vitality.

Across the years since then I have seen those topical preachers petering out and leaving the ministry. If people do not come to church anxious about what happened to the Jebusites, neither do they come yearning to hear a lecturer express his personal opinion on themes which editors, columnists, and radio commentators have been dealing with throughout the week. So, I floundered until personal counseling gradually led me into an approach to preaching which made it an exciting adventure.

Personal counseling does not begin full force in the experience of a young minister fresh from the seminary. He is too callow, inexperienced, immature. Children may flock around him, but adults do not naturally seek his advice. I vividly recall the first serious case of personal need presented to me—a youth from one of the church's finest families, conquered by alcohol and in utter despair. "I don't believe in God," he said to me, "but if *you* do, for God's sake pray for me, for I need him!" That was a challenge to everything I believed and preached. Few experiences in my first pastorate had so deep an effect on me as the battle in which that youth and I for long months engaged. That it ended in victory is one of the satisfying memories of my early ministry. "If you ever find anyone who does not believe in God," the youth said at last, "send him to me. I know."

In retrospect, the relevance of such an experience to preaching seems obvious, but only gradually did I stumble up the road until I saw it. Many other young preachers in those days were stumbling up that same road, discontented with both the prevalent expository and topical sermon patterns but not sure how to replace them. Little by little, however, the vision grew clearer. People come to church on Sunday with every kind of personal difficulty and problem flesh is heir to. A sermon was meant to meet such needs; it should be personal counseling on a group scale. If one had clairvoyance, one would know the sins and shames, the anxieties and doubts, the griefs and disillusionments that filled the pews and could by God's grace bring the saving truths of the gospel to bear on them as creatively as though he were speaking to a single person. That was the place to start—with the real problems of the people. That was a sermon's specialty, which made it a sermon, not an essay or a lecture. Every sermon should have for its main business the head-on constructive meeting of some problem which was puzzling minds, burdening consciences, and distracting lives, and no sermon which so met a real human difficulty, with light to throw on it and help to win a victory over it, could possibly be futile.

As I experimented with this approach, I found that within a

paragraph or two after a sermon started, first one listener and then another would discover that the preacher was bowling down his alley, and sometimes the whole congregation would grow tense and quiet, seeing that the sermon concerned a matter of vital import to every one of them. The preacher was handling a subject they were puzzled about, or a way of living they were dangerously experimenting with, or an experience which had bewildered them, or an ideal they were striving for, or a need they had not known how to meet.

Any preacher who, with even moderate skill, is thus helping folk to solve their real problems is functioning. He never will lack an audience. He may have little learning or eloquence, but he is doing the one thing which is a preacher's special business. He is delivering the goods which the community has a right to expect from the pulpit.

This did not mean that the Bible's importance in preaching diminished. Upon the contrary, I had been suckled on the Bible, knew it, and loved it, and I could not deal with any crucial problem in thought and life without seeing text after text lift up its hands begging to be used. The Bible came alive to me—an amazing compendium of every kind of situation in human experience with the garnered wisdom of the ages to help in meeting them.

Nor did this *project method* shut out the best values in topical preaching. The problems that came to church on Sunday in the minds and hearts of the worshipers were not simply individual but social, economic, international. The preacher, however, did not need to deliver a lecture on them as though he were a trained specialist in these diverse fields. He could not possibly know enough for *that,* but he could know the inner impact of those problems on his people in their defeatism and disillusionment, their agnosticism and despair, their surrender of Christian principles in the face of life's terrific realism, their reactionary clinging to old prejudices despite new light, and their class-bound loyalties to the wrong side of great issues. Let him start with the people confronting him in the pews and speak as wisely and Christianly as he could to their "business and bosoms," and he might help at least one individual that Sunday.

I have often been asked to deliver lectures on the art of preaching with a view to their subsequent publication in a book, but I have always declined. Many years ago I wrote an article for *Harper's Magazine* on "What Is the Matter With Preaching?" in which I said in gist what I am saying now, but I never expect to write a book about it. This thing that I am saying here is all I have to offer—this and a few corollaries which can be briefly noted.

I found my sermons becoming more and more cooperative enterprises between the preacher and the congregation. When a man takes hold of a real difficulty in the life and thought of his people and is trying to meet it, he finds himself not so much dogmatically thinking for them as cooperatively thinking with them. A preacher can easily play "Sir Oracle," assertive, dogmatic, flinging out his dictum as though to say "Take it or leave it," and such preaching has its appeal to credulous and emotionally impressionable minds. It has lost its influence on intelligent folk, however, and the future does not belong to it.

Later, in my classes at the seminary, I repeatedly used the story of a headmaster in his school chapel who had plunged into the first statement of his sermon theme, when a professor arose from the congregation, mounted the pulpit beside the preacher, and offered a criticism of what he just had said. Excitement reigned. The headmaster answered the objection, but the professor remained in the pulpit, and the sermon that day was a dialogue on a great theme of religion. The boys had never before been so entranced by a sermon. It was, of course, a prearranged affair, an experiment in having the congregation represented in the pulpit.

It certainly takes more than a preacher alone in the pulpit to make an effective sermon. If, however, the people can be there too, so that the sermon is not a dogmatic monologue but a cooperative dialogue in which the congregation's objections, questions, doubts, and confirmations are fairly stated and dealt with, something worthwhile is likely to happen. Sometimes this can be done implicitly through the preacher's evident sympathy and understanding; sometimes it can be made explicit in paragraphs beginning "But some of you will say." Of course this style of preaching requires clairvoyance on the preacher's part into the people's thinking, but any man who lacks this has no business to preach anyway. And of course this method can be exaggerated and become a mannerism, but so can any other. We have plenty of sermons that are sheer propaganda, where preachers set out by hook or crook to put something over on the congregation. We have pugnacious sermons, where preachers wage campaigns, attack enemies, assail the citadels of those who disagree, and are in general warlike and vehement. We need more sermons that try to face people's real problems with them, meet their difficulties, answer their questions, confirm their noblest faiths, and interpret their experiences in sympathetic, wise, and understanding cooperation. This is the only way I could find to achieve excitement without sensationalism. Constructively to help people to meet trouble triumphantly, or to live above the mediocre moral level of a modern city, or to believe in God despite the world's evil, or to make Christ's principles standard in the face of our disordered world is really not sensationalism. If it is well done, however, with no dodging of the difficulties, it can be vitally stimulating and can spoil all somnolent use of sermon time. An auditor, after one Sunday morning service, exclaimed: "I nearly passed out with excitement, for I did not see how you could possibly answer that objection which you raised against your own thought. I supposed you would do it somehow, but I could not see how until you did it." At any rate, it was toward this style of preaching that I set my sights.

No homiletic method is without its dangers, and this one which I espoused has perils aplenty. I presented it once to a group of experienced ministers and collected a galaxy of warnings about its possible perversions. They had endeavored so precisely to deal with a real problem that Mr. Smith had vexatiously waked up to the fact that they were talking about him; or they had tried to be so fair about objections that, overstating the opposing side, they had found neither time nor ability to answer it; or they had been so practical in dealing with some definite problems that they had become trivial, failing to bring the eternal gospel to bear on the issue; or they had been so anxious to deal with felt needs in the congregation that they had forgotten still deeper needs, unfelt but real; or they had so limited the difficulties they preached about to private, psychological maladjustment that they became merely amateur pulpit psychiatrists, neglecting the public concerns of the Kingdom of God. These dangers are real, but such perversions are the fault of unskilled handling, the like of which would wreck any method whatsoever.

My own major difficulty sprang from the fact that starting a sermon with a problem, however vital and urgent, suggests a discussion, a dissertation, a treatise. A sermon, however, is more than that. The preacher's business is not merely to discuss repentance but to persuade people to repent; not merely to debate the meaning and possibility of Christian faith but to produce Christian faith in the lives of his listeners; not merely to talk about the available power of God to bring victory over trouble and temptation but to send people out from their worship on Sunday with victory in their possession. A preacher's task is to create in his congregation the thing he is talking about.

I learned that such direct results could be achieved through personal counseling. It was a great day when I began to feel sure that a sermon could be thus immediately creative and transforming. A good sermon is an engineering operation by which a chasm is bridged so that spiritual goods on one side—the "unsearchable riches of Christ"—are actually transported into personal lives upon the other.

Here lies the difference between a sermon and a lecture. A lecture is chiefly concerned with a *subject* to be elucidated; a sermon is chiefly concerned with an *object* to be achieved. A justifiable criticism of much modern, liberal preaching is that, though it consists of neat, analytical discourses, pertinent to real problems and often well conceived and happily phrased, it does nothing to anyone. Such sermons are not sermons but essays, treatises, lectures. It is lamentably easy to preach about moral courage without making anyone more courageous; to deliver a discourse on faith without creating any of that valuable article in a single life; to argue that man has power to decide and choose without causing anyone then and there to make a momentous decision.

So I went through project preaching and beyond it and began to see how much the old preachers had to teach us. At their best they did achieve results. Their sermons were appeals to the jury, and they got decisions. They knew where the great motives were and appealed to them with conclusive power. I began studying sermons of men like Phillips Brooks—not merely reading them but analyzing sentence by sentence the steps they took toward working in their auditors the miracles they often did achieve—and I concluded that while we modern preachers talk about psychology much more than our predecessors, we commonly use it a good deal less.

After that, preaching became exhilarating. It need never fail to make a transforming difference in some lives. One is not merely making a speech about religion; one is dealing with the profoundest concerns of personality, with incalculable possibilities dependent on what is said that day. My silent prayer rose each Sunday before the sermon started: "O God, some one person here needs what I am going to say. Help me to reach him!" Nothing can make preaching easy, but seen as a creative process which can transform lives, it becomes so stimulating that it reproduces in the preacher the strength it takes from him, as good agriculture replaces the soil it uses.

The supreme reward of the preacher is nothing that the public knows about. It comes in letters like this:

> More than twenty-five years ago a dirty and wretched young man crept into a church one evening and listened to your talk. . . . The drunk young man went out into the night, and the words stayed with him. And things happened. He heeded the words, straightened up, went to night school for years and years until at last he graduated from ——— University, from postgraduate work at ——— University, became nationally and internationally known in his chosen field, and only recently ——— University asked him to write a new book. . . . I am that man.

The early nineteen hundreds saw a stormy upsurge of social reform in the nation, and while our suburban church with a juvenile preacher did little about it, we felt its impact. In 1905 Charles Evans Hughes made his famous investigation of the insurance companies. Later, in the Riverside Church, I had his warm friendship and his family's, but in my memory he appears first as the intrepid investigator who converted the insurance business "from a public swindle to a public trust." The earliest "muckraking" articles appeared in *McClure's Magazine* in 1902, and such was the popular reception of these exposés of public corruption that soon *Munsey's, Everybody's,* the *Cosmopolitan,* and others plunged into the fray. I used to play golf with E. J. Ridgeway, editor of *Everybody's,* thereby hearing some of the inside story, and as a spectator I applauded what Lincoln Steffens, Ray Stannard Baker, and Ida Tarbell, the star "muckrakers," were trying to do.

I was not at home in economics, however, and I was troubled by my unschooled ineptness in an area where there was so much uproar. So I took courses at Columbia in sociology and economics under Franklin H. Giddings and John Bates Clark, getting an M.A. in 1908. My thesis was a firsthand study of the organized labor movement as it had developed in Montclair, from the old Knights of Labor to the new craft unions. The latter—masons, carpenters, plumbers, painters, sheet metal workers, electricians, and hod carriers—were well organized when I came to town, and beginning that year there was a labor war, a combined strike and lockout, which lasted fourteen months. Rereading my Columbia thesis reveals that I made the acquaintance of the major labor leaders in town, attended meetings of the locals, and helped in founding a social headquarters for union men where it was vainly hoped that friendly intercourse might issue in more efficient cooperation. Resentment was seething among the laborers, much of which, in my judgment, was justified. I saw, however, that human nature on the unions' side could be quite as selfish as the human nature exhibited by ornery operators, and as for bringing the union men into the church's fellowship, I made no gains which I recall, save in the case of the head of the carpenters' union.

I note this frustration in trying to save a Protestant congregation from being a class church because it has haunted all my ministry. It constitutes today one of Protestantism's major problems.

In 1912 the *Outlook,* then one of our leading weeklies, sent me to cover the famous textile strike at Lawrence, Massachusetts. I saw there the raw side of the labor situation in our nation. Twenty thousand men and women had been on strike for ten weeks. Forty different languages and dialects were spoken by those workers; in one of the largest mills 67 percent were wholly ignorant of English. Save for a few in the upper brackets, the wages were pitiful, and when a new state law reduced the hours of labor from fifty-six to fifty-four per week and the next pay checks showed that wages were to be reduced accordingly, the workers rebelled. Five hundred Italians broke loose in the Washington Mills and, in one of the worst riots of the strike, stampeded one factory after another.

At the beginning the laborers were unorganized. The Industrial Workers of the World, a radical left-wing syndicalist group—we should call them communists now—had barely three hundred members among the workers at the start, but they saw their chance, took over, and before the strike was finished, more than ten thousand members were in their ranks. Like the communists now, they found their best opportunity in the worst social conditions.

In my report for the *Outlook* I tried to play fair with both sides of the angry struggle. Concerning much of the writing that had been done about the situation, which was attracting nationwide attention, I said: "The main endeavor has been to find someone to blame." I did my best to avoid that attitude. One could easily understand the position of the mill owners. "As a class," I wrote, "they are not less kindly and conscientious than other men, nor are they so blind to their own interests as to desire a body of discontented workmen." They did face competition with factories in other states where working hours were longer and wages lower. They could produce figures to show that some of their mills were losing money and that others were paying wages out of capital surplus. And while, after the strike, the factories were humming again with wages raised from 5 to 15 percent, they could argue that this was made possible by an upswing in the market.

This ability of each side to defend itself, however, did not lessen the total tragedy.

Two of the strike leaders, Ettor and Giovanitti, were thrown into prison. I visited Ettor there. He was held on a phony charge of homicide, although the evidence was conclusive that when the crime was committed, he was two miles away. The authorities jailed him, however, for he was too flaming a personality to be left at large. A genial, magnetic young fellow, twenty-seven years old, born in New York City and educated in the public schools, he was what we would call a left-wing radical. As we sat together in the Lawrence jail, he said to me: "They tell us to get what we want by the ballot. They want us to play the game according to the established rules. But the rules were made by the capitalists. *They* have laid down the laws of the game. *They* hold the pick of the cards. We never can win by political methods. The right of suffrage is the greatest hoax of history. Direct action is the only way. . . . No class of people ever gave up the chair of privilege until somebody tipped the chair over." So, in 1912, in the United States, a young American was proclaiming what we now think of as Russian communism. After the police, on a freezing January day, had played their fire hoses on a crowd of strikers, Ettor said: "There is being kindled in the heart of the workers a flame of proletarian revolt which no fire hose in the world can ever extinguish."

The great majority of the workers—even those who joined the I.W.W.—did not agree with Ettor's theories and commonly did not know what they were. I talked with many of the strikers. All they wanted was enough income to live on, and all they welcomed in the I.W.W. was organized leadership in winning their strike. Because of what I saw in Lawrence, I understand much more clearly than I otherwise could have understood what it is that even in America gives communists their chance—the desperate plight of some of the underprivileged on one side, and on the other, the starry-eyed, idealistic sympathy of some of the intelligentsia, who think that Ettor's road is the only way out.

While, however, there were dangerous extremes on the left wing of the strikers, there were dangerous extremes also on the right wing of the stockowners and operators. Said one lady on Commonwealth Avenue in Boston: "The strikers should be starved back to work." Cried one Boston lawyer: "The militia should have been instructed to shoot. That is the way Napoleon did it. The strikers should have been shot down. *I stand for law and order!*" This persuasion that any means was justified in crushing the laborers came to its most outrageous exhibition in the action of John J. Breen, son of an ex-mayor of Lawrence, who, so his conviction ran, secretly planted dynamite in the Syrian colony of the town in order to bring discredit on the strikers. The court only fined him five hundred dollars. Who paid Breen to plant the dynamite? the strikers wondered. What would the sentence of a striker have been if he had done it? As a matter of fact, surprisingly little violence was used by the strikers.

The more I talked with the aggrieved laborers, the more apparent it became that while higher wages were a major issue, a deeper problem in human relationships lay underneath the economic issue. "They treated us like dumb cattle," said one of the men. The evidence backed up that charge. A friend of mine who knew the mills thoroughly—his interests all on the side of the employers, not of the workers—said to me: "I myself have seen a foreman go cursing and blaspheming through a department to fire a workman without explaining why, until my blood boiled."

One of the workers, a trusted and highly paid man, told me that in his department there were only English-speaking girls—decent, self-respecting young women from American-trained families—but that the overseer habitually addressed them with oaths that would not bear repeating. I asked one of the most highly paid women in the mills to tell me the names, which she herself had heard, with which the foremen commonly addressed the workers. She started in but I asked her to stop. Nothing much more brutal and obscene could be imagined. One of the well-paid women operatives—twenty dollars a week—who became the foremost woman leader of the strikers explained to me why she, who had nothing to complain of for herself, had joined the strike: "I have been getting madder and madder for years at the way they talked to those poor Italians and Lithuanians." And one man, not a laborer but altogether on the owner's side of the issue, said to me: "The manufacturers had it coming to them, and they got it!"

At any rate, I came home sympathizing in a way with all the parties in the tragedy but boiling with indignation at the gross betrayal of all that democracy stands for which the factories in Lawrence illustrated. That was *not* America! In the four decades and more since then, admirable progress has been made throughout the nation in the relationships between employers and employees, but anyone who supposes that organized labor was not indispensable in achieving it does not know what he is talking about.

Twenty-five years after the Lawrence incident I said this:

> Whatever may be the details of the struggle of the American laboring man for a larger share in the products of industry, and whatever the rights and wrongs of the present troubled scene, it is a safe affirmation, backed by long history, that a century from now it will be clear that the laboring man was right about the main matters. That is, he was not receiving a just share of the products of industry, and he had a right to collective bargaining on a scale that was denied him. Again, the truth is not that the privileged fail in estimating the situation because they are bad, and the laboring men see it more truly because they are good. The truth is that it is the man who is being hurt who feels where the shoe pinches.

I said *that*, however, in the Riverside Church to a congregation made up of professional and business people, with very few if any manual laborers present. I have often dreamed of two other opportunities—one in which I might be minister in a country church, seeing what I could do with the rural problems, and the other in which I might be pastor of a congregation of workers in a factory town. Vice-Admiral Woods of the British Navy, who received the Distinguished Service Order for his conduct in World War I, later retired from the Navy, took a theological course, became a priest in the Church of England, and was sent at his own request to a parish in the dockyard section of London's East End. At the beginning his congregation numbered seven; at the end the crowds could not get in. I take off my hat to him!

Meanwhile, in Montclair I watched the national campaign for large-scale social and political reforms gaining headway, with Theodore Roosevelt and his *square deal* in the forefront. Having succeeded President McKinley—assassinated in Buffalo in 1901—T. R. was elected President in 1904; then, having retired in favor of Mr. Taft in 1908, he fought for the nomination in 1912, and failing to secure it, he formed his Bull Moose party and staged an uproarious campaign. Behind the intrigue and clamor of politics the issues at stake were the regulation of railroads, breaking up trusts, workmen's compensation laws, social welfare legislation for women and children in industry, extension of civil service, pure food and drug laws, governmental responsibility for slums, factory conditions, shorter hours, better wages, regulation of insurance companies, banks and saving institutions, limitation on the use of injunction in labor disputes, income taxes, the postal savings bank, and parcel post. The choice on such issues seemed clear to me. When Theodore Roosevelt in 1912 pictured an immigrant steelworker bargaining with the United States Steel Corporation and asked what the American doctrine of equality meant in that situation, when he backed laws on housing, hours of labor, and workmen's compensation against the judicial decisions which had nullified them, I was all for him. I still recall the disapproval I faced in conservative Montclair when I spoke at a mass meeting supporting his candidacy.

Such social liberalism was to me essentially Christian, and Walter Rauschenbusch, whose *Christianity and the Social Crisis* appeared in 1907, furnished welcome force to this conviction. I was strongly influenced by him. He was an inspiring person to meet—an impressive six-footer, charming in his friendliness, handling his deafness with such patience and skill that he seemed all the more engaging because of it, and obviously a man of dynamic energy. He is remembered now as the author of influential books and as a famous professor at the theological seminary in Rochester, but to understand his passion for the Christian social gospel, one must go back to that decade, beginning in 1886, when he was pastor of a little church in "Hell's Kitchen" in New York City. There, in the overcrowded, health-destroying, crime-breeding slums, was lighted his burning conviction that a merely individualistic gospel, taking no responsibility for the social conditions that condemn multitudes to physical and Moral ruin, was both practically futile and profoundly un-Christian. His social outlook came, as he said, "through personal contact with poverty, and when I saw how men toiled all their life long, hard, toilsome lives, and at the end had almost nothing to show for it; how strong men begged for work and could not get it in hard times; how little children died."

Henry Van Dusen, president of Union Theological Seminary, said once that Walter Rauschenbusch had exerted "the greatest single personal influence on the life and thought of the American church in the last fifty years." He certainly made a momentous appeal to the social conscience of the Christian churches in the early nineteen hundreds. Undoubtedly my early preaching caught some of its flavor from his influence. None of us, however, then foresaw what lay ahead, nor guessed how much more resistant to the Kingdom of God human nature is than we supposed. For the dark shadows were closing over Europe, and World War I was at our doors.

Along with Walter Rauschenbusch another personality deeply influenced me—Rufus Jones, the Quaker. His book, *Social Law in the Spiritual World,* was published the year I came to Montclair, and reading it was a memorable event in my life. After that I devoured everything he wrote. I was far from being a Quaker then, so far as war was concerned, but in the message of the Society of Friends, especially as Rufus Jones interpreted it, I found such vitality—what William James called "a religion of veracity rooted in spiritual inwardness"—combined with such fearless and practical application of Christian principles to social problems, that I was gripped by it.

I little guessed then what warm friendship I was to enjoy in later years with Rufus Jones and his family. He was a radiant spirit concerning whom we in our household would say what a colleague at Haverford College said: "To meet him was to feel set up for the day." He did more than believe in the *inner light;* he possessed it. Moreover, along with this vital inwardness that made his life luminous was a social passion that made him the principal founder of the American Friends' Service Committee, whose extraordinary program of worldwide usefulness has won multitudes of contributing supporters and has gained such recognition as the Nobel Peace Prize for the Quakers.

Rufus Jones wrote fifty-seven books. It was a labor of love when after his death I prepared an anthology of his writings, the title of which seems to me still to tell the truth: *Rufus Jones Speaks to Our Time.*

No picture of my eleven years in Montclair would be true to the facts if it left out the play and fun which eased the days and kept my spirits buoyant. Music and the theater helped a lot—I never can forget that evening when first I heard Fritz Kreisler or that enchanted night when I saw Sir Henry Irving play Shylock—and golf helped too. One Saturday I picked up a game with a stranger, and we finished with a tie, so that he suggested another game the next morning to settle the matter. I said that I never could play on a Sunday because I had a job which compelled me to work that day. "What kind of job is that?" he asked. "What the hell do you do on Sunday mornings?" When I told him that that was a good question, that I had often asked it myself, and that he would have to come to the First Baptist Church some Sunday morning to discover the answer, we became fast friends.

The community was kind to me, and my reminiscences of that far-off time are full of humor as well as of labor. One friendly family talked so favorably about me that their Negro maid became interested too and was urged by her mistress to come and hear me. In those days I had a head of bushy, curly hair, and the maid's report about that Sunday service centered on that. "Fo' the Lawd, ma'am," she said to her mistress, "his very hair do proclaim him to be a man of Gawd."

It was that " 'ayrick 'ead of 'air" which gave me the best chance I ever had to get back at a toastmaster. A bald-headed presiding officer introduced me at a banquet as "the man with the crocheted hair," to which I responded, "Mr. Toastmaster, I would far rather have hair that is crocheted than hair that is nit." That story must have spread, for not long ago one of my old students, meeting me by chance, looked at my thinly covered head and remarked sadly: "Neither crocheted nor nit!"

Happy and fortunate though my years in the Montclair pastorate had been, I was growing ready to leave. The reasons were inward, not outward. The church gave every indication of being loyally united behind my ministry, and everything a church could do to persuade a minister to stay was done. I felt sure, however, that I had done in Montclair all I was likely to do, and I urgently desired the stimulus of a new situation.

In 1908 Union Theological Seminary had appointed me lecturer on Baptist Principles and Polity and in 1911 had made me an instructor in homiletics. When in 1915 the seminary invited me to a full-time position there, I accepted and became Morris K. Jesup Professor of Practical Theology.

Chapter 2

What Is the Matter With Preaching?

HARRY EMERSON FOSDICK

ONE MIGHT THINK that such a subject would presuppose preachers as an audience and that an article on it should appear in a magazine devoted to their special interests. On the contrary, there are only about 200 thousand preachers in the United States, but there are millions who more or less regularly enjoy or endure their ministrations. Whatever, therefore, is the matter with preaching is quantitatively far more a concern of laymen than of clergymen. Moreover, if laymen had a clear idea as to the reasons for the futility, dullness, and general ineptitude of so much preaching, they might do something about it. Customers usually have something to say about the quality of goods supplied to them.

Of course, there is no process by which wise and useful discourses can be distilled from unwise and useless personalities, and the ultimate necessity in the ministry, as everywhere else, is sound and intelligent character. "You cannot carve rotten wood," says a Chinese proverb. Every teacher of preaching sometimes feels its truth when he tries to train his students. Whether the grade of intelligence now represented in candidates for the ministry is lower than it used to be cannot easily be determined. As we grow older, we tend to idealize the state of things in our youth and to suspect the progressive deterioration of the human race. One

---

Note: Reprinted from *Harper's Magazine* (July, 1928) by permission of the author and of Harper & Bros., publishers.

theological professor, aged seventy, obviously did this when he told his classes that each new generation of students had known less than their predecessors and that he was curiously hoping to live to see the next, which he was certain would know nothing.

The best brains today are naturally drawn into occupations other than art, literature, music, education, and religion. These spiritual interests are not the crucial and distinctive concerns of our era. We are magnificent in scientific and commercial exploits but mediocre in affairs of the spirit, and one result is the draining of most of our virile minds into scientific invention and money-making. The ministry of religion suffers along with other kindred callings which serve the souls of men with goodness, truth, and beauty. This relative and, I think, temporary inferiority of spiritual callings, however, does not necessarily mean an absolute decline in the intellectual quality of religious leadership, and there is no reason why we should not have much better preaching than we ordinarily get.

One obvious trouble with the mediocre sermon, even when harmless, is that it is uninteresting. It does not matter. It could as well be left unsaid. It produces this effect of emptiness and futility largely because it establishes no connection with the real interests of the congregation. It takes for granted in the minds of the people ways of thinking which are not there, misses the vital concerns which are there, and in consequence uses a method of approach which does not function. It is pathetic to observe the number of preachers who commonly on Sunday speak religious pieces in the pulpit, utterly failing to establish real contact with the thinking or practical interests of their auditors.

Even in the case of a preacher poorly endowed, this state of affairs is unnecessary. No one who has any business to preach at all need preach uninteresting sermons. The fault generally lies not in the essential quality of the man's mind or character but in his mistaken methods. He has been wrongly trained, or he has blundered into a faulty technic, or he never has clearly seen what he should be trying to do in a sermon and so, having no aim, hits the target only by accident.

No bag of tricks can make a preacher, but if I were to pick out one simple matter of method that would come nearer to making a preacher than any other, it would be the one to which this paper is devoted.

II

Every sermon should have for its main business the solving of some problem—a vital, important problem, puzzling minds, burdening consciences, distracting lives—and any sermon which thus does tackle a real problem, throw even a little light on it, and help some individuals practically to find their way through it cannot be altogether uninteresting.

This endeavor to help people to solve their spiritual problems is a sermon's only justifiable aim. The point of departure and of constant reference, the reason for preaching the sermon in the first place, and the inspiration for its method of approach and the organization of its material should not be something outside the congregation but inside. Within a paragraph or two after a sermon has started, wide areas of any congregation ought to begin recognizing that the preacher is tackling something of vital concern to them. He is handling a subject they are puzzled about, or a way of living they have dangerously experimented with, or an experience that has bewildered them, or an ideal they have been trying to make real, or a need they have not known how to meet. One way or another they should see that he is engaged in a serious and practical endeavor to state fairly a problem which actually exists in their lives and then to throw what light on it he can.

Any preacher who even with moderate skill is thus helping folk to solve their real problems is functioning. He never will lack an audience. He may have neither eloquence nor learning, but he is doing the one thing that is a preacher's business. He is delivering the goods that the community has a right to expect from the pulpit as much as it has a right to expect shoes from a cobbler. And if any preacher is not doing this, even though he have at his disposal both erudition and oratory, he is not functioning at all.

Many preachers, for example, indulge habitually in what they call expository sermons. They take a passage from Scripture, and proceeding on the assumption that the people attending church that morning are deeply concerned about what the passage means, they spend their half hour or more on historical exposition of the verse or chapter, ending with some appended practical application to the auditors. Could any procedure be more surely predestined to dullness and futility? Who seriously supposes that as a matter of fact, one in a hundred of the congregation cares, to start with, what Moses, Isaiah, Paul, or John meant in those special verses or came to church deeply concerned about it? Nobody else who talks to the public so assumes that the vital interests of the people are located in the meaning of words spoken two thousand years ago. The advertisers of any goods, from a five-foot shelf of classic books to the latest life insurance policy, plunge as directly as possible after contemporary wants, felt needs, actual interests, and concerns. Even moving picture producers, if they present an ancient tale, like Tristan and Isolde, are likely to begin with a modern girl reading the story. Somehow or other, every other agency dealing with the public recognizes that contact with the actual life of the auditor is the one place to begin. Only the preacher proceeds still upon the idea that folk come to church desperately anxious to discover what happened to the Jebusites. The result is that folk less and less come to church at all.

This does not mean that the Bible has either lost or lessened its value to the preacher.* It means that preachers who pick out texts from the Bible and then proceed to give their historic setting, their logical meaning in the context, their place in the theology of the writer, with a few practical reflections appended, are grossly misusing the Bible. The Scripture is an amazing compendium of experiments in human life under all sorts of conditions, from the desert to cosmopolitan Rome, and with all sorts of theories, from the skepticism of Ecclesiastes to the faith of John. It is incalculably rich in insight and illumination. It has light to shed on all sorts of human problems now and always, and as for the personality of Jesus, if Rodin, the modern sculptor, could feel that Phidias, the Greek sculptor, could never be equalled—"No artist will ever surpass Phidias—for progress exists in the world but not in art. The greatest of sculptors . . . will remain forever without an equal"—it is surely open to even the most radical of Christians to adore Christ as Master and Lord.

What all the great writers of Scripture, however, were inter-

---

* See Chapter 9 for a discussion of Dr. Fosdick's use of the Bible in preaching.

ested in was human living, and the modern preacher who honors them should start with that, should clearly visualize some real need, perplexity, sin, or desire in his auditors, and then should throw on the problem all the light he can find in the Scripture or anywhere else. No matter what one's theory about the Bible is, this is the searchlight, not so much intended to be looked at as to be thrown upon a shadowed spot.

That much insight into contemporary human problems which almost all preachers use in thinking about the practical applications at the end of their sermons might do some good if it were used, instead, at the beginning of their sermons. Let them not end but start with thinking of the auditors' vital needs, and then let the whole sermon be organized around their constructive endeavors to meet those needs.

III

An increasing number of preachers, too modern by far to use the old, authoritative, textual method which we have just described, do not on that account light on a better one. They turn to what is called topical preaching. They search contemporary life in general and the newspapers in particular for subjects. They discover that in comparison with dry, textual analysis there is such attractive vividness in handling present-day themes, such as divorce, Bolshevism, America's foreign policy, the new aviation, or the latest book, that they enjoy their own preaching better, and more people come to hear it. It is at least a matter of contemporary and not archeological interest.

The nemesis of such a method, however, is not far off. Most preachers who try it fall ultimately into their own trap. Watch the records of any considerable number of them and see how large a proportion peter out and leave the ministry altogether. Instead of starting with a text, they start with their own ideas on some subject of their choice, but their ideas on that subject may be much farther away from a vital interest of the people than a great text from the Bible. Indeed, the fact that history has thought it worth while to preserve the text for so many centuries would cause a gambling man to venture largely on the text's superior vitality.

Week after week one sees these topical preachers who turn their pulpits into platforms and their sermons into lectures, straining after some new, intriguing subject, and one knows that in private they are straining after some new, intriguing ideas about it. One knows also that no living man can weekly produce first-hand, independent, and valuable judgments on such an array of diverse themes covering the whole range of human life. And deeper yet, one who listens to such preaching or reads it knows that the preacher is starting at the wrong end. He is thinking first of his ideas, original or acquired, when he should think first of his people. He is organizing his sermon around the elucidation of his theme, whereas he should organize it around the endeavor to meet his people's need. He is starting with a subject, whereas he should start with an object. His one business is with the real problems of these individual people in his congregation. Nothing that he says on any subject, however wise and important, matters much unless it makes at the beginning vital contact with the practical life and daily thinking of the audience.

This idea that we are applying to preaching is simply the project method, which is recognized as the basis of all good modern teaching. The old pedagogy saw on one side the child as a passive receptacle and on the other side a subject, like mathematics or geography, waiting to be learned and so seeing the situation, proceeded to pour the subject, willy-nilly, into the child. If he resisted, he was punished; if he failed to assimilate it, he was accounted stupid. No good teacher today could tolerate such an idea or method. The question now is why the child should wish to know geography and what practical interest in the child's life can be appealed to in the endeavor to have him desire to know geography. Modern pedagogy starts not with the subject but with the child. It adapts what is to be learned to the learner rather than vice versa. Even the food which the child eats for breakfast, coming from the ends of the earth, is used to fascinate his interest in other lands, and we find our children getting at their mathematics by measuring the cubic space of the front parlor or estimating the distance per second which they have walked in an hour.

All this is good sense and good psychology. Everybody else is using it, from first-class teachers to first-class advertisers. Why should so many preachers continue in such belated fashion to neglect it? The people often blindly know that there is something the matter with the sermon although they cannot define it. The text was good and the truth was undeniable. The subject was well chosen and well developed, but for all that, nothing happened. The effect was flat. So far as the sermon was concerned, the congregation might as well have stayed home. It may have been a "beautiful effort," as some kindly woman doubtless told the preacher, but it did no business in human lives. The reason for this can commonly be traced to one cause: the preacher started his sermon at the wrong end. He made it the exposition of a text or the elucidation of a subject instead of a well-planned endeavor to help solve some concrete problems in the individual lives before him. He need not have used any other text or any different materials in his sermon, but if he had defined his object rightly, he would have arranged and massed the material differently. He would have gone into his sermon via real interest in his congregation and would have found the whole procedure kindling to himself and to them.

IV

The meaning of this method can best be seen in some of its corollaries. For one thing, it makes a sermon a cooperative enterprise between the preacher and his congregation. When a man has got hold of a real difficulty in the life and thinking of his people and is trying to meet it, he finds himself not so much dogmatically thinking for them as co-operatively thinking with them. His sermon is an endeavor to put himself in their places and help them to think their way through.

The difference in tone and quality which this makes in a sermon is incalculable. Anyone accustomed to hearing preaching must be aware of two diverse effects commonly produced. One type of minister plays "Sir Oracle." He is dogmatic, assertive, uncompromising. He flings out his dicta as though to say to all hearers, Take it or leave it. He has settled the matter concerning which he is speaking and is not asking our opinion; he is telling us. This homiletical dogmatism has its own kind of influence on credulous and impressionable minds. Such minds are numerous, so that such preaching can go on for years ahead. As Jesus said about the Pharisees, such preachers have their reward.

Their method, however, has long since lost its influence over intelligent people, and the future does not belong to it. The future, I think, belongs to a type of sermon which can best be described as an adventure in cooperative thinking between the preacher and his congregation. The impression made by such preaching easily is felt by anyone who runs into it. The preacher takes hold of a real problem in our lives and stating it better than we could state it, goes on to deal with it fairly, frankly, helpfully. The result is inevitable: he makes us think. We may agree with him or disagree with something vital to us, and so he makes us think with him even though we may have planned a far more somnolent use of sermon time.

Here, too, we are dealing with preaching in terms of good pedagogy. The lecture method of instruction is no longer in the ascendant. To be sure, there are subjects which must be handled by the positive setting forth of information in a lecture, but more and more good teaching is discussional, cooperative. The instructor does not so much think for the students as think with them. From the desire to use some such method in religious instruction has come the forum in modern churches and the questionnaire group after the sermon, where those who wish can put objections and inquiries to the preacher, and discussion groups of all sorts where religious questions are threshed out in mutual conference. The principle behind such methods is psychologically right. We never really get an idea until we have thought it for ourselves.

A good sermon should take this into account. A wise preacher can so build his sermon that it will be not a dogmatic monologue but a cooperative dialogue in which all sorts of things in the minds of the congregation—objections, questions, doubts, and confirmations—will be brought to the front and fairly dealt with. This requires clairvoyance on the preacher's part as to what the people are thinking, but any man who lacks that has no business to preach anyway.

Recently, in a school chapel, so I am told, the headmaster was only well started on his sermon when a professor mounted the pulpit beside him and offered a criticism of what he was saying. Great excitement reigned. The headmaster answered the objection, but the professor remained in the pulpit, and the sermon that day was a running discussion between the two on a great theme in religion. To say that the boys were interested is to put it mildly. They never had been so worked up over anything religious before. It turned out afterward that the whole affair had been prearranged. It was an experiment in a new kind of preaching, where one man does not produce a monologue but where diverse and competing points of view are frankly dealt with.

Any preacher without introducing another personality outwardly in the pulpit can utilize the principle involved in this method. If he is to handle helpfully real problems in his congregation, he must utilize it. He must see clearly and state fairly what people other than himself are thinking on the matter in hand. He may often make this so explicit as to begin paragraphs with such phrases as, "But some of you will say," or "Let us consider a few questions that inevitably arise," or, "Some of you have had experiences that seem to contradict what we are saying." Of course, this method, like any other, can be exaggerated and become a mannerism. But something like it is naturally involved in any preaching which tries to help people to think through and live through their problems.

Such preaching when it is well done always possesses an important quality. It is not militant and pugnacious but irenic, kindly, and constructively helpful. How much the churches need such discourses! We have endless sermons of sheer propaganda where preachers set out by hook or crook to put something over on the congregation. We have pugnacious sermons where preachers wage campaigns, attack enemies, assail the citadels of those who disagree, and in general do anything warlike and vehement. But sermons that try to face the people's real problems with them, meet their difficulties, answer their questions, interpret their experiences in sympathetic, wise, and understanding cooperation—what a dearth of them there is!

Yet not only is such preaching the most useful, it is the most interesting. This is the only way I know to achieve excitement without sensationalism. Constructively to state the problem of meeting trouble victoriously or of living above the mediocre moral level of a modern city, or of believing in God in the face of the world's evil, or of making Christ's principles triumphant against the present international and interracial prejudice is surely not sensationalism, but it is vitally interesting. A breathless auditor came up after one such sermon saying, "I nearly passed out with excitement, for I did not see how you possibly could answer that objection which you raised against your own thought. I supposed you would do it somehow but I could not see how until you did it." There is nothing that people are so interested in as themselves, their own problems, and the way to solve them. That fact is basic. No preaching that neglects it can raise a ripple on a congregation. It is the primary starting point of all successful public speaking, and for once the requirements of practical success and ideal helpfulness coincide. He who really helps folks to understand their own lives and see their way through their spiritual problems is performing one of the most important functions in the modern world.

V

No method of preaching is without its dangers and of course this one which I am espousing has perils in plenty. I presented it once to a group of experienced ministers and collected a galaxy of warnings as to its possible perversions. They thought of times when they had tried it with disappointing results. They had endeavored so precisely to deal with a real problem that Mr. Smith had vexatiously waked up to the fact that they were talking about objections to their thought, that they had overstated the opposing side and then had neither time nor ability to answer it, or they had been so practical in thinking about some definite problem that they had become trivial and had forgotten to bring the wide sweep of the Gospel's truth to bear in an elevating way on the point at issue, or they had been so anxious to deal with felt needs in the congregation that they forgot to arouse the conciousness of need unfelt but real. All these dangers are present in the method which we are suggesting. It can be offensively personal, argumentatively unconvincing, practically trivial, and narrowed to the conscious needs of mediocre people. But these perversions are the fault of just such unskilled handling as would wreck any method whatosever.

The best antidote to making a wrong use of the project method in the pulpit is to be discovered in the ideal of creative preaching. The danger involved in starting a sermon with a problem is that the very word *problem* suggests something to be merely debated and its solution may suggest nothing more than the presentation of a helpful idea to the mind. But we all want something else in a sermon than a discussion even about one of our vital problems, no matter how wise the discussion or how suggestive the conclusion. The best sermons, I still maintain, are preached on the project method, but after all, in the preacher's hands it means something more than the same method in a classroom. It is the project method plus.

What this plus is can easily be seen. When a preacher deals with joy, let us say, he ought to start not with joy in the fifth century B.C. nor with joy as a subject to be lectured on but with the concrete difficulties in living joyfully that his people actually experience. He should have in mind from the start their mistaken ideas of joy, their false attempts to get it, the causes of their joylessness, and their general problem of victorious and happy living in the face of life's puzzling and sometimes terrific experiences. This is a real problem for everybody, and the sermon that throws light on it is a real sermon. But that real sermon must do more than discuss joy—it must produce it. All powerful preaching is creative. It actually brings to pass in the lives of the congregation the thing it talks about. So, to tackle the problem of joy so that the whole congregation goes out more joyful than it came in —that is the mark of a genuine sermon.

Here lies a basic distinction between a sermon and an essay. The outstanding criticism popularly and properly launched against a great deal of our modern, liberal preaching is that though it consists of neat, analytical discourses, pertinent to real problems and often well conceived and well phrased, it does nothing to anybody. Such sermons are not sermons but essays. It is lamentably easy to preach feebly about repentance without making anybody feel like repenting or to deliver an accomplished discourse on peace without producing any of the valuable article in the auditors. On the other hand, a true preacher is creative. He does more than discuss a subject; he produces the thing itself in the people who hear it. As an English bishop said about Phillips Brooks: "He makes one feel so strong." *

Obviously, personal quality is the major factor in producing spiritual power. There is a real reason for the halos which the painters have put about the heads of the saints. They are symbols of something intangible but real—an effluence that ordinary men do not possess, a radiance that is not the less powerful because it is ineffable.

Nevertheless, even a moderately endowed preacher, who never would suggest a halo to anybody, may have some of this power to create what he discusses. Whether he does or not depends a great deal upon whether he sees the objective clearly enough to head for it with precision. If he thinks of his sermon merely as a discussion of somebody's problem, he will play with a series of ideas, but if he thinks of his sermon as an endeavor to create something in his congregation, he will play on motives. There is where much of our modern preaching fails. The old preachers at their best did know where the major motives were. Fear, love, gratitude, self-preservation, altruism—such springs of human action the old sermons often used with consummate power. To be sure, they sometimes outraged the personalities of both adults and children by the way they did it, but for all that, they often showed an uncanny insight into the springs of human action. I often think that we modern preachers talk about psychology a great deal more than our predecessors did but use it a great deal less.

One often reads modern sermons with amazement. How do the preachers expect to get anything done in human life with such discourses? They do not come within reaching distance of any powerful motives in a man's conduct. They are keyed to argumentation rather than creation. They produce essays, which means that they are chiefly concerned with the elucidation of a theme. If they were producing sermons, they would be chiefly concerned with the transformation of personality.

This, however, brings us back to our major issue. If a preacher is to use the project method, as a preacher should, not simply to

---

* See Chapter 21 for an essay on Phillips Brooks and Harry Emerson Fosdick.

discuss the real problems of real people but to create in the people the thing that is discussed, his chief interest must be in the individuals in his congregation. He must know them through and through, not only their problems but their motives, not only what they are thinking but why they are acting as they do. Preaching becomes thrilling business when it successfully achieves this definite direction and aim. A sermon, then, is an engineering operation by which a chasm is spanned so that spiritual goods on one side are actually transported into personal lives upon the other.

VI

Throughout this paper we have held up the ideal of preaching as an interesting operation. That is a most important matter, not only to the audience but to the man in the pulpit. The number of fed-up, fatigued, bored preachers is appalling. Preaching has become to them a chore. They have to "get up" a sermon, perhaps two sermons, weekly. They struggle at it. The juice goes out of them as the years pass. They return repeatedly to old subjects and try to whip up enthusiasm over weatherbeaten texts and themes. Their discourses sink into formality. They build conventional sermon outlines, fill them in with conventional thoughts, and let it go at that. Where is the zest and thrill with which in their chivalrous youth they started out to be ministers of Christ to the spiritual life of their generation?

Of course, nothing can make preaching easy. At best it means drenching a congregation with one's lifeblood. But while, like all high work, it involves severe concentration, toil, and self-expenditure, it can be so exhilarating as to recreate in the preacher the strength it takes from him, as good agriculture replaces the soil it uses. Whenever that phenomenon happens, one is sure to find a man predominantly interested in personalities and what goes on inside of them. He has understood people, their problems, troubles, motives, failures, and desires, and in his sermons he has known how to handle their lives so vitally that week after week he has produced real changes. People have habitually come up after the sermon, not to offer some bland compliment but to say: "How did you know I was facing that problem only this week?" or "We were discussing that very matter at dinner last night," or, best of all, "I think you would understand my case—may I have a personal interview with you?"

This, I take it, is the final test of a sermon's worth: how many individuals wish to see the preacher alone?

I should despair, therefore, of any man's sustained enthusiasm and efficiency in the pulpit if he were not in constant, confidential relationship with individuals. Personal work and preaching are twins. As I watch some preachers swept off their feet by the demands of their own various organizations, falling under the spell of bigness, and rushing from one committee to another to put over some new scheme to enlarge the work or save the world, I do not wonder at the futility which so often besets them. They are doing everything except their chief business, for that lies inside individuals.

If someone utterly "sold" to our American worship of size and our grandiose schemes for saving the world should protest that this means individualistic preaching, he would only reveal his own obtuseness. In one sense, all good preaching and all good public speaking of any kind must be individualistic—it must establish vital contact with individuals. Even if one were speaking on the rings of Saturn, one might as well not begin unless one could cook up some reason why the audience should wish to hear about them. The failure to recognize this fact explains why so much of our so-called social preaching falls flat or rouses resentment. A man who on Sunday morning starts in to solve the economic question or the international question as though his people must have come that day of a purpose to hear him do it deserves almost any unpleasant thing that can happen to him. He may be a Ph.D. in psychology, but I doubt whether he knows enough about the way men's minds do actually act to be a successful grocer's assistant.

His special business as a Christian preacher with economic and international questions is profound and vital, but insofar as he sticks to his last, his interest as a minister is distinct from anyone else's, and it calls for an approach of his own. The world's economic and international situation is not alien to our personal problems. It invades them, shapes them in multitudinous ways; it undoes in us and around us much that the Christian should wish done, and it does much that the Christian most should fight against. Let a preacher, therefore, start at the end of the problem where he belongs. Let him begin with the people in front of him, with what goes on inside of them, because social conditions are as they are, with the economic and international reasons for many of their un-Christian moods, tempers, ideas, and ideals, with their responsibilities and obligations in the matter, and in general with the tremendous stake which personal Christianity has in those powerful social forces which create the climate in which it must either live or die. Such preaching on social questions starts, as it should start, with the individuals immediately concerned, establishes contact with their lives, and has at least some faint chance of doing a real business on Sunday.

Every problem that the preacher faces thus leads back to one basic question: how well does he understand the thoughts and lives of his people? That he should know his Gospel goes without saying, but he may know it ever so well and yet fail to get it within reaching distance of anybody unless he intimately understands people and cares more than he cares for anything else what is happening inside of them. Preaching is wrestling with individuals over questions of life and death, and until that idea of it commands a preacher's mind and method, eloquence will avail him little and theology not at all.

Chapter 3

How I Prepare My Sermons—
Harry Emerson Fosdick

CHARLES A. MCGLON, *Editor*

THE FIRST STEP is the choice of an object—not a subject but an object. A famous Scotch preacher was once greeted by an admirer who exclaimed: "That was a wonderful sermon." "What did it *do?*" retorted the preacher, "What did it do?" Every sermon's central motive should be some definite objective to be achieved. An essayist may be content with the discussion of a subject, but a preacher can be content only with the attainment of an object. I mean not simply some overall aim—such as the presentation of Christian truth and the persuasion of men to accept it—which obviously should be all preaching's purpose, but for each sermon a specific intent. It may be the help of individuals in facing some personal problem, or the answering of a puzzling question in theology, or the persuasion of tempted souls to abandon some popular sin, or the confrontation of some public evil with the Christian ethic, or the winning of wavering minds and consciences to a definite decision for Christ, but I, for one, cannot start a sermon until I clearly see what I propose to get *done* on Sunday morning.*

---

* Cf. Harry Emerson Fosdick: What's the matter with preaching? *Harper's Magazine,* CLVII (July 1928), pp. 134–141; and **Roy C. McCall:** Harry Emerson Fosdick: paragon and paradox, *QJS,* XXXIX (October 1952), pp.283–290.

Note: Reprinted from *The Quarterly Journal of Speech,* Volume XL, Number 1 (February 1954).

To be sure, the object of a sermon always involves a subject. Whatever the aim may be, some truth is relevant to its accomplishment, but the truth, when presented in any given sermon, should be no abstraction but an implement to serve a definite intent. So, having chosen an object, I look for the relevant truth, and at that point the Bible invariably steps in. Sometimes a single passage may sum up the matter, but if I give an exposition of that passage, it is not for the exposition's sake but because I hope to drop the truth, like a pile driver, ramming home the impact to achieve a definite result. Sometimes a sermon may have no single text; the pertinent truth may be so diffused in Scripture that one starts with his object and keeps running into applicable passages one after another. These two factors, however, always are present at the sermon's origin—a definite objective and relevant truth.

With this much clear, I sit down with pen and paper and practice what the psychologists call *free association of ideas*. That is, I jot down haphazardly any idea that comes into my mind, which directly or indirectly bears upon the matter in hand. At this stage I do not consider how the sermon will begin or end or what its structure may turn out to be. I give free gangway to my mind and let it pick up anything within the scope of the sermon's object and subject which it may chance to light upon. If an idea is only a vague intimation with no development or application evident, I do not labor it. If an idea branches out into consecutive suggestions, I briefly note them. I observe no logical continuity in accepting any suggestion that may come but jot it down. This process may go on for hours—*one idea awakening another* and all of them an unorganized jumble and potpourri, without order or logical connection; but, not infreqently, when this stage is finished, I have the basic material, the loose bricks, with which the sermon will be built.

When this process of free association has run its course and is paying no more dividends, I take my mind in hand and face it with definite questions.

1. What have I ever read in general literature—biography, history, novels, poetry—that throws light upon my theme?

2. What have I ever run upon in personal counseling that illustrates the human need with which I am dealing and the **resources to meet it?**

3. Where, beyond the passages I have already thought of, does the Bible—that vast storehouse of experience—illumine the sermon's problem and the way to treat it?

4. What, in my own personal experience, has this theme intimately meant to me, and what—honest-to-goodness!—does it really mean now in my own life?

Such questions as these mean research, without and within, and generally by the time the results are gathered, I begin to see the structural outline of the sermon. When matters go well, I do not deliberately build the structure; it *comes,* emerging out of the material as though by spontaneous suggestion. Sometimes the whole structure appears with imperative clarity; sometimes I see only where I must begin and vaguely perceive the steps that will follow. Some sermons, therefore, are fully outlined before I start writing; on others I commence writing and feel my way, stage by stage, until the outline becomes clear.

Every sermon I have ever preached has been written in full by hand. I think on paper. I recognize, of course, that there are other methods; that there are geniuses to whom the old Negro preacher's advice applies: "Read yourself full; think yourself clear; pray yourself hot; and then let yourself go!" The Henry Ward Beechers can do that and still retain, to an amazing degree, variety and flexibility of style, richness of vocabulary, freedom from repetitious words and phrases, and diversity of ideas. As I have watched

the preachers who do not write, however, I have seen the almost inevitable result: monotonous style, a limited vocabulary with few synonyms, repetitious ruts of thought, and finally a quick change of pastorate to find a congregation unfamiliar with the preacher's now well-worn clichés. Even the Beechers avoid such consequences only because while they do not write their sermons in full, they write articles and books constantly and so gain for their preaching what habitual writing alone can give.

Writing forces careful consideration of phraseology, makes the preacher weigh his words, compels him to reread what he has written and criticize it without mercy, constrains him to clear up obscurities in thought and language, begets discontent with repetitious mannerisms, and allows the preacher, before he mounts the pulpit, to listen, as it were, to his own sermon as a whole and judge whether it would hit his nail on the head were he an auditor.

The familiar criticism of the written sermon is that it lacks spontaneity, but that depends, first, on what kind of sermon has been written, and, second, on how it is delivered. Written and spoken styles are not identical, and the competent preacher, preparing a sermon, learns to write not for readers but for listeners. He writes as though he were speaking, with the direct impact of work on ear always in mind. In his imagination, as he puts pen to paper, the congregation is vividly present—especially some specific type of person whose mind and conscience he proposes to reach—and he writes as he would talk to people face to face, directly, pungently, appealingly. A lawyer does not prepare an appeal to a jury in the same manner used by an essayist inditing a thesis, but rather, determined to get an affirmative decision, he orders and phrases his address with listeners in mind and so conceives and words it that it undercuts prejudices, challenges opposition, evokes emotion, persuades reluctant minds, and gets a decisive vote. No sermon need be so written that it lacks spontaneity.

As for a sermon's delivery, there are many methods, and I have tried three of them—memorizing, speaking from an outline, reading from manuscript. Memorizing I gave up long ago. Speaking from an outline has been my most common practice. But in recent years I have found that one can have the full manuscript in front of him and can read it as though he were not reading but talking, with just as much freedom, spontaneity, colloquial directness, and person-to-person impact as though no manuscript were on the pulpit. Just as one can *write* for listeners, so one can *read* for listeners, combining the advantage of a manuscript's careful preparation with the freedom of face-to-face address.

This brief statement has concerned only the preparation of the preachment not the preparation of the preacher. That second matter runs deep. The best sermon ever written can be murdered by a preacher spiritually unqualified to present it. And many a sermon which would suffer devastating criticism at the hands of homiletical experts has moved human souls to great issues because what the preacher *was* made his words weigh a ton. Nevertheless, our Lord, whose message was driven home by his divine character, was not careless of the form his message took. His parables are more than spontaneous—they are works of art, unmatched in the annals of man's teaching.

Chapter 4

Animated Conversation

HARRY EMERSON FOSDICK

MY IDEAL of a sermon is an animated conversation with an audience concerning some vital problem of the spiritual life. A good minister when he deals with an individual applicant for counsel and help and feels himself in the presence of a real personal problem, oftentimes is at his best and marshals his knowledge, experience, insight, and faith to solve the difficulty before him. My ideal of a sermon is one that carries up this interest and directness of attack on real problems into the pulpit and discusses real questions with real people in a real way.

One upshot of such an approach is that I am always interested rather to get an *object* for a sermon than a *subject*. No sermon seems to me to get well under way until I have clearly in mind some difficulty that people are facing, some question that they are asking, some sin they are committing, some possibility they are missing, some confused thinking they are doing, so that I have before me rather a goal toward which I aim than simply a subject or a text from which I talk.

This point of approach also affects the entire order of development of a sermon. I am not so interested to arrange my thoughts logically as I am to arrange them psychologically. To be sure, there need be no contradiction here; a sermon certainly ought not to be illogical. But a preacher is not a mere essayist illuminating a

---

Note: Reprinted with permission from Joseph Fort Newton: *If I Had Only One Sermon To Prepare.* New York, Harper & Bros., Publishers 1932.

subject in a logical fashion. He is after his audience to create a change in them, and therefore his primary endeavor must be to arrange his thought in a psychological fashion, so that he may start where they are in their thinking and lead them on from one step to another along an inclined plane that is most natural for their feet to mount. I often find that this contrast between a merely logical and a vitally psychological arrangement of thought can make or unmake an entire sermon.

Put in another way, this means that the preacher is primarily interested in personalities, in what is actually happening to them, and all the while has in his mind's eye not primarily a subject he is developing or a text to which he is giving an exposition but people in front of him whom he is trying to help. A sermon, therefore, becomes an engineering operation, building a bridge from one side of the river to the other, and actually carrying over spiritual supplies to those who need them. All the thrill and zest of preaching seems to me to lie in this very fact, and the only preachers who can ever find preaching dull are those that miss it.

Stated in another way, this makes preaching creative. That is to say, it is not the discussion of a matter simply but the endeavor to create something actually by transfusion of faith and light so that people will go out from church changed from what they were when they came in. It is one thing to preach a sermon about patience or joy, and it is another thing to create patience and joy in the congregation. Only the latter is real preaching.

The phrase *animated conversation,* with which I started, would also indicate my ideal of the delivery of a sermon. One must abhor rhetoric and oratory and all manner of pulpit tricks designed merely to do stunts with a congregation. However the delivery of a sermon may rise out of the conversational style into impassioned discourse, it must always be based upon the conversational and return to it. And the total effect ought to be one of talk —plain, straightforward, illuminating, helpful talk—between the preacher and his congregation. The more a preacher can make his sermon an elevated and animated rendition of the sort of thing he would do for an individual soul, when he was at his best, the better the sermon is likely to be.

Put in still another way, this means that the preacher must

always have in his mind what the persons in his congregation are likely to be saying in answer to what he is saying. Probably I carry this too far, for I often introduce opposing personalities into my discourse, saying that very probably this or that or the other thing is being objected to my line of thought. In this way the sermon does cease to be a mere monologue and becomes a dialogue. My ideal would be, so far as possible, to take into account the objections, difficulties, and contradictory experiences that would occur to the person listening to any discourse.

All this does not mean, of course, that a sermon may not be expository. The great texts of Scripture are the classic formulations of abiding human experience. They came out of experience, reflect experience, and are valuable only because they express an experimental fact of abiding poignancy and significance. Therefore, I do constantly use the expository method in trying to dig into the experience that was behind a great text of Scripture. Always, however, the preacher's major interest should not be historical or literary or theological. Everything should be but a mere instrument in his hands for his definite personal goal of doing something creative with the individuals in front of him.

I do not know how much you wanted me to say about practical methods of sermon preparation. The big business, as you may imagine from what I have just said, is the selection of the definite problem that I propose to discuss the next Sunday, the determination of the goal that I am going to drive at; when that is clearly visualized, I count the sermon well on its way. I mean by that, I suppose, what Hugh Black meant when he said to me once that as soon as he was able clearly to write the first sentence of his sermon, he thought that his sermon was at least half done. I should be wretchedly unhappy not to have this whole matter clearly in mind and the initial stages of it stated by Tuesday noon at the latest. On Wednesday, Thursday, and Friday morning I work on the development of my strategy in achieving the goal that I have in mind with the congregation. Uniformly I am through with my manuscript on Friday noon. The next stage is one of the most important of all, for fearful that in working out my subject I may occasionally have forgotten my object and may have got out of the center of focus the concrete personalities who will face me on

Sunday, I sit down on Saturday morning and rethink the whole business as if my congregation were visibly before my eyes, often picking out individuals and characteristic groups of individuals, and imaginatively trying my course of thought upon them, so as to be absolutely sure that I have not allowed any pride of discussion or lure of rhetoric to deflect me from my major purpose of doing something worthwhile with people. This process often means the elision of paragraphs that I liked very much when I first wrote them and the rearrangement of order of thought in the interest of psychological persuasiveness. My sermon is always ready for the pulpit Saturday noon.

Chapter 5

Personal Counseling and Preaching

An Understanding of Personal Counseling Can Give Tone, Direction, and Significance to Preaching Which Our Generation Critically Needs

HARRY EMERSON FOSDICK

THE RELATIONSHIP between personal counseling and preaching is a two-way street. Any preacher who in his sermons speaks to the real condition of his people, making evident that he knows what questions they are asking and where their problems lie, is bound to be sought out by individuals, wanting his intimate advice. And any pastor who, with intelligence and clairvoyance, practices such personal counseling, is bound to find his sermons, in content and form, insight and impact, profoundly affected. The right kind of preacher is coerced to become a personal counselor, and the right kind of personal counselor gains some of the most necessary ingredients of preaching.

One does not mean to say that a man cannot be an excellent preacher without being an excellent personal counselor, and vice versa. Gifts differ. Certainly there are expert counselors who cannot preach, and I suppose that there are powerful preachers who do little or no individual counseling—although how that latter thing can be true, I only with difficulty see. Our statement about

---

Note: Reprinted from *Pastoral Psychology,* Vol. 3, No. 22 (March, 1952).

this relationship, however, is not negative but positive. For some of us, at least, the two functions of the ministry are mutually indispensable to each other.

The only way I see to make this statement vital is to make it autobiographical, and I may as well be frankly that. When I began my ministry I did not know how to preach. I had been trained to stand up and talk in public, so that, however little I had to say, I could at least say it, but how my first parishioners endured those early sermons I do not see. In reminiscence I can discern several factors which helped me out of that morass of homiletical frustration and bewilderment, but one factor is primary. Perhaps I now overemphasize my first victorious experience in personal counseling, but it certainly was crucial.

A young man from one of the church's finest families, falling victim to alcoholism, sought my help. I recall my desperate feeling that if the Gospel of Christ did not have in it available power to save that youth, of what use was it? When months of conference and inward struggle ended in triumph, when that young man said to me, "If you ever find anyone who doesn't believe in God, send him to me—I know!", something happened to my preaching that courses in homiletics do not teach. *This* was the kind of effect that a *sermon* ought to have. It could deal with real problems, speak directly to individual needs, and because of it transforming consequences could happen to some person then and there. From that day on the secret prayer which I have offered, as I stood up to preach, has run like this: Somewhere in this congregation is one person who desperately needs what I am going to say; O God, help me to get at him!

Personal counseling has its routine aspects, its drudgeries and boredoms, but ever and again it becomes thrilling. A real problem is presented and a real victory gained. The Gospel works. One sees a miracle take place before one's eyes. A life is made over, a family is saved, a valuable youth turns about in his tracks and heads right, a potential suicide becomes a happy and useful member of society, a sceptic who had thought that life comes from nowhere, means nothing, and goes nowhither, accepts the Christian faith and is "transformed by the renewing of his mind." Such experiences in the consultation room—indubitable experiences of sometimes almost incredible regeneration—must have a profound effect when the counselor steps into the pulpit.

For one thing, personal counseling deepens the preacher's clairvoyance. He learns a lot about human nature which otherwise he could not have known. Books on nervous disorders are useful, but now he has *seen* what the books talk about. Newspapers tell him the news, but now he has confronted at first hand what the news is doing to real people inside. He gains that elemental factor without which all preaching is futile—insight into what actually is going on in the lives of those to whom he preaches.

For another thing, personal counseling deepens the preacher's confidence in the gospel of Christ and in the power which it makes available. He intimately faces frustration, despair about the world, abyssmal sin, fear, and the endless disasters of egocentricity, and he actually watches the miracle of transformation wrought. *It can happen*—not just because the Bible says so or because it is orthodox to think it but because he has seen it and has helped to mediate the truth and power that did it. Nothing so much as this experience, I suspect, can send a man into the pulpit sure that preaching can be personal consultation on a group scale and that someone's life that morning can be made all over.

For another thing, personal counseling tends to shift the preacher's mind from obsession with his sermon's subject to a purposeful concern about its object. A famous Scotch preacher was once greeted after service by an admiring friend who exclaimed, "That was a wonderful sermon," and the preacher turned on him. "What did it *do?*" he said; "What did it *do?*" Far too many sermons are harmless discussions of a subject, intelligent as it may be, well thought out and well delivered but lacking any purposeful drive to achieve an object. I do not see how a pastor experienced in counseling can preach like that. When he goes into the pulpit, he is after something with definite, deliberate intent. When he lifts a great truth, he intends, like a pile driver, to drop it on something. He has a subject, of course, but when he chose his subject, he had an object. He proposed that somebody that morning should face his Damascus Road.

We are not saying that personal counseling by itself can make a good preacher. Obviously it cannot. But it can give tone and direction and significance to preaching which our generation critically needs.

During a long ministry I have watched with interest two familiar types of sermon. The first is the expository model—elucidation of a Scriptural text, its historic occasion, its logical meaning in the context, its setting in the theology and ethic of the ancient writer; and then, at long last, application to the auditors of the truth involved. That a vital preacher can use that model with excellent effect goes without saying, but is there not something the matter with the model? To start with a Biblical passage and spend nearly all the sermon on its historic explanation and exposition presupposes the assumption that the congregation came to church that morning primarily concerned about the meaning of those venerable texts—which, in my experience, is a condition contrary to fact. Long ago I wrote petulantly: "Only the preacher proceeds still upon the idea that folk come to church desperately anxious to discover what happened to the Jebusites."

In revolt against the expository model the topical preachers arose. They searched contemporary life in general and the newspapers in particular for subjects. Instead of concentrating on textual analysis, they dealt with present-day themes about which everyone was thinking. I watched those topical preachers with a dubious mind. Week after week, turning their pulpits into platforms and their sermons into lectures, they strained after new intriguing subjects, and one knew that in private they were straining even more strenuously after new intriguing ideas about them. Instead of launching out from a great text, they started with their own opinions on some matter of current interest, often much farther away than a good Biblical text would be from the congregation's vital concerns and needs. Indeed, the fact that history had thought it worthwhile to preserve the text for centuries would cause a wise gambler to venture confidently on the text's superior vitality. If people do not come to church to learn what happened to the Jebusites, neither do they come yearning to hear a lecturer express his personal opinion on themes which editors, columnists, and radio commentators have been discussing all the week.

Jesus dealt primarily with individuals, and after that he spoke to the multitude. Does not that indicate a third approach to preaching which our generation needs? At any rate, it has been a godsend to me. People come to church with every kind of difficulty and problem flesh is heir to. A sermon is meant to meet such needs—the sins and shames, the doubts and anxieties that fill the pews. This is the place to start, with the real problems of the people. This is a sermon's specialty, which makes it a sermon—not an essay, an exposition, a lecture. Every sermon should have for its main business the head-on, constructive meeting of some problem which is puzzling minds, burdening consciences, and distracting lives, and no sermon which so meets real human difficulty with light to throw on it and power to win victory over it can possibly be futile. Any preacher who, with even moderate skill, is thus helping people is functioning, delivering the goods which the community has a right to expect from him. Even when he addresses a multitude, he speaks to them as individuals and is still a personal counselor.

Of course, these three approaches to preaching are not mutually exclusive. When one tries to bring the truth of the gospel to bear on personal needs, the great texts of the Bible beg to be used, and their exposition can be the backbone of the sermon. And when one deals seriously with personal perplexities, one runs straight into social, economic, and international problems which loom in the background and penetrate the foreground of every life. Nevertheless, the orientation of a sermon is profoundly affected when one approaches the pulpit as though one were beginning a personal consultation.

To plead for such an approach without pointing out its dangers would be unfair. I once presented this approach in a group of experienced ministers and collected a galaxy of warnings about its possible perversions. They had endeavored so precisely to deal with a real problem that Mr. Smith woke up to the fact that they were talking about him; or they had been so practical in dealing with some definite problem that they had become trivial, failing to bring the eternal gospel to bear on the issue; or they had been so anxious to deal with felt needs in the congregation that they had forgotten still deeper needs, unfelt but real; or they had so limited the difficulties they preached about to private, psychological maladjustments that they became merely amateur pulpit psychiatrists; or they had been so concerned to help people that they had become soft nursemaids of sick souls and had omitted all the stern, thunderous, prophetic affirmations of God's truth which our generation ought to hear. Unskilled mishandling of any homiletical method can wreck it.

The most familiar and deplorable danger in attempting to make sermons personal consultations on a group scale is, I think, the limitation of the preacher's scope. If his field of private counseling is confined pretty much to neurotic disorders, his pulpit may all too easily reflect the fact. Every Sunday he will be telling people how to overcome anxiety and fear and achieve peace of mind. He rides a hobby, attracts an audience of nervous patients, and in the pulpit becomes a homiletical neurologist. This is a pathetic perversion of what we are trying to say. We are supposed to preach to "all sorts and conditions of men," and no minister's private consultations include them all. His insight must run beyond his individual experience in the consultation room. He has other ways of gaining clairvoyance into human need, and he should use them all. His scope, like the Bible's, should include all human life, personal and social, and the whole message of the gospel.

Nevertheless—while any approach to preaching can be misused—it is a great day in a minister's life when, having seen what miracles can be wrought by Christ's truth and power brought to bear on individual souls, he mounts his pulpit sure that a sermon, too, can be thus a medium of creative and transforming effects. No longer on Sunday is he merely making a speech about religion; he is engaged in an engineering operation, building a bridge by which a chasm is spanned so that spiritual goods on one side—the "unsearchable riches of Christ"—are actually transported into personal lives on the other.

At this point the old preachers have much to teach us. At their best they did achieve results. Their sermons were appeals to the jury, and they got decisions. They knew where the powerful motives were and appealed to them with conclusive effect. While we modern preachers talk about psychology much more than our predecessors did, we commonly use it a good deal less ably.

As the experience involved in personal counseling can thus

minister to a preacher's power, so preaching can open up to the pastor hitherto unguessed opportunities for individual usefulness. One of the best tests of a sermon is the number of people who afterwards wish to see the preacher alone. It was a notable day in my own experience when, feeling that pastoral calling from house to house was not filling the bill, I announced a consultation hour for those who wished privately to talk with me. That first day I found myself facing a suicidal case, with fourteen others awaiting their turn. That was a generation ago, before the development of personal counseling clinics in Protestant churches had begun. Our churches are on their way now to meet that kind of need, which by many of our ministers had been long unguessed. Unfortunately some ministers who did not see that need were right; they did not evoke the need in their parishes. Their sermons were not of a kind to make hungry and distracted souls want to see them alone. One of the most hopeful movements in Protestantism today is the growing tie-up between preaching and personal counseling—the first so directed that it leads inevitably to the second, and the second so used that it gives individual force and impact to the first.

John Wesley is known as a preacher who customarily addressed audiences of twenty thousand people. He certainly spoke to the multitude. But Wesley was always a tireless personal counselor, and his whole "Society" was organized with a view to the care and supervision of individuals. Surely this factor in Wesley's habit and experience is basic in any explanation of his preaching power. How else can one account for John Nelson's statement concerning the first sermon he heard Wesley preach, before a great audience at Moorfields? "When he did speak," wrote Nelson, "I thought his whole discourse was aimed at me."

Chapter 6

The Christian Ministry

HARRY EMERSON FOSDICK

I

THE MINISTRY of the Protestant churches offers today a more diversified opportunity than it ever has offered before. Roman Catholicism always has been careful to put to use among its clergy a wide variety of talents. Taking any devoted and promising youth discoverable within its circle, Roman Catholicism has not only trained him but has eagerly watched the development in him of special gifts. A remarkable comprehensiveness has characterized the Roman clergy in finding place for many types of ability, so that mystics and administrators, preachers and statesmen, financial experts, scholars, and skilled confessors of souls have all found scope for their several specialties.

The Protestant ministry has been commonly associated with a more narrowly defined function. Two forms of service, pastoral visitation and preaching, have occupied the center of attention. To be sure, the clergyman in a Protestant parish has been supposed to exercise a wide variety of gifts, often extending the gamut from being janitor to being censor of public morals, and including among his many attempted functions money raising, religious education, expert recreational service, civic leadership, and organizational administration. Nevertheless, this diversity of

---

Note: Reprinted with permission from *The Atlantic Monthly* (January, 1929).

endeavor has been centered in the minister's chief business: being a preacher and a pastor.

In particular, the Protestant minister has been expected to preach. Here the contrast with Roman Catholicism is marked and significant. Only a few priests of the Roman church are supposed primarily to be preachers. The center of Roman worship is the sacrament of the Mass; the center of Protestant worship is the sermon. This difference has historical explanations into the theory of which we need not enter but into the practical consequences of which any youth considering the ministry runs headlong. The call to be a Protestant clergyman has always been primarily a call to preach.

A decisive change in this regard is observable today. For one thing, the universal tendency to specialization has inevitably invaded the churches. No one man can be a scholarly theologian, an effective preacher, an expert in religious education, a practical administrator, and a skilled confessor of souls. In spite of their historical bent the Protestant churches are bound increasingly to select young men with a view to particular gifts and to train them in the exercise of their specialties.

Furthermore, the pressure of our centralized population is slowly but surely forcing us to fewer but larger churches, with more diversified functions and with staffs of clergymen representing more varied abilities. This is marked in cities where means of rapid communication have broken down old parish lines and outmoded small local congregations. What with subways, buses, and automobiles, it is frequently easier to go five miles to church than it used to be to go five blocks, and in consequence the inevitable tendency is to combine local congregations into ever more centralized churches and then to staff these larger churches with a diversified ministry.

While this tendency may be marked in the cities, it is, if anything, more significant in rural districts, where already community churches can be seen, displacing or combining sectarian congregations and so making possible, instead of a half-dozen poor preachers, one or two good ones, with additional ministers whose function lies in various forms of communal service and religious education.

To be sure, there is plenty of resistance to this movement, but time and tide are with it, and it cannot be stopped. Dr. Carroll estimates that last year there was an increase in the number of church members of 573,723 and a decrease in the number of churches of 1470, which, if it is correct, is a hopeful sign. Within the next few years we may expect, I think, an acceleration of this tendency, with fewer and larger churches doing a much more diversified business and with forms of ministry other than preaching taking an increasingly important place in the régime.

What part the radio will play in this programme no one can foresee, but it seems destined to perform a real function. Nothing can ultimately displace the living voice or make a sermon from a stranger at a distance an adequate surrogate for the address of a friend at home, but that an increasing amount of the church's preaching will be done over the air is certain, and already such preaching is being at least occasionally received, not simply by individuals in their families but by congregations in their churches.

The upshot of all this is seen in our theological seminaries, where one commonly finds students, both men and women, preparing for the ministry of the churches with no idea of preaching. that is not their specialty, They are headed for religious education, child guidance, psychiatry applied to character building, recreational directorships, service for special groups such as students, pastoral oversight, religious journalism, teaching in the colleges, and various forms of organizational work from the financial superintendence of individual congregations to expert service in interdenominational cooperation.

It is true that in these fields the churches at present are not prepared to absorb and use the abilities that young men and women sometimes present to them. Nevertheless, the situation is developing, and the prospect is hopeful. Many youths who feel neither the ability nor the wish to preach are going, as they supremely desire to go, into the service of their generation's spiritual life. They will be ministers of religion and servants of the church. The result will be a far richer and more varied leadership for the forces of organized faith and a far more satisfying career for many young men and women who, not commercially minded, desire above all else to make a contribution to religion.

This does not mean that the preacher's function will either disappear or be essentially diminished. It does mean, however, that it will cease to monopolize the attention of the church and that, more and more, preachers will be picked for their special skill. Protestantism has relied too much on preaching and has indulged in too large a quantity of it. Many of our churches have had reality pretty well washed out of them by the constant deluge of hastily prepared talk. From the minister's point of view, the resultant strain has often been intolerable and the consequences upon his own life disastrous. Nothing, I think, can stop the movement toward fewer preachers, delivering fewer sermons in larger churches, with the radio at the disposal of at least the pick of them.

This prospect ought to exert a powerful influence on many youths who are considering the ministry. Some who do not want to preach at all will be saved from the obsession that they must preach if they are to be ministers of organized religion. Others, who do wish to preach and to preach well, will be saved from the terrifying prospect of endless Sundays each with two scrappily thrown-together discourses appended to an immeasurable quantity of midweek religious talk.

Under this new régime which youths now entering, the ministry should help to inaugurate, where fewer and better sermons are the rule, the preacher will once more come into his own. Indeed, the gist of the appeal to young men and women today on behalf of the ministry lies, here as elsewhere, not in asking them to serve the ecclesiastical *status quo* but in summoning them to change it. No one has any business to go into the ministry who is satisfied with the churches as they are. We have too many complacent ministers now. We need more who are unwilling merely to sustain the routine of religious performance as the ordinary church has developed it but who, for all that, believe in organized religion, in public worship, and in the possibilities of preaching.

II

A youth choosing the Christian ministry today and planning primarily to be a preacher should aim first at recovering the accent of reality in the pulpit. The parson used to be what the name implies, the leading person in the community. Preëminent in education and information, backed by the authority of his vocation from God, he held a unique and dominant position. Today the minister is not preëminent in either education or information, and his opinions on any subject are accorded no more respect than in themselves they are worth. People look for light to books and magazines, to lectures and the drama, and the pulpit obviously faces a competition never before experienced. This fact is sometimes taken by churchmen as a discomfiting symptom and is commonly proclaimed by the church's enemies as a sure prelude to the minister's downfall.

As a matter of fact, it is the best thing that ever happened to preaching. It forces the wise preacher to quit his reliance on ecclesiastical authority, to cut out cant, bombast, hokum, or whatever else represents the cheap substitution of wordiness for genuineness, and to make of his sermons a forthright endeavor to deal in a real way with the real problems of real people.

To be sure, plenty of preaching shows small indication of such beneficent consequence, and that is a major reason why in many cases church attendance dwindles. That also is a happy augury. People will no longer go as a matter of form where reality is not to be found as a matter of fact, and while the immediate effect is troublesome to the churches, the ultimate outcome will be salutary.

What the young man or woman headed for the pulpit should remember is that preaching can fulfill an indispensable function in the community. The preacher can tackle the real questions which the people are asking about right and wrong, God, the soul, and immortality. He can face honestly the problems which perplex them in their loves and hates, prejudices, troubles, successes, and failures, both individual and social; he can meet their inward needs as genuinely as the grocer feeds or the physician heals their bodies.

Thus, to cut through the conventionalities of homiletical tradition, to break away from slavish subjection to formal textual exegesis, and to make of the sermon a contribution to the thinking of the people about their spiritual problems calls for more than a standardized mind. In appealing for this type of ministry, therefore, one would insist that we do not need more preachers but better ones. A preacher, even in his youth, gifted with some clear convictions about the meaning of personal and social life at their best can approach in a straightforward fashion the questions which people are asking, the problems they are facing, and the experiences that perplex them in private life or social situations. He can speak out his honest thought with no pretense that he knows more than he does know, meeting fairly the objections that may be raised and endeavoring always to help the people to think and live their own way through. He can with intelligent, tolerant, and constructive intent genuinely make the most of his best for the sake of others and bring to bear on real life the light and power of religion as Christ has revealed its meaning. If he does this, he will find an eager following. He may even become to many what one layman recently called his minister—"our animated conscience."

III

The youth headed for the pulpit should also rightly appraise his immense opportunity as a director of public worship. The Protestant minister, in particular, should take account of the limitations to which overemphasis on the sermon has subjected the evangelical churches. The Roman Catholic goes to church to worship, and the center of that worship is a sacrament. Now, the value of a sacramental symbol as a center of worship lies in part in its inclusiveness: all sorts of people, from the very ignorant to the very learned, can get something out of it. The philosopher and the longshoreman may kneel together at the Mass and each extract from the performance what each brings the capacity to see and feel. But, while philosophers and longshoremen may thus be included in the benefits of a symbolic act, they rarely can be seen together listening to a sermon. A sermon is selective; it appeals to a certain mental stratum; it automatically excludes from its range of interest other types of mind than the kind from which it comes. This is one reason why Protestant churches in America, centering their worship in a sermon, have so largely become class organizations—religious clubs appealing to a narrowly selected group of ideas and traditions.

So long as patriotism is expressed by saluting the flag, everybody can indulge in that symbolic act, and each can find in it his own meaning. If, however, patriotism's expression should be thought of as listening to discourses on the Constitution, that would eliminate wide ranges of the nation's population, whoever was engaged as the expositor.

I do not mean that preaching can be or should be minimized, but alongside the sermon the present renaissance of beauty in worship should be recognized as one of the chief concerns of the ministry. There are three main avenues to fellowship with God: goodness, truth, and beauty. Protestantism has been strong on the first two. Goodness—the ethical stress of evangelical Christianity has been untiring, and while at times belated in its forms and perversely directed in its tendencies, its zeal and determination can be counted on. Truth—the doctrinal interest of the Protestant churches has been tremendous, and while often blinded by fanaticism and ignorance, the evangelical interest in religious truth is ineradicable. Beauty, however, has had no such place in the Protestant tradition. Yet for multitudes beauty is the major roadway to fellowship with God.

To recover this lost accent in our churches, to make religion not simply moral and intelligent but beautiful, an affair of joy and festival as well as of goodness and truth, is crucially important, and the man in the pulpit can further this movement and direct it.

To many youths public worship has largely lost serious meaning simply because the actual worship of the churches has been so abominably conducted. Our public prayers would often be blasphemous if they were not ridiculous instead, and the ugliness of much of our church architecture is carried out with appalling consistency in the corresponding ugliness in the conduct of the service. Public worship, however, can be and sometimes is exhilarating, exalting, cleansing, and ennobling. It does actual business in human souls. It causes people who have been looking down to look up. It reorients life, redirects energy, freshens ideals, restores equilibrium, and liberates spiritual resources.

A minister may well recall each Sunday the words of ex-President Eliot of Harvard, who, speaking of the days when Phillips

Brooks led the worship in Harvard chapel, said, "Prayer is the greatest achievement of the human soul." *

IV

Again, the preacher should magnify his opportunity for intellectual leadership. The present distaste of university communities for conventional religion, the common abstention of students from religious practices, the familiar professions of agnosticism to be heard on the campuses, and the still more common confessions of utter bewilderment are often written up as disconcerting and dangerous symptoms of a wayward age. As a matter of fact, they constitute a great opportunity to the minister.

If he is alive to the situation, he will quit his reliance on creedal authority, and instead of standing outside the turmoil and confusion of this generation's endeavor to find an intelligible religion, he will get inside. There is little in the situation that can be called unprecedented. This generation, like others before it, but in accentuated fashion, is facing a new world view. The cosmos in which we live, with its size, its evolutionary process, its law-abiding uniformity, both physical and psychological, its unity of structure, making incredible the old discriminations between natural and supernatural—such major matters, with many attendant factors, have outmoded our old formulations of religion and have forced us to revise and enlarge our conception of God.

Like all important matters, the consequent bewilderment can be taken hold of by one of two handles. It can be approached as a disaster or tackled as an opportunity. The intelligent and adventurous minister will certainly see in the religious questions being asked and the religious problems being faced by earnest minds today not a catastrophe but a chance for leadership and an open door to a more credible faith. This generation is not irreligious; it is intensely concerned with religion; but it will not, in its intelligent areas, be content with creedal conventionality. It cannot patiently harbor a modern worldview on one side and on the other a formulation of religion which contradicts it.

---

* See Chapter 20 for an essay on Phillips Brooks and Harry Emerson Fosdick.

The present rebellion against religion is therefore in a deep sense a confession of concern for religion. The outstanding need is light and leadership. Give us more first-class brains in our pulpits —nothing can take the place of that!

Instead of using the well-dug channels of commercial life as river beds for their lives, let high-grade men set themselves, as many of them are initially minded to set themselves, to the task of honest and constructive thinking on religion. If one type of church will not have them, let them shake the dust of it from their feet and turn to another. There are free churches where no ecclesiastical overlordship spoils the autonomy of local congregations, and even in more highly articulated denominations there is much more liberty than is usually supposed. Certainly there is as much freedom as the average editorial writer, college professor, lawyer, or politician enjoys and often much more. Freedom to express one's self in all these fields is commonly a matter of the individual himself, his strength of character, his courage, his ability of mind, and his personality quality of wisdom and fair play. If some churches are closed to intelligent thought, the argument is not that they must be left as hopeless but that they must be opened.

One way or another, the man who has something to say will be heard. And the crying need, which constitutes one of the most challenging calls to the ministry, is for first-rate minds to help clarify and reconstruct the thinking of the churches.

V

No youth should enter the ministry today without a clear intent to help harness religious dynamic for the solving of our social problems. The opportunity is very great. Say what evil one may about the churches, they are still the reservoirs of moral enthusiasm and serious ethical interest to a degree not true of any other institution. These enormous resources of spiritual power often lie dormant or when aroused, are misdirected, but they are there. Few matters of such moment face American civilization as the unleashing of this power and its sensible and effective guidance to some good purpose.

While, therefore, many high-minded youths of the new generation should and will go in for the engineering side of philanthropy, economic reform, politics, and internationalism, others must deal with the question of spiritual dynamics. In the churches, with their faith, their ideals of the Kingdom of Righteousness, their millions of well-intentioned and morally earnest people, lie resources of power without the impulsion of which no great cause can be brought to victory in this country.

Here again, the great need is leadership. The mass of our church members are neither bad-spirited nor willfully reactionary on social questions, but they are often uninstructed. They have done too little thinking on the major problems of our economic and international life; they have not seen clearly the relationship between these problems and the religious ideals which they profess; they have never had the social implications of Christianity made concretely real to them in terms of their attitudes toward militarism, war, racial prejudice, and economic injustice.

If they only knew it, preachers have it in their power to work so salutary a change in the whole social ethic of America that the consequences would run out to the ends of the earth. But no third-rate preachers can do this. The opportunity calls for high-grade men. The pulpit supremely needs teachers. And in no realm is patient, constructive, kindly, courageous teaching more needed than in the application of the Christian ethic to our social, economic, and international affairs.

Altogether, the pulpit is one of the most crucial points in the whole line of civilization's advance. That the churches are in a very unsatisfactory condition this paper has taken for granted. They cannot and they should not stay as they are. But, so far from taking that as an excuse for the white feather, a clear-eyed churchman must surely see it as a critical problem and a challenging opportunity. We cannot permanently evade the problem of the church. Some kind of church or other there is bound to be. If we allow the churches to be dominated by ignorance, bigotry, sectarianism, and a perverted ethic, our entire American society will suffer irreparable loss. Such churches will even put laws on our statute books denying freedom of scientific teaching and in countless ways will hamper freedom, discourage idealism, drive spiritually-minded men into atheism, make religion a byword among the intelligent, and cripple the most hopeful movements of philanthropy and social advance.

To build at the center of American life the right kind of churches, homes of the best spiritual life of our communities, and power houses for human service is a task without the fulfillment of which American life can never develop its possibilities. And the man who must lead in this reconstruction of organized religion is the preacher.

Chapter 7

To Those Interested in the Profession of the Ministry

HARRY EMERSON FOSDICK

THE CHRISTIAN MINISTRY during these next few years cannot reasonably appeal to soft minds desiring a merely conventional profession. The changes immediately ahead are likely to be radical and disturbing. They will, I think, involve the collapse of much of our traditional ecclesiastical organization and program, and the necessity of creating new if our communities are to be adequately churched at all. All this is going to be uncomfortable to formal and stereotyped clergymen. Already, many of them are growing confused and dizzy as the religious situation becomes increasingly chaotic. Under these circumstances, I can think of no more unhappy place than the Christian ministry for a young man who does not belong there.

For men and women, however, who are built of stout timber and who desire above all else to make a spiritual contribution to their generation, the situation in the churches is the more alluring and challenging just because it is so disturbed and fluid. Always the greatest consequences have come out of the most upset situations. The crux of our entire religious problem in America is leadership. The old order is changing, giving place to new, and

---

Note: Reprinted from Lockhard, Earl G. (Ed.): *My Vocation.* New York, H. W. Wilson Co., 1938 pp.251–259.

wherever leaders are present with intelligence and character, the hope of a better day for religion in general and its organizational expressions in particular is keen and buoyant. The call is out for creative personalities who will lay hold on this problem with spiritual insight and constructive statesmanship.

To a youth, therefore, considering the Christian ministry in terms of safety, respectability, salary, and professional routine, I should say, "Stay out." But if a youth is at all responsive to Sir Philip Sidney's advice to his nephew, "Young man, if you see a good fight anywhere you had best get into it," I should commend the ministry to him as the scene of one of the most crucial conflicts in our generation.

This does not mean that pugnacity is the minister's attitude. Not pugnacity but pedagogy is the greatest need. This does mean, however, that to surrender obsolete forms of sectarian organization and program, which have lost their pertinency and power, to reinterpret Christian truths so that this generation can apprehend them and live by them, and to create for our communities centers of spiritual life, which will function seven days a week and be the dynamic source of the best hopes and ideals of the town, require foresight, courage, high-grade ability, and genuine statesmanship.

America has been specializing in the accumulation of things by which to live and has too largely forgotten the spiritual ends for which to live. The old challenge is critically pertinent to America's life today: What shall it profit a man or a nation to gain the whole world and lose the soul? In the meeting of this need our present churches, bound by traditions no longer meaningful and separated into sects that have no pertinence for living problems, are laboring under tremendous handicaps. Nevertheless, the best hopes of the nation still are in them; their people at their best represent a depth of faith and a latent moral power without which nothing worthwhile doing in America is likely to be done. The need is leadership. With the right leaders we can change the nation's spiritual tone in a generation and win victories that at present seem incredible.

To discuss the church problem in America as though it were a question of church or no church is unrealistic. The question is not

To Those Interested in the Profession of the Ministry 71

whether we are to have churches but rather what kind of churches we are to have. This is one of the most important questions that America faces. A nation's homes, schools, and churches are its three basic, deliberate, character-producing agencies. If in this land now all were well with these three agencies, no one can measure how well it would be with our people, and all three of these are inevitable. The family life, the educational life, and the spiritual life of American communities will continue to be organized. The question is whether they will be organized well or ill, efficiently or inefficiently.

Personally, I think that there is bound to be a great mortality among sectarian churches in the next twenty-five to fifty years. The old type of church, centered denominationally in the peculiarities of some sect, has outlived its usefulness and cannot minister to the deepest needs of the American people. As the old type of church dies out, however, a new type comes in. The decisive element in the new kind of church is not sectarianism but the interest of the community. To belong to the whole community, to serve the best life of the entire community, to welcome without regard to denominational lines the finest spiritual life of the community, trying to make the church worthy at least of those signs the electric companies used to put over their stations —PUBLIC SERVICE, LIGHT AND POWER—that idea already is approximated by the best of the churches. The future, I am confident, belongs to it. To the building of such churches the Christian leadership of the days to come is challenged.

As for the basic needs of personal religion and its ethical and social applications, there never was a time when the better sort of people were more conscious of its indispensableness. We are facing one of the most perilous portents in the history of the world, the emergence, that is, of a thoroughly secularized, materialistic civilization implemented by the powerful agencies of scientific invention but losing the abiding spiritual values which alone give to life essential dignity and worth. Whatever may be the attitude of intelligent people toward many traditional elements in religion now grown obsolete, the peril involved in this portent of a completely materialistic and secular society is becoming increasingly evident to thoughtful folk. Here lies the minister's great opportunity. Man does not live by bread alone, and this generation is finding it out. Leadership in the recovery of the abiding spiritual values of life is indispensable. Such is the challenge of the Christian ministry!

PART TWO

Essays on Harry Emerson Fosdick's Preaching

Chapter 8

A Young Preacher Listens to Fosdick

THE REV. SAMUEL H. MILLER *

IT IS TWILIGHT and Sunday. I have been sitting in my home listening to a voice—a voice of prophecy in a land of much preaching. The service is over, the radio is turned off, and I want a little time for meditation, for I am convinced that somehow that voice left me different. I have untangled a snarl in the many skeins of life. I have crossed a barrier into a vaster land. Pent-up energies have been released that were log-jammed by confusion. But how? That interests me as a preacher. If another man does it for me, can I do it for others? Where does the secret of that effectiveness lie by which I am led with such naturalness, as I believe, to be a better man?

To be sure, there is a particular value in a radio service in that it strips worship of every nonessential. There is a limitation to the grandest cathedral, and distraction in the noblest appearance of priest or preacher. Truth needs no accessories when the imagination is untrammeled. Gestures and symbols often become barriers rather than gateways. But a voice and twilight, mind related to mind by thought—this is elemental, spiritual.

Yet this very fact makes it necessary for the thought alone to be responsible for any effectiveness. Fiery gestures, an inspired countenance, vehement emphasis, and charming idiosyncracies are all

---

* Dean of the Harvard Divinity School.
Note: Reprinted from *The Homiletic Review*, CI (February, 1931), pp.114–115.

valueless. Many speakers are engaging with these aids but futile without them. Thanks to radio, violent action can not make up for lack of genuine thought.

Here undoubtedly is one of the sources of Doctor Fosdick's influence. There is such an inherent power of spirit and truth in his preaching that fistic emphasis and grand gestures could add but little. The dynamic is not so much in him as in the thing of which he speaks. Through his clear words I see it plainly. Through the unobstructed channel of his straight thinking I come face to face with it. In the illuminating phrase of Cromwell, "he speaks *things.*"

This genius to reveal a situation or a truth in definite and distinct outline furnishes a wide base for firm spiritual building. To see a thing as it is, to have a hazy experience lifted into conscious clarity, to have a blurred situation put into focus so that its various parts stand out distinctly is one-half the battle of life. To state the problem so that a new light breaks from the clouds and reveals mountainous ideals, treacherous swamps, barren wilderness, and straight paths—this is a ministry of itself.

All this—the reliance upon the thought value rather than upon any oratorical accessories, the revelation of the thing itself, and the focusing of indefinite notions is the foundation of the vaster structure of Doctor Fosdick's fine spiritual service. Having thus cleared the ground and marked the boundaries of further operations, the structure of his sermon rises like a cathedral of pointing pinnacles, thrust and balance, allureness and mellow beauty.

The characteristic constantly impressing me as I listen to Doctor Fosdick's preaching is its utter confidence in the intrinsic power of goodness to produce its like in human life. I am not exhorted, urged, pressed—but the good and the true is unveiled before my eyes that I may see it. My soul leaps up intuitively and finds reality. I take it in, and it becomes mine. Then at last, it is me. I have not been rudely pushed into the sanctuary of a new experience but stimulated and attracted by the dynamic appeal of goodness, beauty, or truth. It is the difference between external pressure and inner motive, between exhortation and explanation.

Exhortation may have its place, but as one looks back to the gospels it becomes plainly evident that John the Baptist was the exhorter and Jesus the explainer; John the preacher and Jesus the teacher; John pointed in frenzy to the kingdom, Jesus helped men attain it; John's preaching thundered with the flail and the ax of God fervidly urging men to repent, Jesus' preaching comprised simple parables revealing and explaining the relationship of God to man and man with man. Certainly no one would ever accuse Jonathan Edwards of being a "milk and water" Christian, yet when he considered the revivalist he wrote such words as these: "The man Christ Jesus, when he was upon earth, had doubtless as great a sense of the infinite greatness and importance of the eternal things and the worth of souls as any have now; but there is not the least appearance in his history of his taking any such course or manner of exhorting others."

Shorn of the external compunction of church or creed, exhortation thus becomes the last resort of those who lack the inner authority of truth. It is close kin to high-pressure salesmanship in the wake of which there is so much regret—and often real tragedy. Souls are put under verbal pressure only to gain relief by escape or acquiescence. Like the guides of European art galleries, preachers may be divided into two classes—those who lead one into the presence of a great masterpiece and then step aside while the soul drinks deep of its beauty and those who stand over one and chatter like magpies in the mad attempt to urge belief in its splendor. For him who has ears to hear and eyes to see, music and mountains, goodness and God are not increased by the empty thunder of much urging. And for him who has no ears to hear it and no eyes to see it, the beauty is not there. Some preachers use their sermons like clubs and beat their listeners into submission, while others use theirs like batons and draw forth melody and sweet sound of which the worshiper never suspected himself capable.

No one ever learns to appreciate fine art by the talkativeness of its devotees, but he can learn to appreciate it if someone explains its symmetry and color. So with the Christian life. Mere exhortation profits little, but an explanation of its balance and design and its heroic colors and royal shadows commends itself at once to understanding. What criminal folly to urge a novice who knows next to nothing of driving an auto to get in and "step on the gas—harder—and harder"! If he is fool enough to do it, the machine roars and bucks and ends in a crash. If he comes out of it alive, his nerves are fagged, and he is determined that no one will ever get him to do it again. That is the very thing much of our preaching does. "Get in," we say, "Be good—be good—better and better," without explaining the process by which such progress can be made. When traffic gets into a snarl and cannot move, stepping on the gas does not help much.

And when all the mixed desires and varied interests of a man's life become tangled and the soul stops, mere exhortation, however moving it may be, will scarcely save the day. The tangle must be unraveled until things move no longer at cross purposes but according to an orderly principle. It is guidance, not more gas, that is wanted.

Doctor Fosdick does this very thing and does it with a surgical precision that defies analysis. Explaining and adjusting concepts and desires and ideals, he brings a new sense of integrity out of inner conflicts and unity from an ill-defined chaos. One rises a better man, not because he was frantically gesticulated at or pummeled with steam-hammer words but because he understood, and understanding, he became. "Ye shall know the truth, and the truth shall make you free."

Surely a young man may be forgiven his feeling of awe as he stands at the beginning of his ministry and hears the preaching of a Fosdick, every sermon a work of art, revealing the spiritual trinity of God in beauty, truth, and goodness. How wisely they start from where people are; what clarity of outline and meaning as they proceed; what an accumulation of content and implication is gained by those repetitive phrases, which begin as particulars but grow until they become symbols of a universal; what simplicity is effected by the visualization of the most abstract principle; what swift, sure applications are made of general truths and moral ideals; and finally, what a clincher is the closing prayer that lifts the whole experience of the sermon into the light of God by a brief sentence or two that drives to the heart of our common need. Others may bemoan the muddle we are in and cry for the good old times, but I thank God I live today, when preaching as best I can, I have the high privilege of tuning in at twilight reverie a voice as clear in meaning as it is distinct in diction that "setteth forth many fair lineaments of divine truth and saith very lofty things touching a perfect life."

Chapter 9

How Dr. Fosdick Uses the Bible in Preaching

(Based on "The Hope of the World")

EUGENE MAY *

FROM HIS SERMONS, even if we knew nothing further about Dr. Fosdick, we could tell that he is a pragmatist in philosophy. This is important to the subject because a pragmatist begins with present experience and tries to understand and interpret that experience by all the resources available. In his sermons one becomes aware that he is taking into consideration the physical, mental, and social elements as factors in the present situation and also the experience of the race. It is in the review of the experience of the race that he comes to the experiences that are recorded in the Bible. He makes selections from this source of experience and shows a high appreciation for it by a wholehearted choice and expression. The validity of the Bible by this approach is in its functional relation to experience and its capacity to make a beneficial difference in the conduct of life.

Dr. Fosdick is scientific, critical, fearless, and honest. While he begins with the immediate and present situation and in his sermons is talking to the needs of people, the first purpose of his sermons is not to please people. His expressions on social issues

---

* Pastor of First Christian Church, Bluefield, West Virginia.
Note: Reprinted from *The Pulpit,* XXI (May, 1950), pp.118–119.

must be irksome to many, as are his pronouncements about war. His method is persuasion, and he does not appeal to authority except the authority of demonstrable truth. And when he quotes from the Bible, he does not assume that these quotations have authority because of their source but because the principle is true and its truth is demonstrable in life now. He would have people come to faith in Jesus as the Son of God not by intellectual acceptance of creed or dogma but as the disciples did—by living with Jesus.

I believe most people reading Dr. Fosdick's sermons would get the idea that he applies Jesus' words, "a little leaven leaveneth the whole lump." However, probably they would also agree that he brings out of the oven a very nice loaf. Curiosity and a desire to be accurate in judging the extent to which he used Biblical material prompted me to keep the following table as I read, which probably is no more accurate than a Gallup poll, and I do not claim too much for it as a method of inquiry. Nevertheless I pass it on as of possible interest: Direct quotation—135; Reference not direct quotation—99; Text used—11; Text but not used—4; No text—2.

I

The 135 direct quotations were well selected and relevant to the subject. The extent of this use of the Bible varied in his sermons from one sermon in which he used 16 direct quotations (*Crucified by Stupidity*) to another in which he used no direct quotations (*Modern Civilization's Crucial Problem*).

The 99 times that he used Biblical language but not in direct quotation were also well selected and relevant to the subject and indicated the natural expression of one who knew and valued the language of the Bible.

There were 11 sermons where it could be said that the main thought came from the text, as in *The Service of Religious Faith to Mental Health* in which this text was used: "For God hath not given us the spirit of fear; but of power, and of love, and of a sound mind." In his sermon *The Conquest of Fear,* he uses a different text for each of the three points. First point, Clean Living, text—"I was afraid . . . and I hid myself"—the words of

Adam when he had transgressed; second point, Faith, text—"I know how to be abased, and I know also how to abound . . . I can do all things through him that strengtheneth me"—words of Paul indicating that his faith was an adequate resource for life; third point, Love, text—"Perfect love casteth out fear."

In his sermon *Christianity More Than Duty—Not Weight But Wings,* he uses as a text, "The bed is shorter than that a man can stretch himself on it; and the covering narrower than that he can wrap himself in it," and the theme of the sermon is that by reducing religion to the least we can get by with, we make ourselves uncomfortable. It seems in this that the theme is the outgrowth of the text or at least that the text was a good choice for the theme.

There were four sermons where, in my opinion, the text was not used or used merely as an illustration, as in *The Soul's Invincible Surmise,* where the subject was taken from Santayana, and the text was, "He endured, as seeing him who is invisible." Although four well-selected quotations are used, the sermon is based on the theory of immortality found in philosophy and not on the Biblical belief in the resurrection or the immortality discourses of Paul.

There were only two where one could definitely say that no text was used, an example of which is *Through the Social Gospel into Personal Religion.* There was one sermon, *The Sermon on the Mount,* that I will call an expository sermon. In it he devoted the major portion of space to interpreting Biblical material.

This leaves eight sermons where I could not form an opinion as to whether or not a text was used. It is obvious that lacking a definite standard in judging the use or the proper use of a text, there would be a wide divergence of opinion as to the extent of its use, and doubtless the author of these sermons, as well as anyone else reading them, would disagree in many instances with the division I have made.

II

Dr. Fosdick uses both quotations and references to Biblical language as illustrations of the idea of the sermon, and in no

How Dr. Fosdick Uses the Bible in Preaching 83

instance did I notice that he used the Bible authoritatively. His hope for acceptance of the ideas advanced seems to be based on their appeal to the reason of the hearer by their basic soundness. He would want the hearer to say that it is true because it is an accurate analysis of the way it has been in my experience.

I have a feeling that the more radical the idea, the more he uses Biblical references, as in the sermon *The Peril of Worshiping Jesus* in which he quotes directly 11 times and makes 6 references to Biblical language, while his average use is $5\frac{1}{2}$ direct quotations and four references.

Dr. Fosdick does not use the Bible merely to justify his own ideas. He is not an apologist for the Bible or for himself. He holds that some of the Bible simply is not relevant to life today and some is outgrown by moral and spiritual progress; but, when he uses it, one has the sense that he is using it fairly and according to the best interpretation possible. Although we know from other sources that he is thoroughly critical in his study of the Bible, there is little evidence in his sermons of dissection. He does not parade the tools with which he works. It is more like a statue being unveiled after the chips are swept up and the tools put away.

On the title page of the book *The Hope of the World,* the author describes what he has endeavored to do in the sermons contained therein by calling it, "Twenty-five Sermons on Christianity Today." I think that is an accurate statement. His dominant concern is with present life and with what he hopes it will become, with Christianity as it operates or could operate to meet the needs of individuals and the social order of today.

It seems obvious to me that he starts with needs and uses the resources of the past, the experience of the race—including the Bible—to meet those needs and to direct life toward ideal ends. These sermons seem to be initiated to a very large degree by the questions asked by living people. I imagine that even as the sermons were prepared in the quiet of his study, the faces of these people appeared before the typewriter and their anxieties and comments entered into the writing. In meeting these needs, he has used the Bible to a surprising extent. While he quotes from

Shakespeare, Emerson, Lincoln, Shaw, Stevenson, Karl Marx, and others, his quotations from all combined would not approach the extent of space that he gives to quoting the Bible.

In addition to the uses of the Bible listed under specific uses in the foregoing paragraphs, he makes a large use of essentially Biblical ideas such as his statement that "a vital Christian faith . . . confers on one resources of inner, spiritual power" (p.173). He says in another book (*Living Under Tension,* p.7), "The more the temporal outweights the eternal in any statement, especially in a sermon, the less permanence its message has. . . . The church of Christ has a special function, (and) ought to be more than the voice of any government or the echo of any popular opinion and passion." In order to approach these ideals in preaching he uses essentially Biblical ideas.

III

Dr. Fosdick cannot be accused of bibliolatry or literalism. In his opposition to war, he appeals to the life and spirit of Jesus rather than to a text quoted as dogma. In the sermon *Six Ways to Tell Right From Wrong,* he does not name the Bible as one of the six ways but did advise, as one test, that conduct be carried before the most admired personality—the Man of Galilee. He says (p.147) that the Bible cannot always be taken literally but that it should be taken seriously.

I believe that Dr. Fosdick prefers to be a guide into unborn tomorrow rather than a merchant of dead yesterdays, that he cares more about new ideas than he does about conformity to custom, that he cares more about the world as it should be than he does about conformity to it as it is, and that he cares more about the people whom he is teaching than he does about the subject he is trying to teach. And feeling this way, he sees the Bible not only as the greatest instrument for influencing people in a helpful way but also as an unique instrument.

We know that thousands of people both in his church and on the air hear him gladly. I believe that one who hears him would say, "This man knows people, knows me, knows God, knows what it's all about," rather than "He knows his Bible." But if they gave it serious further thought, they would see that in the natural and unobtrusive way in which he uses the Bible, he knows it too and loves it. They would turn to him in trouble and find him a source of strength and faith. In his messages the authority of the Bible and the authority of experience to evaluate and direct life are happily blended. It seems that for Dr. Fosdick the past is water behind the boat against which the rudder pushes; experience is the energy and the prow dividing the waters of the present. He manages to use the two in progress toward the more abundant life.

Chapter 10

Harry Emerson Fosdick and Reinhold Niebuhr: A Contrast in the Methods of the Teaching Preacher

ERDMAN HARRIS [*]

THIS PAPER must begin with an acknowledgment of the respect and affection which the writer holds for both Harry Emerson Fosdick and Reinhold Niebuhr. The writer realizes that both men have made inestimable contributions to the religious life of this generation. He believes that an analysis of their methods of work should be helpful to any engaged in the task of preaching and teaching today. He is interested not only in the *why* and the *what* of religious instruction but also in the *how*. His contention is that the two men under discussion represent an interesting *contrast* in their approach to the problem of the public presentation of Christianity and that others may learn how to secure more effective results by an examination of that contrast. It goes without saying that the methods employed by each man *are* extraordinarily effective. It would be foolish to try to imitate either. One can learn from another not by copying but by having his attention called to certain principles of study, style, or

---

[*] Chairman of the Department of Religion, Lawrenceville School, Lawrenceville, New Jersey.

Note: Reprinted from *Religion in Life*, Vol. 12 (1942–1943), pp.389–400.

A Contrast in the Methods of the Teaching Preacher 87

delivery. One can learn from Fosdick and Niebuhr to be, more effectively, himself.

This paradox is true in the musical realm. The composer Saint-Saens could imitate the style of his predecessors and contemporaries so felicitously that he could fool most of his listeners into believing that they were actually hearing unfamiliar compositions by Bach, Mozart, Beethoven, or Brahms. He knew the methods by which they gained their effects—but he also could compose in his own right. Actually, his knowledge of other composers helped him to be *original*, to compose soundly and successfully. The landscape painters of Canada, formerly known as the Group of Seven, learned much from each other and belonged to a single school—though the work of each is creative and original and can be distinguished by those at all familiar with the work of the group.

Furthermore, as we shall see, the contrast between the methods of Fosdick and Niebuhr is not so sharp but that we can find Niebuhrian accents in Fosdick and Fosdickian accents in Niebuhr, and where the two men differ, one feels like echoing Niebuhr's dedication of "Beyond Tragedy" to Sherwood Eddy and William Scarlett: "There are diversities of gifts but the same spirit. And there are differences of administrations but the same Lord!" And I think Niebuhr borrowed that from someone else.

To make my problem simpler, I am not primarily contrasting the message of Fosdick with the message of Niebuhr. On the matter of their message, one thing ought to be recognized. As one reads their books afresh, as I have done recently, he is impressed with the balance and comprehensiveness of their Christian witness. Both have an unusually full-orbed gospel. Neither is really one-sided. Listen to this passage:

"Essential human nature is much the same wherever it is found, and it is as false and dangerous to glorify the proletariat as it is to play sycophant to the privileged. Sin is 'no respecter of persons.' Its demonic, corrupting power runs through all classes, and no realistic mind can suppose virtue to be preponderant in any special group, even the downtrodden." Who said that? That was spoken by Doctor Fosdick in 1936.

"When our class is favored, when it receives support and distinction from the *status quo,* we are almost irresistibly tempted to mass and marshal our thought in support of it. *Most of our thinking about social questions is done not individually or rationally but by pressure of class interests.*" That is Doctor Fosdick again.

"This unescapable fact, which again and again in Christian history has called modernism to its senses, we face: we cannot harmonize Christ Himself with modern culture. What Christ does to modern culture is to challenge it." Fosdick again; and in case anyone should think that all of this side of his thinking has been called out by the overwhelming bitterness of these latter years, listen to this, spoken in 1921:

"We are handling the same unescapable experience out of which the old doctrine of original sin first came, we are dealing with the same fundamental fact which Paul was facing when he said: 'As in Adam all die': that humanity's sinful nature is not something which you and I alone make up by individual deeds of wrong but that it is an inherited mortgage and handicap on the whole human family."

Now listen to this, by way of contrast:

"Modern humanism was as truly religious in some of its affirmations as in some of its criticisms. It affirmed that men possessed a common humanity in their common needs. That great spirit of early humanism, Shakespeare, expresses this idea perfectly in the mouth of Shylock: 'Hath not a Jew eyes? Hath not a Jew hands, organs, dimensions, senses, affections, passions; fed by the same food, hurt with the same weapons, subject to the same diseases, healed by the same means, warmed and cooled by the same winter and summer, as a Christian is? If you prick us do we not bleed? If you tickle us do we not laugh? If you poison us do we not die, and if you wrong us shall we not have revenge?' High cultural elaborations, including religious ones, are always in danger of forgetting this simple fact. It is not only 'in Christ,' that is ultimately, that men are one; they are one immediately in creation. 'God has made of one blood all the nations of men.'" That is Professor Niebuhr in 1936.

Or again: "It makes a difference whether men are good or evil and whether they do good or evil. In spite of all moral relativism we know fairly well what good and evil are. Utilitarian moral schemes may justify egotism to a larger degree than the gospel ethic. But there is no system of morals which does not in some way or other give moral preference to the other-regarding rather than the self-regarding act. We know that it is good to restrain the sinful tendency of the self—to live its life at the expense of other life—and to strengthen the impulses by which it is bound to other life. Love is the law of life and not merely some transcendent ideal of perfection." That is Professor Niebuhr again. And this and kindred passages should be sufficient to meet the strictures made by a critic that Niebuhr tends to minimize the moral distinctions among men in the interests of his main contention that all men stand equally under the judgment of a righteous and holy God. The trouble is that too many critics of both Fosdick and Niebuhr make up their minds on the basis of certain isolated and colorful utterances and do not take the trouble to study the complete architecture of their thought, which appears when one studies the nine major books of Niebuhr and the eighteen works of Harry Emerson Fosdick.

That is all I shall write about the specific moral and theological content of their approach. I am more interested here in examining their methods. And here we do find some interesting contrasts. Let us examine *two* of them.

We may approach the first through a study of one difference between Shakespeare and Ibsen as dramatists. Just for fun the other evening, I reread the long article on Shakespeare in the *Encyclopedia Britannica*. Shakespeare apparently had this in common with Gilbert and Sullivan and most preachers, that he wrote to meet a deadline. But that has nothing to do with the one simple point I have in mind. My point is that as far as we can gather, Shakespeare himself was not so much interested in suggesting interpretations of life and culture radically different from those who saw his plays. He wrote, in this order apparently, *Romeo and Juliet, Hamlet, Othello, Lear* and *Macbeth,* to name just five tragedies, including the four major ones. Those five tragedies are, of course, a mine of apt quotations. There is, however, no evidence that Shakespeare tried to challenge the basic assumptions of the most farsighted of his Elizabethan audience. People came to *Othello* for the most part believing that jealousy was a bad thing. Shakespeare set that conviction before them in such matchless form that people were even more convinced than before that their own half-formed or unconsciously accepted standards were true. I all but vowed the last time I saw *Othello* that I never wanted to see it again. I always have a peculiar feeling as I witness the play that I may lose control of myself in the closing moments and, seeing Othello approach Desdemona's bed to strangle her, will rise in the audience and cry: "Stop! you fool, she isn't guilty! Investigate Iago." Shakespeare, in one sense, was a teacher, but largely because he set forth familiar ideas in a new and convincing form. And in this connection a wise remark was made by Albert Schweitzer when he said: "Just as a tree brings forth each year the same leaves but leaves which are forever new, so must all permanently useful ideas be born again in thought."

Ibsen's dramatic method was different because his intent was different. If Shakespeare could count on 90 percent of his audience's agreement with his basic assumptions, Ibsen could count on 90 percent disagreement when his plays were first produced. What Ibsen did was to challenge the assumptions of his Victorian audience head-on.

One can see this clearly by rereading *A Doll's House* or *Ghosts* or *An Enemy of the People*. In *The Wild Duck* Ibsen takes a fling at the idea that honesty of speech is the best policy and shows how (or tries to show how) a marriage which was proceeding successfully on the basis of a closed closet containing a figurative skeleton was spoiled and embittered by opening the closet and viewing the skeleton. Ibsen's ideas do not seem particularly shocking to us today. But they did in his day. They might not have been so shocking at certain earlier epochs, but they were in his own time. His primary teaching device was to startle his hearers out of their complacency and persuade them to examine the assumptions on which they had been proceeding.

This dramatic contrast fails to do justice to analogous contrasts in preaching in that all preachers are propagandists whereas some dramatists are not. But the application to preaching is this: some

A Contrast in the Methods of the Teaching Preacher 91

ministers are chiefly intent in their sermons on getting their hearers to take the ideals which they already believe in verbally but which they have placed temporarily in cold storage and get them out of cold storage, warm them up, and use them again. Other preachers are chiefly intent upon showing that the ideals and ideas by which people have been nourishing their lives must themselves be modified or scrapped. Every preacher worth his salt uses *both methods,* but if one examines the bulk of a minister's utterances you will usually find that he considers his task chiefly the one or the other.

In spite of the fact that Doctor Fosdick has been a champion for many advanced and sometimes unpopular causes, the bulk of his preaching has been devoted to the task of challenging his congregations to make certain ideals and ideas, which they hold in cold storage or to which they give mere lip service, or which they know are a part of the rich Christian heritage, genuinely ruling in their hearts. One of the best examples of this type of preaching is to be found in a sermon entitled "The Cross and the Ordinary Man: a Palm Sunday Sermon," which appears in a collection entitled *Successful Christian Living* and published in 1937. It is a remarkably cogent sermon. Here is a paragraph from the introduction to it:

> This morning we seek some element in the experience of the cross so universal that it must be real to us in our daily life. Note, then, that what Jesus did when He went to the cross was something that no one could have required of Him. No laws could be passed coercing a man to sacrifice himself like that, and were such laws passed they could not be enforced. In going to the cross Jesus was taking on Himself something that no one could demand. He was moving—that is, in the great realm of unenforceable obligations.

Doctor Fosdick then tells the story of a wireless operator who kept at his post on a burning ship far beyond the time which could have been required of him even by the high tradition of the sea and tells of his saying, "I intend to stand by my post"—a decision which no one could have demanded of him. The sermon proceeds: "Even our ordinary life is pretty much made up of two things: enforceable and unenforceable obligations, on the one side, conduct that the laws of court or custom can demand; and on the other, the ways of living that no laws and no codes of custom ever can require." Doctor Fosdick quotes Lord Moulton's appeal to the English people: "The greatness of a nation lies in the number of its citizens who can be trusted to obey self-imposed law."

Now this concept is perfectly simple. When it is stated, it is immediately accepted by any intelligent person. The genius of the sermon is that it illustrates and drives home this generalization by thirteen of the most cogent examples any preacher could collect and sends many of the congregation out with the consciousness that they have not been faithful in their obedience to unenforceable laws and the conviction that they ought to do better. It is a fine specimen of what one might call without misunderstanding, as I have defined it, a Shakespearean sermon. Twenty-four of the twenty-five sermons in the volume, *Successful Christian Living,* are more or less of this character.

Reinhold Niebuhr is much more akin to Ibsen. While Harpers was publishing Doctor Fosdick's *Successful Christian Living,* Scribners was publishing Professor Niebuhr's *Beyond Tragedy,* a collection of fifteen essays based upon sermons preached during the few years immediately preceding 1937. These volumes are, therefore, contemporaneous. As one studies the fifteen chapters of *Beyond Tragedy,* he is bound to be impressed by the difference in approach. None of them can be summarized by a simple, reasonable, understandable aphorism. None of them involve what I have called the Shakespearean technique of taking a theme which many would assume as true and then bringing it home with vividness and poignancy. Especially at the time they were delivered, these sermons challenged the fundamental assumptions on which modern Christians were basing their world view and their way of living. To numbers of listeners the sermons were provoking, not to say startling or shocking. Their keynote is the *paradox,* and the first sermon begins with this sentence: "Among the paradoxes with which St. Paul describes the character, the vicissitudes and the faith of the Christian ministry, the phrase 'as deceivers, yet true' is particularly intriguing."

Niebuhr then proceeds to say that every apologist for Christianity teaches the truth by deception. The hearers say, "What is that again?" Niebuhr maintains that "We are deceivers yet true when we say that God created the world." Later he says: "We are deceivers yet true when we say that men fell into evil." Later on still he says: "We are deceivers yet true when we declare that Christ will come again at the last judgment." He clarifies considerably what he means by all this, but his explanations sometimes irritate and provoke a modern man whose desire is to make his philosophy of life reasonable to himself and others. Niebuhr then proceeds, in the other sermons, to challenge, one by one, many of the affirmations of a liberally trained college graduate. Often he appears to go too far. His transvaluation of values seems too radical. The whole volume is a remarkable example of what I might define as Ibsenian preaching.

If someone says that Doctor Fosdick has also, in his day, done his share of Ibsenian preaching, I will admit there is much truth in this. Doctor Fosdick has, at various times, taken up the cudgels for ideas which were unpopular at the moment to his hearers. He fought valiantly for the freedom of biblical criticism against the literalists. He has preached a social gospel which caused some listeners to brand him as pink if not red. I have heard him defend Prohibition during Prohibition to a congregation by no means universally sympathetic. But his famous sermon on "Shall the Fundamentalists Win?" was preached to a congregation which very largely agreed with him. And the overwhelming bulk of his homiletical work has been Shakespearean rather than Ibsenian. Parenthetically, it is interesting to note that both Doctor Fosdick and Dr. Niebuhr are chiefly interested in expounding the Christian tradition. They both believe that the minister's main task is to help people place themselves intelligently and consciously in the Christian stream of thought and life. Both are thoroughly steeped in the tradition they are eager to see carried on and enriched. As I understand the situation, however, Doctor Fosdick is convinced that many of the products of modern thought—especially in the realm of science—have a useful contribution to make to any full-orbed gospel for the modern world; Doctor Niebuhr is not so sure. Or, if Niebuhr, because of the breadth of his thought were willing to admit this up to a point in private conversation and at moments in his writing, he nevertheless stresses those places where even the best in modern thought has derailed the religious thinking of the modern man. Thus, we find that what I have called the predominantly Shakespearean character of Doctor Fosdick's thought and method stems partly from his progressivism, whereas the predominantly Ibsenian character of Niebuhr's thought and method stems partly from his traditionalism, or from his desire to see what he regards as the basic insights of biblical and traditional Christianity recovered and restated as a challenge to modern thought.

Let me set forth a *second* contrast between the techniques of Doctor Fosdick and Doctor Niebuhr as teaching preachers. In the early 1900's Doctor Fosdick worked in a Bowery mission. Percy Hayward, who wrote a biographical sketch of him for a symposium, maintains that this experience helped to teach him the habit of expressing himself simply and clearly. Whether this be the case or no, one of the outstanding characteristics of Doctor Fosdick as both a teacher and a preacher is his crystal clarity. He can say all sayable things and express all expressible things more succinctly than almost any other preacher alive. His lectures on the "Modern Use of the Bible" are models of forthright, closely knit style. Take, for example, the second paragraph of this exceedingly influential book:

> To more ministers than one likes to think, the use of the Bible is a difficult enigma. Some reveal this by avoiding wide areas of the Scripture altogether. All the king's horses and all the king's men could hardly drag them into dealing with certain passages that used to be the glory of our fathers' preaching. Others make their embarrassment clear by their use of texts—no longer treasuries of truth from which they draw the substance of their message but convenient pegs on which they hang a collection of their own thoughts. Others reveal their discomfort and confusion when they try to discuss biblical problems, such as miracles. They are ill at ease in handling these scriptural categories, reminding one of a comment which Longfellow once made on a preacher: 'I could not tell what he was driving at, except that he seemed desirous not to offend the congregation.' Still other preachers cut the Gordian knot by practically surrendering the Bible as the inspiration of their thought and teaching, save as by courtesy they use it in some oblique and cursory fashion to point a moral, or adorn a tale.

No one has put that problem more clearly; the care taken to make the verbiage come out clean and apt is characteristic of Doctor Fosdick's entire written work.

A Contrast in the Methods of the Teaching Preacher

Let us take a passage in which he is trying to explain a difficult point:

> Christ was human, and He must be divine in what sense He can be divine, being assuredly human. Many moderns do not know that throughout its early history the Church fought some of its most serious theological battles to maintain its hold on this humanness of Jesus. Suppose I should say that Docetism was an early heresy that nearly tore the Church asunder and that it concerned who Jesus was. Would you not naturally suppose that the Docetists must have doubted His deity? Upon the contrary, they asserted that He was God but they did not believe that He was man. They said that He only seemed to be born with a body, to possess flesh and blood, to suffer and to die. And the Church fought the Docetists tooth and nail and drove them out. Were I to say that a heretic, Apollinaris, convulsed the Church with his idea of Jesus' nature, would you not suppose that he must have doubted His deity? Upon the contrary, he asserted that, but he denied that Jesus had a human soul and a human will, and the Church withstood him and cast him out. Throughout the early centuries some of the most serious battles in the Church were fought in the endeavor to keep a firm hold on the real humanity of Jesus.

Doctor Fosdick goes on to ask what, then, the divinity of Jesus means and he answers: "In the first place, it is an assertion primarily not about Jesus, but about God." He then illustrates this point, follows it with the assertion, "In the second place, it is also an affirmation about Jesus." After setting this forth with exceedingly apt illustrations, he ends, "Finally, the divinity of Jesus is an affirmation not only about God and about Jesus, but about man." The whole sermon is a clear statement of what a clear-headed and reverent liberal may believe about Christ.

Now let us turn to Niebuhr's sermonic presentation of some of the same concepts:

> The idea of eternity entering time is intellectually absurd. This absurdity is proved to the the hilt by all the theological dogmas which seek to make it rational. The dogmas which seek to describe the relation of God the Father (the God who does not enter history) and God the Son (the God of history) all insist that the Son is equal to the Father and yet not equal to Him. In the same way all doctrines of the two natures of Christ assert that He is not less divine for being human and temporal and not less human and temporal for being fully divine. Quite obviously it is impossible to assert that the eternal ground of existence has entered existence and not sacrificed its eternal and unconditioned quality without outraging every canon of reason

Reason may deal with the conditional realities of existence in their relationships, and it may even point to the fathomless depth of creativity out of which existential forms are born. But it cannot assert that the Divine Creator has come into creation without losing His unconditioned character. The truth that the Word was made flesh outrages all the canons by which truth is usually judged. Yet it is the truth. The whole character of the Christian religion is involved in that affirmation. It asserts that God's Word is relevant to human life. It declares that an event in history can be of such a character as to reveal the character of history itself.

Later on, Niebuhr preaches:

In Christian thought Christ is both the perfect man, 'the second Adam,' who had restored the perfection of what man was and ought to be; and the Son of God who transcends all the possibilities of human life. It is this idea which theology sought to rationalize in the doctrines of the two natures of Christ. It cannot be rationalized, yet it is a true idea. . . . . There is no sharp line between the infinity in man and the infinity beyond man, and yet there is a very sharp line. Man always remains a creature, and his sin arises from the fact that he is not satisfied to remain so. He seeks to turn creatureliness into infinity, whereas his salvation depends upon subjecting his creaturely weakness to the infinite good of God. Christ, who expresses both the infinite possibilities of love in human life and the infinite possibilities beyond human life, is thus a true revelation of the total situation in which life stands.

Niebuhr is sometimes misunderstood, but in passages like this it is not misunderstanding but understanding at all that is the problem of the average listener. When studied, Niebuhr's idea becomes clear. Heard, it does not convey a clear idea. But it is a characteristic of the man to make few concessions to the listener. And the approach has this to be said for it, that as the preacher is dealing with a complex and ultimately unstatable series of concepts, it is unwise to try to simplify because such simplification easily becomes oversimplification. Doctor Fosdick has been accused of oversimplification, but there is at least this to be said, that he gives his listeners a clear concept of something sublime which though in Niebuhr's terms may be a deception, nevertheless helps to shed as much light as the individual can receive upon the problems of theology.

In the realm of painting we have a similar problem. Reality is complex. The artist must always select. The Dutch painters set forth their conception of life and character with simple clarity. The modern French painters used their pigmentation to suggest the almost infinite complexity of the scene they were trying to capture. The Dutch artists had neat, tidy, reasonable minds. The French painters were far too impressed with the inexpressibility of their subjects to bring their paintings into sharp focus. Who can say that the one approach is better than the other? Alexander Pope expressed truths clearly by a rigid and meticulous process of careful exclusion, so that his lines have the character of sculpture, and one can hardly imagine how they could be phrased in any other way:

> Vice is a creature of such frightful mien
> As to be hated needs but to be seen,
> But, seen too oft, familiar with her face,
> We first endure, then pardon, then embrace.

Clear, curt, complete! T. S. Eliot not so, in much of his writing. Most modern anthologies carry many stanzas which suggest far more than they express or give one a sense of the rational insolubility of life's problems.

So some lecturers and preachers are not happy unless they can make the difficult more easy and the obscure clear. Doctor McGiffert, of Union Seminary, had this capacity to a high degree. Other preachers and lecturers are so anxious that their hearers shall not think that a problem is settled when it is clearly analyzed and a reasonable formula for its solution suggested that they tend to leave their expression only slightly less confusing than reality itself. Both tendencies have their own peculiar dangers, as well as their obvious virtues.

I should like to venture this as a general comment on the subject: The test of all preaching and teaching is what happens to the listener or student as a result. Something or other must happen. Occasionally nothing does because there has been no active response. A lecture or a sermon must be interesting—I hesitate to say entertaining, but at least interesting. After interest has been aroused and a line of thought presented, the point of the talk should be made clearly enough so that the hearer can tell someone else about it afterwards. More important, a sermon or lecture should live on in the memory, for a while at least, and challenge the one who heard to think about it from time to time.

Occasionally, however, a lecture or a sermon is given which sets in motion a discussion that lasts for a considerable period. The speaker may not have been as clear as one usually expects a speaker to be; he makes his hearers reach up, he puzzles them, he intrigues them, and he leaves it to others to help clarify some of the points raised.

When Professor Niebuhr spoke at the Lawrenceville School, there were two reports published in the school paper, one a news item and the other a column headed "The Man Who Came to Chapel." The column began: "To a large part of Lawrenceville, Professor Niebuhr's lecture at first seemed to be an amazing plunge into profundity which elicited much interest and less comprehension." It ended with the statement: "Regardless of what can be proved, the lecture gave us a hefty piece of something to chew on." The columnist, however, did get many of the important points of the lecture and said, in passing: "To the extent to which the speaker was hard to understand, however, he indirectly complimented his audience by refusing to elucidate every point (a process which some may have found almost too extensively used by the preceding speaker in the series)."

It is said that an embryonic composer once came to Mozart to ask him how to write a symphony. Mozart replied that he did not think it wise for a novice to start with a symphony but rather with something less ambitious, possibly some ballet music. "But," the man protested, "you wrote a symphony yourself when you were thirteen." "Yes," responded Mozart, "but I did not have to ask anyone how to do it." There are many things in life which cannot be taught. I do not suppose that one can really teach another to preach. One can guide the development of a learner as a coach does, but one cannot even make a tennis player by teaching him merely the proper methods of hitting the ball. That is one of the great difficulties in a department of education, which is designed to teach teachers to teach.

One has to work out his own method, at the long last, so that what he does represents himself doing the best of which he is capable. But just as a composer may stimulate his creative faculties by acquaintance with the counterpoint of Bach and the orchestration of Brahms, so may preachers and teachers learn more about their work by studying the work of others. And of those whose work furnishes such a rewarding study, the men whom I have been discussing may, in my opinion, be listed very close to the top.

Chapter 11

Harry Emerson Fosdick: Realist and Idealist

EDGAR DEWITT JONES

THE MOST PREEMINENT PULPIT of the Christian faith in America, if not the world, is that of Dr. Harry Emerson Fosdick in Riverside Church, New York City. Given a ten-million-dollar cathedral, complete to the smallest detail, occupying a commanding site on a magnificent boulevard, a dynamic personality, possessing homiletic genius of a high order, safeguarded and empowered for the most efficient use of his preaching talent—and the possibilities stagger the imagination. Given another factor, the backing of a multimillionaire, John D. Rockefeller, Jr., by name, and no strings or conditions attached, but on the other hand the full liberty of prophesying—given these and you have the most extraordinary preaching opportunity of modern times.

Millions knew Dr. Fosdick through his books before the world knew him through his pulpit achievements. Those little volumes, *The Meaning of Prayer, The Meaning of Faith, The Meaning of Service, The Manhood of the Master,* and *The Challenge of the Present Crisis,* had a ministry all their own, vital and inspiring. The writing of these books was something more than the preparation of manuscripts—a great man was in training for a mighty service. Baptist though he is, and of course an independent, Fosdick became the minister of First Presbyterian Church, New York

---

Note: Reprinted with permission from *American Preachers of Today.* Indianapolis, Bobbs-Merrill Co., Inc., 1933, pp.26–37.

City, whereupon his pulpit fame grew apace. His sermon entitled "Shall the Fundamentalists Win?" produced the livest kind of controversy. The newspapers gave the subject much space and played it up to the fullest. The denominational journals turned a barrage of criticism on the preacher, all of which but contributed to Dr. Fosdick's reputation and provided a sounding board that made his every utterance the more distinct and sent his name the world around.

As a preacher Dr. Fosdick combines realism with idealism. His pulpit material is modern, and he has the courage to use accepted facts in Biblical criticism, sociology, and economics. His power of clear statement is probably unexcelled in the American pulpit today. He can take a theme, say an appraisal of modern Protestantism, and in a series of pungent paragraphs bare to the bone every weakness, uncover and expose every blemish of organized Christianity, so that when he finishes there seems nothing left worth preserving. As you listen, you become alarmed, apprehensive, indignant. You say to yourself, "This man has gone too far; he has given his case away." You are humiliated and chagrined, when lo! Fosdick begins an assessment of the world's debt to Protestantism and what remains that is of priceless value and marshals brilliantly the reasons for conserving the same. He becomes constructive; the man speaks with the fire of the crusader. Your heart beats faster, your cheeks are warm, something stirs within you in response to the preacher, and you feel that a real discipleship of Jesus Christ in these modern days is the mightiest challenge and the grandest thing in the world.

Listening to Dr. Fosdick, you do not think of the orator or the rhetorician. Yet his sermons are powerful and the result of painstaking toil. He does not go in for polish and literary beauty as does Joseph Fort Newton or Frederick F. Shannon. He does not range over so wide a field as Cadman, nor has he the charm of conversational eloquence of a Jefferson. He has not the serenity of a Gaius Glenn Atkins, nor the epigrammatical fire of Lynn Harold Hough. He is an able speaker who makes few gestures, talks right on and always to the point; comes to close grips with life; uses effectively illustrations taken not from books solely but from the daily experiences of men and women as they meet pain, disappointment and temptation. He is never *detached* or *remote* in his preaching. It is difficult to think of Fosdick as ever vague or *mystical*. No hangovers of theology trouble him, no traditions weigh him down. He is a free man in a free pulpit. Physically there is nothing extraordinary about him, yet he is an arresting personality. His hair, once so abundant, is beginning to thin a little but still stands up like a mop. Dr. Fosdick exudes vitality. Much worn as the word is, *dynamic* best describes the man and his preaching.

How did Dr. Fosdick become the great preacher he is? By the hardest kind of work, unceasing, laborious toil, painstaking industry. For thirty years, approximately, since the days of his first pastorate in Montclair, New Jersey, he has spent the mornings of five days a week in his study. No messages get to him there, no telephone calls can reach him, no visitors are admitted. In such seclusion he "toils terribly" over his sermons. This long practice, self-discipline, persistent, purposeful life program, is the answer to the question, how did Fosdick become the great preacher he is?

Does he do any pastoral work? Practically none; in fact, he regards social visitation as a waste of precious time. But he responds to urgent requests from ill and ailing parishioners who ask to see him personally. He writes numerous notes of commendation for services rendered, remembers to do the courteous deed in person where no one could represent him or serve by proxy. Yet he is jealous of his time, duplicates no service, makes no unnecessary motion, is as finely disciplined as the head of a mammoth bank or industry but keeps human, simple, patient, long-suffering.

Outside demands would crush this preacher if he permitted a tithe of them to sap his time and vitality. He goes from his pulpit only four times during the active preaching year and then to speak at various colleges in the country where he feels there is a special reason for his appearance. Yet Dr. Fosdick is not a scholarly recluse. He is accessible to those who have need to see him. The chinks of his busy afternoons are filled by carefully scheduled appointments, made at fifteen-minute intervals. Many of his evenings are spent with the organizational life of his church. Here he keeps in close and vital touch with the body of his congregation,

Harry Emerson Fosdick: Realist and Idealist

assisted of course by an efficient and personable staff of expert associates, secretaries, and staff visitors. He takes long and restful vacations, which are, however, devoted to reading, study, and writing.

The budget of the Riverside Church is a wonder—both in its planning and carrying out is indeed worthy of the most carefully directed business concern in the country. Here is an institution that balances its budget even in hard times. True, owing to the depression, the budget of Riverside Church for May 1, 1932, to April 30, 1933, was decreased 100 thousand dollars, but nevertheless it totals 322 thousand dollars. Nor is this all: this budget is balanced to a penny between current expenses and benevolences and missions; thus, 161 thousand dollars for self and 161 thousand dollars for others—the ideal that thousands of churches everywhere have dreamed about but few attained. Dr. Fosdick preaches an annual budget sermon which in its own way is as pungent and masterful as any of his famous discourses that are heard by throngs and widely circulated through various publications.

I asked the Rev. Eugene C. Carder, Dr. Fosdick's able associate, to give me a *close-up* of the minister of Riverside Church. He told me that it was a joy for him to stress his admiration for Dr. Fosdick as minister, first, last, and all the time, assuring me that he never deviates from the main track, which is preaching. The heart of what Dr. Carder said in praise and interpretation of Dr. Fosdick is compressed in this most revealing paragraph:

> The more I see of this man, the more convinced I am that he is essentially a conservative. He does not now nor never has owned an automobile. That is not due primarily to the fact that he lives in New York where taxicabs are to be had on every corner. Few New Yorkers have resisted the temptation to join the great majority and buy a car some time or other. He just is not susceptible to the influence of the crowd. A circumstance connected with the furnishing of his study and its present equipment amuses me every time I go in there to talk with him. I was chairman of the committee that furnished the building here and had a hand in selecting all of the furnishings, furniture, lamps, and so forth, in his study. In due course the desk was set in place and the equipment put on it, bookcases arranged, table, and what-not. He has been working in that study for two years now and insofar as I can see there hasn't been a thing moved an inch from the place where it was put when we first set the room up. He simply moved in on top of

the furniture we had placed there and went to work. Mr. Gandhi achieves his reputation for not being dependent upon things by divesting himself of all things, even his clothes. Dr. Fosdick achieves an even more significant independence of things by sitting down in the midst of all kinds of things, of everything he could possibly want, and proving himself to be absolutely independent of them by altogether ignoring them and doing his work, doing his work not because of them but in spite of them. From this point of view, he is the most independent spirit I have ever known. I confess he is a great challenge to me at this particular point.

I put the inevitable question to Dr. Fosdick, "How do you prepare your sermons?" He answered with pithy brevity: "I choose a subject early in the week, work on it hard, think about it all I can, write it out in full, draw off an outline of it for Sunday morning, and do as well as I can, talking from the outline."

Asked his opinion of present-day preaching, Dr. Fosdick placed in my hands a reprint of his article from *Harper's Magazine* of July, 1928—"What is the Matter with Preaching?"*—saying, "This will give you my idea about sermons, what they are for, and how to get at them." This pamphlet is solid stuff, made luminous by the use of short staccato sentences, direct and unconventional statements; the whole atmosphered with a buoyant enthusiasm for the preacher's task. Reading and reflecting on this treatise, for such it is, I speculated on the great good that might be accomplished if a copy could be put in the hands of every young man in America who is thinking of the ministry as a career. Two paragraphs, only, do I quote, but they are sufficient to indicate the style and the passion of the author and something of the tang he has imparted to type.

> Throughout this paper we have held up the ideal of preaching as an interesting operation. That is a most important matter, not only to the audience but to the man in the pulpit. The number of fed-up, fatigued, bored preachers is appalling. Preaching has become to them a chore. They have to 'get up' a sermon, perhaps two sermons, weekly. They struggle at it. The juice goes out of them as the years pass. They return repeatedly to old subjects and try to whip up enthusiasm over weatherbeaten texts and themes. Their discourses sink into formality. They build conventional sermon outlines, fill them in with conven-

---

* See Chapter 2.

tional thoughts, and let it go at that. Where is the zest and thrill with which in their chivalrous youth they started out to be ministers of Christ to the spiritual life of their generation?

Of course, nothing can make preaching easy. At best it means drenching a congregation with one's life blood. But while, like all high work, it involves severe concentration, toil, and self-expenditure, it can be so exhilarating as to recreate in the preacher the strength it takes from him, as good agriculture replaces the soil it uses. Whenever that phenomenon happens, one is sure to find a man predominantly interested in personalities and what goes on inside of them. He has understood people, their problems, troubles, motives, failures, and desires, and in his sermons he has known how to handle their lives so vitally that week after week he has produced real changes. People have habitually come up after the sermon not to offer some bland compliment but to say: 'How did you know I was facing that problem only this week?', or 'We were discussing that very matter at dinner last night,' or best of all, 'I think you would understand my case—may I have a personal interview with you?'

Somebody has said that Dr. Cadman is preaching to people over sixty, Fosdick to those over forty, and Niebuhr to those in their middle twenties. A statement of this kind needs to be qualified, and yet there is something in it. If Fosdick's appeal is to middle life instead of flaming youth, then I should say that those in mid-channel who continue to hear or read Fosdick will find it difficult to think complacently the thoughts they used to think and are due for a rebirth at a period when most people are in a mental groove. I incline to the belief, however, that Fosdick, as was Beecher, is able to preach to all ages with almost equal power.

Has Dr. Fosdick no critics? What a foolish question. Anybody who ever does anything and does it especially well is a fair target. The very fact that he has achieved unusual prominence, and in his own field preeminence, would guarantee a crop of critics. But quite apart from the captious and the chronic critic, there are of course the extremely conservative churchmen who look upon the minister of Riverside Church not as a rebel-saint but just a rebel. There are a few also among the radicals in the ministry who are disposed to chide Dr. Fosdick for not being radical enough. Some who read this will recall a rather caustic article in the *Christian Century* by the venturesome Reinhold Niebuhr entitled, "How

Adventurous Is Dr. Fosdick?"—a play of course upon the latter's book, *Adventurous Christianity*. Another case at point is Mr. Douglas Bush's leading article in *The Bookman* for March, 1932, which refers to "Well meaning liberals like Dr. Fosdick present a faith so stripped of dogmatic encumbrance that they may be thought to have thrown out the baby with the bath water." Such criticisms are inevitable and do not matter. In truth they may render one valuable aid. Was it not Donatello who claimed that his art suffered when he worked in an atmosphere of constant praise?

It should be said to the credit of Northern Baptists that while many of the conservatives among them fear and criticize Dr. Fosdick's liberalism, they do not rule him out of their list of great convention speakers. He appears occasionally on their national programs and is accorded the fullest liberty of utterance. Salvos of applause greet his presentation and resound throughout the hall when he concludes his address. Many of his Baptist brethren, quite apart from doctrinal interpretations, seem to take a pride in this internationally famed preacher nurtured in their denomination and who is a daring exponent of *soul liberty,* a basic Baptist principle. Here indeed is a modern prophet not without honor among his own people, despite wide differences of theological opinion, culture, and outlook. One could wish that all Christian communions were as wise and fraternal as to give a hearing on their platforms to able men quite regardless of their liberalism or conservatism. Until that time comes, there is something farcical in talk of Christian unity and sardonic in the passing of resolutions looking to the reunion of the divided house of God.

One of my preacher friends, who is also an intimate friend of Fosdick, confided to me that he never fails to pray each day for Harry Emerson Fosdick—prays for his success, his health, his ever-widening fame! Said this friend, "Modernism has its stake in Fosdick. If he should fall, Modernism would fall. If he keeps going, rising in power and influence, Modernism will rise with him and prosper even as he prospers. Therefore I pray daily for Harry Fosdick. He must not fail." Very fine, but I refuse to believe that any cause worthy of living depends upon any man, however potent his ministry or necessary he may seem in the progress of emancipatory movements. Yet I can understand and appreciate this friend's concern and greatly admire his prayerful support of one of our day's most prophetic souls. Such support, I doubt not, means more to Dr. Fosdick than the pristine splendor of the cathedral in which he preaches and the terrible money power that encompasses him about.

Chapter 12

Harry Emerson Fosdick: Titan of the Pulpit

EDGAR DEWITT JONES

> ... the essential nature of a sermon as an intimate, conversational message from soul to soul makes it impossible for printing to reproduce preaching, and unlike the traditional child, sermons should be heard and not seen.
> ———Harry Emerson Fosdick, in the Foreword to
> *The Hope of the World,* his first volume of sermons (1933)

Dr. Fosdick is the only one of the living lecturers in the Yale Series included here among "The Titans," and few will question his right to be in this classification. As I conversed once with a distinguished editor, publicist, and churchman on the American pulpit, he remarked: "Harry Emerson Fosdick is the Henry Ward Beecher of our day." Many will agree with this statement, including some who fail to see eye to eye with Dr. Fosdick and his theology. Not, of course, that he resembles the renowned Brooklyn preacher in temperament, method, or extraordinary oratorical power, although this Titan of the pulpit is an effective public speaker of distinctive style.

My editor-friend went on to say that just as Beecher influenced the preaching of his day for good, making it more human and sentient, so had Dr. Fosdick bettered the pulpit of our day both in sermon content and delivery. This observation makes sense. Con-

---
Note: Reprinted with permission from *The Royalty of the Pulpit*. New York, Harper & Bros., 1951, pp.101–107.

sider the ramifications of his ministry at Riverside Church, New York City. His published sermons, seven volumes in all, besides his other books, outsell, I have been informed, those of any other contemporary American preacher. They are also read and prized in Great Britain, on the Continent, in Australia, and in other countries abroad. The peoples of other countries think of Dr. Fosdick as first among American preachers, just as they think of Dr. Niebuhr as first among our theologians.

While yet a fledgling in the ministry Dr. Fosdick set up for himself an exacting standard of preaching excellence, and come rain or shine, he has maintained that standard for nearly half a century. His sermons follow an orderly construction and abound in quotable sentences often of an epigrammatic flavor. Notwithstanding the touch of grandeur that distinguishes the Fosdick pattern of speech and the lofty plateau upon which his preaching moves, he is not averse to a colloquialism or a humorous chuckle. His vocabulary is ample but not lavish. He rarely uses an exotic word, although he probably knows a lot of them. Instead, good, strong, lusty words are this preacher's delight. His sentences, long or short, are clear; the illustrative material fresh, and the realms of literature, art, and music are drawn upon with discriminating nicety.

There is also a down-to-earth quality in Fosdickian preaching. Who could imagine a Phillips Brooks preaching "On Catching the Wrong Bus"; but Dr. Fosdick did, and with zest. The sermon appears in his *On Being Fit to Live With,* and even in print it is warm, human, sagacious. Not even Beecher so much as dreamed of preaching on "The Decisive Babies of the World," but one of Dr. Fosdick's finest sermons is on this theme. That he was indebted to the historian, Creasy, for the inspiration in no way detracts from the sheer genius of substituting "Babies" for "Battles." Every alert preacher who reads this sermon wonders why he was too dumb to perceive the fine gold in that homiletic hill. Still, all may not be lost to the hard-pressed pastor. It will be recalled that Oscar Wilde, dazzled by a phrase on the lips of his friend, Whistler, the painter, sighed and remarked, "I wish I'd said that," and Whistler replied, "You will, Oscar, you will."

In answer to my questionnaire which I sent to all the living lecturers in the Lyman Beecher Lectures, Dr. Fosdick said in part:

> I have no idea, either, how much time I spent in immediate preparation. For years I had been giving at Union Theological Seminary a year-long course on the same subject I used at Yale. What I did, therefore, was to take advantage of the lectureship at Yale to arrange, condense, write out carefully, and prepare for publication the material I had been working on for a long time.

So it happens that to date Dr. Fosdick is the only lecturer in the long list to devote his series to the Bible exclusively, as Dr. Jefferson did in 1910 on the Church. Many of the other lecturers gave space both to the Bible and to the Church; uniquely Drs. Jefferson and Fosdick deal solely, one with the institution and the other with its textbook. I think it was a source of disappointment that this master preacher did not choose to take preaching as his subject at Yale. Later he was pressed to return for another series of a homiletical nature, but he could not find the time for the kind of preparation he always gives to the task ahead.

It turned out, however, that the interest in the Fosdick series on *The Modern Use of the Bible* was marked and sustained. So great were the throngs which came to hear him that officers were detailed to keep the crowd from storming the chapel when the doors were thrown open. This thing of policing a throng waiting to hear a Lyman Beecher lecturer had never occurred before, nor since, although capacity audiences have greeted several of the lecturers, and in a few instances standing room was at a premium.

The fact that the Fundamentalist-Modernist controversy was rampant at the time and that Dr. Fosdick was in the center of it and subject to heavy attack naturally added interest to the occasion and helps to account for the intense interest in the course.

Dr. Fosdick's lectures appeared in book form the year they were delivered, 1924, and enjoyed a huge circulation. The volume belongs in that comparatively small list of the published lectures which deserve classification as *best sellers*. The chapters were read from manuscript by Dr. Fosdick, who is adept in that method of preaching. Up to that time only one lecturer in the course had dealt with the Bible from the modern critical view, and then with only a part of it—Dr. George Adam Smith, whose subject in 1889 was *Modern Criticism and the Preaching of the Old Testament*—a fact which Dr. Fosdick commented on in the opening paragraph of his first lecture.

Rereading these lectures twenty-five years after their delivery, they appear as fresh, crisp, and pertinent as on that day I first opened the book and read far into the night that followed. As I read I glanced occasionally toward my book shelves, and my gaze fell on Dr. William Newton Clarke's *Sixty Years with the Bible,* a volume which came to me when I needed the reflections of that great yet humble scholar. These two books have much in common, and it is good news to some of us that Dr. Fosdick looked upon Dr. Clarke as a "saint."

There is a paragraph in Dr. Fosdick's first lecture which goes to the heart of the matter, thus:

> The man who ministers . . . must have an intelligible way of handling the Bible. He must have gone through the searching criticism to which the last few generations have subjected the Scriptures and be able to understand and enter into the negations that have resulted. Not blinking any of the facts, he must have come out with a positive, reasonable, fruitful attitude toward the Book. Only so can he be of service in resolving the doubts of multitudes of folk today. If they can see that the Bible is not lost but is the more usable the better it is understood, that the new knowledge has not despoiled it but has set its spirit free for its largest usefulness, that its basic experiences are separable from its temporary forms of thought, and that in its fundamental principles of life lie the best hopes of the world today, they are set in liberty from a great fear that their faith is vain. In the end, like many of us, they may see more in the Scriptures now than ever they saw under the old regime.

Dr. Fosdick is a constructive critic always and employs a method that is direct, honest, and courageous. But one may follow such a plan and still deal solely with negations. It is different with this New York preacher-professor. He places the emphasis on the affirmative and holds that liberalism by itself or as a cult is not enough. Neither liberalism nor conservatism availeth anything but a new creature. Take his subjects in order: I. The New Approach to the Bible; II. The Old Book in a New World; III. The Ancient Solution; IV. Abiding Experiences in Changing

Categories; V. Miracle and Law; VI. Perils of the New Position; VII. Jesus, the Messiah; VIII. Jesus, the Son of God. Now, controversial issues emerge in every one of the eight chapters. He meets them head-on but always with humility and a total absence of intellectual pride and doctrinaire vanity. Thus, he speaks in a passage which is of the pattern of the whole:

> Here, then, is the first essential of intelligent Biblical preaching in our day: a man must be able to recognize the abiding messages of the Book, and sometimes he must recognize them in a transient setting. No man will ever do this well if he does not divest himself of vanity and pride and clothe himself with humility as with a garment. He must see that many of our ways of thinking are very new; that they, too, are transient, and that many of them will soon be as outmoded as our forefathers' categories are.

If any theological student sitting through the first five lectures found himself heady with the new wine of interpretation from new bottles, the sixth lecture on "Perils of the New Position" must have had a sobering effect upon him. "Now abide three perils of liberalism—irreverence, sentimentality, and ethical disloyalty to Jesus—and the greatest of these is ethical disloyalty to Jesus." Thus endeth the chapter on the perils of the position for which the lecturer had so ably argued.

What Dr. Fosdick taught the theological students at Yale he taught the congregation to whom he preached, and the standards he set up for the young men at New Haven, he, himself, lived by. In this set of lectures delivered six years after World War I, and seventeen years before America's entrance into World War II, Fosdick declared: "The late war violated everything Jesus taught and, pouring the whole world into almost irremediable confusion, has provoked widespread impatience with purely theological speculations about Christ."

In July, 1928, Dr. Fosdick wrote an article which appeared in *Harper's Magazine* on the subject, "What Is the Matter with Preaching?" * It attracted wide attention and elicited many comments, most of them favorable. Among other things he said:

---
* See Chapter 2.

Harry Emerson Fosdick: Titan of the Pulpit

Recently, in a school chapel, so I am told, the headmaster was only well started on his sermon when a professor mounted the pulpit beside him and offered a criticism of what he was saying. Great excitement reigned. The headmaster answered the objection, but the professor remained in the pulpit, and the sermon that day was a running discussion between the two on a great theme in religion. To say that the boys were interested is to put it mildly. They never had been so worked up over anything religious before. It turned out afterward that the whole affair had been prearranged. It was an experiment in a new kind of preaching, where one man does not produce a monologue but where diverse and competing points of view are frankly dealt with.

Any preacher, without introducing another personality outwardly in the pulpit, can utilize the principle involved in this method. If he is to handle helpfully real problems in his congregation, he must utilize it. He must see clearly and state fairly what people other than himself are thinking on the matter in hand. He may often make this so explicit as to begin paragraphs with such phrases as, "But some of you will say," or "Let us consider a few questions that inevitably arise," or, "Face frankly with me the opposing view," or, "Some of you have had experiences that seem to contradict what we are saying." Of course, this method, like any other, can be exaggerated and become a mannerism. But something like it is naturally involved in any preaching which tries to help people to think through and live through their problems.

A publisher of New York City, whose friendship I prize, once described to me the first time he heard Dr. Fosdick preach and the effect of the sermon upon him. He was a graduate student at Chicago at the time, and Dr. Fosdick was the preacher at the Sunday Evening Club. Orchestra Hall was packed, and although the youth came early, he had difficulty in finding a seat. "For the first time in my life," the publisher said, "I was to see the man who had written *The Meaning of Prayer,* a book that had meant much to my college roommate and me, and to hear the preacher whose name like Abou Ben Adhem's, led all the rest. Even though I was ready for the unusual I didn't expect the extraordinary. Here were ideas presented so cogently and vigorously that my mind could not hold them all, so like a torrent they came. The choice of words was often so apt that it was sheer delight to sense how apposite to the idea was the word chosen to express it. This aesthetic pleasure I remember having experienced years earlier when as a boy I had heard William Jennings Bryan lecture from a

Chautauqua platform. The title of Dr. Fosdick's sermon I heard in Chicago I have long since forgotten but I shall never forget the impact made by his preaching."

I have recalled this conversation from a memory still aglow with the enthusiasm of the publisher describing to me the experience. If anything, my account of the incident has lost, not gained, in vividness.

Exciting preaching which is not merely emotional but also highly intelligent and spiritually powerful never lacks for a hearing. Already the name of Fosdick is being ranged alongside the names of Henry Ward Beecher * and Phillips Brooks ** on this side of the Atlantic, and with Frederick William Robertson on the other. Riverside Church, New York City, is destined to take its place in the history of preaching with Plymouth Church, Brooklyn; Trinity Church, Boston; and Trinity Chapel, Brighton, England.

Dr. Fosdick is now minister emeritus of Riverside Church. In semiretirement he is still a busy person. His latest book, *The Man from Nazareth,* is enjoying a wide and enthusiastic reading.

---

* See Chapter 19.
** See Chapter 20.

Chapter 13

Harry Emerson Fosdick:
A Study in Sources of Effectiveness

ROY C. McCALL *

FOR MORE THAN TWO DECADES Harry Emerson Fosdick was "the most important popular figure in the Protestant pulpit." He combined "in his person the rare art of the preacher with the spirit of the earnest student if not of the academic scholar."[1] Although a dissident minority once held that he "is no authentic representative of the Christian religion,"[2] certainly he was during his active ministry "a conspicuously successful preacher . . . whose good report . . . filled the whole city";[3] "one of the most popular and distinguished clergymen of America."[4]

In England he was regarded as "the true successor of Phillips Brooks," one who made the English "prouder than ever" of their "communion in language with the United States." His was "real eloquence," the kind which for three days kept "Scotland . . . sitting at his feet."[5]

---

* Roy C. McCall (A.B. University of Redlands 1930, M.A. 1931, Ph.D. 1936, University of Iowa) is President of the College of the Desert.

Note: Reprinted from Loren Reid (ed.) : *American Public Address*. By permission of the publisher, University of Missouri Press, Columbia, Missouri. Copyright 1961, by the Curators of the University of Missouri.

[1] *Christian Century*, LII, 20 (November, 1935), p.1480.
[2] *Catholic World*, CXXXIV, 799 (October, 1931), p.100, editorial comment.
[3] *Current Opinion*, LXXVII (December, 1924), pp.756–757.
[4] *American Magazine*, XCVII (January, 1924), p.32.
[5] *Fosdick and the Fundamentalists*. New York, League for Public Discussion, 1925.

His radio broadcasts, begun with one station in 1926, became soon the major attraction of National Vespers, which opened in 1927 and eventually was carried nationwide every Sunday over NBC. In 1936 was initiated the mimeographed service which made his vesper sermons available by mail to all who requested them, and until necessity forced retrenchment during the war, his broadcasts were carried by short wave to England, Africa, New Zealand, and Australia.[6] Sermons, lectures, and essays bound into books sold in excess of a million copies during the twenties.[7]

Dean Karl Onthank of the University of Oregon tells of going two hours early to get a good seat in an assembly hall at Columbia University where Fosdick was scheduled to speak, only to find the place packed and people standing outside. Everett L. Waid, longtime president of the Art Students League of New York City, reports that when he was an usher at the First Presbyterian Church of New York, the staff was forced to close the doors against hundreds nearly every Sunday. It was during this period that Fosdick preached the sermon "Shall the Fundamentalists Win?" which caused the storm that eventually drove him from that pulpit and built "a sounding board behind" him so that his "message reached farther than [he] ever dreamed it could." [8]

Dr. Loren Reid, professor of speech at the University of Missouri, writes: "I remember vividly a series of lectures that Fosdick gave at Grinnell College about 1926 or 1927. Every morning one week he gave a chapel lecture; the chapel period was lengthened from its usual twenty minutes to an hour in order to feature his talk. Morning classes were correspondingly shortened. I recall that many, many of us actually ran to chapel in order to be sure of a seat."

"He received 125,000 letters a year from his radio talks alone." [9] One contemporary said of him: "The most preeminent pulpit of the Christian faith in America, if not in the world, is that of Dr. Harry Emerson Fosdick in Riverside Church." [10]

---

[6] Mrs. Dorothy Noyes, for twenty-three years Fosdick's secretary.

[7] *Current Biography.* New York, 1940, p.309.

[8] *Farewell Sermon to First Presbyterian Church of New York,* March 1, 1925, published and distributed by Ivy Lee, p.29.

[9] *Time,* XLV (June 18, 1945), p.56.

[10] Edgar DeWitt Jones: *American Preachers of Today.* Indianapolis, Bobbs-Merrill Co., Inc., 1933, p.27.

When in 1924 ninety thousand ministers of the United States were asked to select the twenty-five outstanding preachers of the land, Fosdick was named among the twenty-five.[11]

Whether such a man stood highest in popularity and influence among Protestant preachers of his age, there is little doubt that his eminence justifies examination of the causes that have rendered him outstanding in the art of preaching. To what extent were his achievements attributable to intellect, to training, to conviction, to empathy with the dominant needs of mankind?

CHARACTER, CONSCIENCE, AND CONVICTION

In the theological controversy which developed among the Presbyterians following Fosdick's sermon "Shall the Fundamentalists Win?," his "sanity and poise" were judged remarkable.[12] When a committee invited him in the interest of peace to subscribe to the creed of the Presbyterian Church, Fosdick replied: "After two years of vehement personal attack from a powerful section of the Presbyterian Church, I face now an official proposal which calls on me either to make a theological subscription or else leave an influential pulpit. Any subscription made under such circumstances would be generally, and I think, truly interpreted as moral surrender. I am entirely willing that my theology should be questioned; I am entirely unwilling to give any occasion for the questioning of my ethics." [13]

In an appraisal of what was wrong with the preaching of his time, Fosdick wrote: "There is no process by which wise and useful discourses can be distilled from unwise and useless personalities, and the ultimate necessity in the ministry, as everywhere else, is sound and intelligent character." [14]

Whether hearing Fosdick's voice unexpectedly from a neighbor's radio on a Sunday during the twenties and thirties or reading one of his sermons in any later decade, the recipients of Fosdick's preaching all testify to a sense of his strong conviction. His sermons seemed to be tearing "off the grave-clothes of Christi-

---

[11] *Literary Digest*, LXXXIV (March 21, 1925), pp.31–32.

[12] *Current Opinion*, LXXVII (December, 1924), p.757.

[13] Letter to Edgar Whitaker Work, quoted in pamphlet, *The First Presbyterian Church of New York and Doctor Fosdick*. New York, 1924, p.38.

[14] Harry Emerson Fosdick: "What is the matter with preaching?" *Harper's Magazine*, CLVII (July, 1928), p.133.

anity, accumulated through the ages by musty theologians . . . to reveal the religion of Jesus in all its imperishable freshness and pertinency . . . dissolving the incrustations of Christianity and . . . challenging the local parsons of thousands of communities to shake themselves out of their lethargy." [15]

The boy who as a returning junior at Colgate wrote his mother, "I'm throwing over my old idea of the universe! I'm building another—and leaving God out!" later considered his ideas too radical to allow him to attempt the career of minister.[16] At the height of his preaching career he wrote:

> Every problem that the preacher faces thus leads back to one basic question: how well does he understand the thoughts and lives of his people? That he should know his Gospel goes without saying, but he may know it ever so well and yet fail to get it within reaching distance of anybody unless he intimately understands people and cares more than he cares for anything else what is happening inside of them. Preaching is wrestling with individuals over questions of life and death, and until that idea of it commands a preacher's mind and method, eloquence will avail him little and theology not at all.[17]

Likewise in his farewell sermon to his congregation at the First Presbyterian Church, where he chose to be ousted rather than yield his principles, he boldly set forth his declaration of independence and devotion, as well as the major premises on which his preaching career was built:

> These are the things we have stood for: tolerance, an inclusive Church, the right to think religion through in modern terms, the social application of the principles of Jesus, the abiding verities and experiences of the Gospel. And these are right. I am not sorry we tried this experiment. It was worth trying. We have listed a standard that no one will pull down. We have started an issue that no man or denomination is strong enough to brush aside.
>
> The future belongs to the things we have been standing for. Some day the whole Church will swing around to them, take them for granted, wonder why they ever seemed new or strange, and what is the heresy of one generation will become the orthodoxy of the next. We say farewell to each other, but let no man say farewell to the things we have been standing for! [18]

---

[15] *Literary Digest*, CVII (November 1, 1930), pp.20–21.
[16] *Current Biography*, p.309.
[17] Fosdick: "What is the matter with preaching?" p.141.
[18] *Farewell Sermon* . . . p.23.

A Study in Sources of Effectiveness 119

Such was the man who rode "rough-shod over ecclesiastical decrees and won a hearing which no decree could suppress" [19] because he "wouldn't live in a generation like this and be anything but a heretic." [20]

A PRODIGIOUS AND METICULOUS WORKER

In 1933 Edgar DeWitt Jones wrote of Fosdick: "For thirty years . . . he has spent the mornings of five days a week in his study. No message can get to him there, no telephone calls can reach him, no visitors are admitted. In such seclusion, he 'toils terribly' over his sermons." [21] He "used to burn up the logwood in the morning and the chips at night, and the first sometimes made a slow blaze and the latter a thin one." [22] In his view, "nothing can make preaching easy. At best it means drenching a congregation with one's lifeblood." [23] Consequently, the general process of sermon preparation caused him "to read every first-rate book that comes out in almost every field." He wrote:

> Early in my ministry I made it my practice to take some special subject, . . . and then to read every worthwhile thing that has been written in the last fifty years about it. . . . Without such consecutive, continuous, well organized study I do not see how any man can grow in his ministry in general or in his preaching in particular. . . . I read all the time, and read omnivorously.[24]
>
> Wanting to know what I really thought about immortality, I broke my question into as orderly an arrangement as I could manage, and announced a series of Sunday evening sermons on the subject. Then I was in for it. I read everything pro and con I could lay my hands on and under the coercion of teaching others taught myself everything I could learn from books and searched my mind for what I thought.[25]

The more specific process of composition required that he write out "every word of every sermon. . . . I do not see how anyone can keep strength of thought and variety and facility of language

---

[19] *Literary Digest*, LXXXIV (March 21, 1925), p.31.
[20] *Farewell Sermon* . . . p.28.
[21] Jones, *op. cit.*, p.29.
[22] Autobiography, a Manuscript, prepared by Fosdick for his grandchildren, and loaned to the author. Referred to hereafter as Autobiography.
[23] Fosdick: "What is the matter with preaching?" p.140.
[24] Letter of November 23, 1945, to G. E. M. The identity of the recipient is so indicated at Fosdick's request. Referred to hereafter as Letter to G. E. M.
[25] Autobiography.

and illustration if he does not discipline himself to the severe task of writing everything he says."[26] "I write with meticulous care and make many corrections."[27]

INDIVIDUALIST

The following characteristics of Fosdick's spoken and written works had caused the writer to assume that the great preacher was schooled in classical rhetoric: (a) the admirable symmetry of Fosdick's sermons, lectures, and essays; (b) his consistent conformity with the classical pattern of organization; (c) his clear and forceful style, rich in imagery and abundant with antithesis, alliteration, and climax; (d) an obvious pattern of decreasing intellectual appeal, increasing emotional charge, and decreasing length in the progression through the sections of the body of the sermon. In addition, Fosdick's father, principal of a Buffalo high school, was a professor of Greek and Latin, which subjects his son mastered early and read in the original with facility.

A startling discovery, therefore, was learning that Fosdick had "read no textbooks on rhetoric since Genung's *Rhetoric,*" except to note some passages in Phillips' *Effective Speaking,* which "seemed to make sense" and were therefore suggested reading for his students in homiletics at Union. Richard Whately's inductive arrangement and Alan H. Monroe's motivated sequence sounded "awfully academic" to him. He further mused: "While books have profoundly influenced me, the influence of two kinds of books has been minor, books about preaching and sermons." His speech training in high school and college, while intensive, was nonetheless almost exclusively in the mechanics of delivery. Brought up in the tradition of elocution, he "mowed 'em down," as he expressed it, with recitation during his grammar school days —though in his second experience he forgot his "piece" and gave up—was elected president of his debating society in high school but was too overcome with fear and embarrassment to express his thanks for the honor, and in college, where "old fashioned oratory still held sway," he was "drilled for four years on gesture and inflection," practiced "breathing for power," and "won every

---
[26] Letter to G. E. M.
[27] Interview.

first" in his course. In later years he "completely abandoned the theory of elocution, never studied effects of oral delivery in advance," and held to the ideal of "animated conversation" as the best mode of delivery. Although early in his preaching career he sought help from the husband of his church organist at his office in Carnegie Hall and through singing exercises gradually worked some huskiness out of his voice, he never "wished to put on a show," hated tricks, "always wanted to talk sense in the pulpit," and looked upon preaching "not as just a speech on Sunday, not just a topical address, but a message to people who needed it." [28]

INFLUENCE OF THE AUDIENCE

Undoubtedly the most significant element in Fosdick's theory and practice of public address is his emphasis on the audience, not only as the focal point of all preaching but also as influencing method in both composition and delivery. He reports that in his early experiences at Montclair, New Jersey, he had great difficulty with himself. "I can recall many hours of complete despair about myself. I didn't know a thing about preaching when I went to Montclair. I really don't know how I got away with it." [29]

> My greater difficulty during my years at Montclair was not with others but with myself. I did not know how to preach. Doubtless part of the trouble was due to my still unsteady nerves, but much of it was still downright ignorance of how to tackle the preparation of a sermon. What saved me, I suspect, was the fact that I had been trained to stand up and talk in public, so that, however little I had to say, I could at least say it. In those years I made it a matter of profound pride—which I now deprecate—never to take a scrap of paper into the pulpit but to preach entirely without notes. While my sermons were therefore immature, often violating the primary canons of homiletics, they were at least not formal, pedantic, and stereotyped but direct talks.[30]

During this period two occurrences combined to awaken him to the audience factor in preaching and to strengthen his conviction concerning its relation to rhetorical technique. The first of these was his successful counseling of a man in dire difficulty. At approximately the time a year's intensive work had revealed to him

---
[28] Interview.
[29] Interview.
[30] Autobiography.

"what could be done with an individual when you sat down with him and brought to bear upon him the resources of the Christian Gospel,"[31] one of his sermons unexpectedly "caught fire." He writes:

> Probably my memory exaggerates the precise occasion when improvement began. One Sunday morning, quite unexpectedly, in the midst of my sermon, the idea I was dealing with caught fire. I had a flaming few minutes when I could feel the congregation's kindling response. I am sure they were as much surprised as I was. I had never preached like that before, and I went home sure that preaching could mean that kind of moving and effective communication of truth.[32]

From this point forward his first concern and constant guide was "clairvoyance as to what is going on in John Doe," and out of this concept developed his philosophy of "personal counseling on a group scale," or the "project method" of preaching, intended always to "work a miracle on some individual in the congregation." Each sermon from that time on was conceived as a project in counseling the members of his congregation in terms of their personal needs. All his sermons delivered before that conviction struck, he later destroyed. This method, which finds its expression in the introductory portion of every sermon in the determination that all listeners shall say to themselves, "He's bowling down my alley,"[33] remained the strongest guiding force in his preaching to the end of his active ministry.

> Every sermon should have for its main business the solving of some problem—a vital, important problem. . . .
>
> This endeavor to help people to solve their spiritual problems is a sermon's only justifiable aim. The point of departure and of constant reference, the reason for preaching the sermon in the first place, and the inspiration for its method of approach and the organization of its material should not be something outside the congregation but inside. Within a paragraph or two after a sermon has started, wide areas of any congregation ought to begin recognizing that the preacher is tackling something of vital concern to them. . . .
>
> Any preacher who even with moderate skill is thus helping folk to solve their real problems is functioning. . . .

---

[31] Interview.
[32] Autobiography.
[33] Interview.

What all the great writers of Scripture were interested in was human living, and the modern preacher who honors them should start with that. . . .[34]

He strenuously objects to "topical preachers who turn their pulpits into platforms and their sermons into lectures. . . ." He says: "One who listens to such preaching or reads it knows that the preacher is starting at the wrong end. . . . He is starting with a subject whereas he should start with an object. His one business is with the real problems of these individual people in his congregation." [35]

THE BASIS FOR STRUCTURE

When asked why nearly all his sermons contained three ideas subordinate to the main theme, Fosdick replied that audiences can not grasp more than three at one sitting; four, perhaps, if the speaker exercises special care in keeping the outline constantly before them. "I preached a sermon at Montclair once with six points," he said. "It came out like a broom, in a multitude of small straws." [36]

When pressed on the question of whether he designed his sermons so that his first point was longest and strongest in intellectual appeal, whereas his last point was shortest and strongest in emotional appeal, he professed no consciousness of such method but said it made sense in terms of the audience's increasing familiarity with the subject as well as their growing fatigue and the speaker's naturally increasing emotion. The questioner gained the impression, however, that such design was, in Fosdick's mind, possibly too studied to allow the complete genuineness, openness, sincerity, and earnestness compatible with the minister's purpose. He says: "Tell them the truth you want to tell them right off. . . . Climax is achieved by showing them the Matterhorn in the beginning, reshowing it, reshowing it, and each time the Matterhorn gets bigger." [37]

As for his sources of ideas and illustrations, he says: "One gets a

---

[34] Fosdick: "What is the matter with preaching?" pp.134–136.
[35] *Ibid.*
[36] Interview.
[37] Interview.

theme in his mind and broods over it;[38] his reading contributes to it, his intimate personal experiences in dealing with the problems of other people enrich his thought about it. . . . I get my illustrations from all sorts of places; primarily from personal life, from keeping my eyes open and watching things go, from my reading.[39]

Transitions, which he consistently makes with fine care, arise, he says, "largely from the speaker's sense of audience needs."[40] Figuratively expressed, the members of the audience are carried along ". . . by showing them the Matterhorn in the beginning, reshowing it, reshowing it. . . ."

SOURCES OF STYLE

Fosdick's style is inimitably clear,[41] forceful, easy, unaffected, intimate without being personal, vivid without being florid, full of imagery without straining at figures or even being noticeably figurative. He considers writing "indispensable to preaching if it is going to grow, and not to slump as the years pass,"[42] and credits his wife with being his "best literary critic," who deserves credit for "the absence of numberless words, phrases, sentences, and paragraphs" because "she ruthlessly cut out the excess verbiage"[43]

---

[38] "Brooding" is reminiscent of Henry Ward Beecher's method, but Fosdick's careful writing out of his sermons is quite the opposite. Beecher said: "I brood it and ponder it, and dream over it. . . . I don't dare to . . . put it down on paper. If I once write a thing out, it is almost impossible for me to kindle to it again. I never dare nowadays, to write out a sermon during the week; that is sure to kill it." Lyman Abbott and S. B. Halliday: *Life of Henry Ward Beecher*. Hartford, American Publishing Co., 1888, p.211. Fosdick studied both Beecher and Brooks and feels that he was unconsciously strongly influenced by both. (Interview.)

[39] Letter to G. E. M.

[40] Interview. The following sentence taken verbatim from "The Deathless Hope that Man Can Not Escape," printed in *A Great Time to Be Alive*. New York, 1944, p.233, is typical: "From one more major source rises this deathless hope—not alone from the way we ourselves are constituted, nor from our love of other people, but from our personal fellowship with God." Note that the sentence (a) clearly reiterates the central theme, (b) obviously restates both points already developed, and (c) definitely states the third point which is next to be developed.

[41] "His power of clear statement is probably unexcelled in America today." Jones, *op. cit.*, p.28.

[42] Letter to G. E. M.

[43] Harry Emerson Fosdick: *On Being a Real Person*. New York, Harper & Bros., 1943, p.14.

and literally "purged" his style.[44] Although he insists that "the essential nature of a sermon as an intimate, conversational message from soul to soul makes it impossible for printing to reproduce preaching,"[45] both listener and reader gain the impression that his sentences spring from a full heart, unimpeded by consciousness of technique or striving for any effect other than driving home his message. Such spontaneity is consistent with his unwavering integrity and selflessness, lost in his eagerness to reach the audience but at the same time subconsciously depending on all the best he has read and practiced until it has become an integral part of him in action. He suspects that he was influenced most by Phillips Brooks, whom he greatly admires, by his reading of the classics in the original[46] and by "a background of great English literature, poetry, history, sociology, and so forth" without which no one could "be a competent preacher."[47]

Note the consistency and naturalness with which the three phases of the following analogy occur: "The idea I was dealing with caught fire. I had a flaming few minutes when I could feel the congregation's kindling response."

A good example of antithesis: "Who at that far off time could have dreamed that humanity would climb from the Galilee man to the Man of Galilee?"[48]

Again: "It is not Christ's message that needs to be accommodated to this mad scene; it is this mad scene into which our civilization has collapsed that needs to be judged and saved by Christ's message. This is the most significant change distinguishing the beginning of my ministry from now. Then we were trying to accommodate Christ to our civilization; now we face the desperate need of accommodating our scientific civilization to Christ."[49]

For combined metaphor and alliteration, the following is typi-

---

[44] Interview.
[45] Harry Emerson Fosdick: *The Hope of the World.* New York, Harper & Bros., 1933, p.7.
[46] Interview.
[47] Letter to G.E.M.
[48] Harry Emerson Fosdick: *A Pilgrimage to Palestine.* New York, Macmillan Company, 1927, p.29.
[49] *A Great Time to Be Alive,* pp.20–21.

cal: "Here is a home economically imprisoned, no financial elbow-room, the natural desires of family life confronting everywhere the prohibitions of penury." [50]

"The mind always walks as uneasily in new ideas as the feet in new shoes." [51]

Whether his style be judged unconsciously eclectic or consciously skillful, it must finally be declared distinctively Fosdick, the lance with which he became "a preacher who reaches the heart through the intellect." [52]

DISCIPLINED SPONTANEITY

In his early preaching he "memorized his sermons with no great difficulty" but later "took notes into the pulpit—notes only" and finally the complete manuscript because he considered "clairvoyance too difficult a matter to be extemporized." The manuscript which he had written "with meticulous care" and "many corrections" had now, without any attempt to memorize it, become so much a part of him that, "I forget that I am reading," hardly more than glancing at the pages now and then, sometimes changing or departing from the manuscript but always profiting from the discipline of having written it as he would like to say it.[53]

Impatient to meet his audience face to face, he often had to take sedatives on Saturday night in order to get his rest for Sunday's adventure. "Not anxiety, but tension that was a stimulus" caused him to be "aroused." "Any man who isn't tense before he speaks can't speak. Fear is not something to be feared, but something to be sublimated." [54]

In the actual delivery of his sermons, Fosdick, who had been schooled in gesture and posture, inflection and power, cast out consciousness of such physical factors as insincere and artificial, and allowed the welling thoughts within as aroused by the visible audience to dictate the behavior of voice and body. His bearing is

---

[50] *Ibid.*, p.134.

[51] Harry Emerson Fosdick. *Adventurous Religion.* New York, Harper & Bros., 1926, p.244.

[52] Wm. G. Shepherd: *Great Preachers as Seen by a Journalist.* London and Edinburgh, New York, and Chicago, 1924, p.9.

[53] Interview.

[54] Interview.

best described as restrained and dignified but expressively consistent with the thought and mood of his message; his voice might well be classed as high and thin and somewhat monotonous in its cadence but always suggestive of earnestness and conviction; his articulation was overly precise and perhaps came nearest to justifying being termed artificial of any of his traits; and yet the sum total of what one heard by radio or in the cathedral was distinctive, a national trademark which, when combined with his written style, enabled listeners always readily to identify him.

His personal magnetism cannot be overrated. Whether his radiance was of the spirit or a happy combination of physical features, good health, and unbounded energy—or both—can not be declared. Only those who have met him face to face know that friendliness encompasses all those near him; only those who have heard him speak know the experience of being arrested and held by an intangible power.

SUMMARY

Thus, Fosdick, a consummate artist in public speaking, achieved his art without artifice. A scholar who sought cause and effect in all relations of life and made himself conversant with beginning, end, and middle of every subject he discussed; an evangelist who attempted to reconcile the spiritual and the scientific, history and the present, he disdained help from books on public speaking, forged his own theory of oral communication out of his daily experience, and practiced what the pedagogues have preached but could not produce. Such was the man who "could preach in a theatre or a car-barn and get his audience." [55]

---

[55] *Literary Digest*, LXXXI (June 21, 1924), p.33.

Chapter 14

Harry Emerson Fosdick:
The Growth of a Great Preacher

ROBERT D. CLARK *

I

LATE IN DECEMBER of 1918, the pastoral relations committee of the First Presbyterian Church of New York announced that Harry Emerson Fosdick, Professor of Practical Theology at the Union Theological Seminary, had accepted a call as associate minister and permanent preacher.

No one thought at the time of comparing him to Henry Ward Beecher or Phillips Brooks; no one anticipated that he would soon become the center of the nation's most spectacular quarrel on religious doctrine, nor did any guess that he was about to take his place as America's most prominent radio preacher, or that John D. Rockefeller would build a million-dollar skyscraper church for him, or that his slender volumes on prayer and faith and service written for Y.M.C.A. study groups would sell over a million copies.

But even in 1918 people recognized that Harry Emerson Fos-

---

* President of the University of Oregon.

Note: Reprinted with permission from Harry Emerson Fosdick. By Robert Clark, from *A History and Criticism of American Public Address.* Prepared under the auspices of The Speech Association of America, Marie Kathryn Hochmuth (Ed.), New York, Russell & Russell, 1955.

dick was a great preacher. As supply minister at the First Presbyterian Church in the fall of 1918, he had attracted attention and prompted the pulpit committee to extend a unanimous call to him. When he was announced to preach, the people crowded the church, and when he stepped to the pulpit they listened eagerly. A small, wiry man, quick in his movements, he impressed them with his energy and his earnestness. With his hands tightly gripping the collar of his gown, he spoke with scarcely a gesture, save for the vigorous and emphatic bobbing of his dark, busy head.[1]

But he spoke directly and urgently, with his black eyes searching the faces of the people. He spoke sharply and critically, and yet hopefully, and the recurring upward inflection in his voice, the persistent suggestion of a ministerial tone served only to temper the occasional asperity of his criticism and the imperative challenge in his voice.

Fosdick was forty years old in 1918. Born in 1878 in Buffalo, New York, he had been reared in a Baptist home. His father was a school teacher, for twenty-five years the principal of a public high school. Young Harry and his brother and sister were steeped in the traditions of religion and learning.

Although the elder Fosdick was a liberal in theology, the tenets which he had come to accept had not yet filtered down to the Sunday school and the children's books through which his son secured most of his religious instruction. Young Harry was nurtured on three volumes of Bible stories, written especially for the young. *Line upon Line* and *Precept upon Precept* told the stories of the Old Testament; *The Peep of Day* recounted those of the New. They were pictures of violence and death as well as of courage and sacrifice, of a vengeful more than a loving God, of a jealous, watchful tyrant who sat on his great white throne, marking down all the wrongdoings and even naughty thoughts of men and women and of little boys and girls. On that final day of judgment he would open his great book, seek out those who did not love him, bind them in chains, and throw them into a lake of fire. There they might gnash their teeth and weep and wail

---

[1] Helena Huntington Smith: Respectable heretic. *Outlook and Independent*, CLIII (October 9, 1929), p.209.

forever, but they should not have one drop of water to cool their burning tongues.[2]

When he was seven, young Fosdick cried himself to sleep in dread of hell, and when he was nine he was ill from "panic terror" lest he had committed the unpardonable sin. Years afterward the Reverend Dr. Fosdick remembered with "resurrected wrath" the long Sunday evening sermon which had persuaded him and a few others to sign a pledge never to drink sweet cider, and the time he had missed his only opportunity to hear Edwin Booth in *Hamlet* because some pious brethren had stirred up his sensitive conscience on the evils of the theater, and the many times when, with agonizing scruples, he had refused to dance the Virginia Reel or to read George Eliot's novels.[3]

If his religion was solemn, his play at least was "right." The family lived for a number of years in a small rural community several miles from Buffalo. Harry roamed the woods, fished in Plumb Bottom and Cayuga Creek, made mud dams, and joined his gang in building a shanty. His father now and then took him fishing on the Niagara, and he learned to love the falls with a fearful and awesome love—the rush of the river as it split and whitened on the jutting rocks, the roar of the cataract, the fateful plunge over the cliff, the boiling water in the stream below. He loved the quieter aspects of nature too, the delicate flowers of the woods which contrasted so strangely with the garish floral patterns in the parlors of the homes he knew. And he thought the calm radiance of a summer dawn not unlike the quiet way his mother moved through her simple, household tasks.[4]

While he was thus engrossed with church and outdoor sports, he also found much time to read—biography and history, the novels of Dickens and Thackeray, and the dime-novel adventure

---

[2] Harry Emerson Fosdick: Morals secede from the union. *Harper's Magazine*, CLXIV (May, 1932), pp.682–683.

[3] Fosdick: Are Religious People Fooling Themselves? *ibid.*, CLXI (June, 1930), p. 62; Fosdick: The trenches and the Church at home, *Atlantic Monthly*, CXXIII (January, 1919), pp.30–31.

[4] Autobiography (Typescript, cited by permission of the author), pp.11, 14, 26, 27; Living for the fun of it. *American Magazine*, CIX (April, 1930), p.56; *The Hope of the World*. New York, Harper & Bros., 1933, p.105; *Successful Christian Living*. New York, Harper & Bros., 1937, p.215.

stories written by his father's younger brother. When he was ready for high school, the family moved back to Buffalo. He attended the school where his father was principal and studied Latin and Greek under his direction. But his most influential teacher was a young instructor who introduced him to literature—Browning, Wordsworth, Whitman—and read aloud with him the whole of Lecky's *History of European Morals*. Under this young man's critical eye he learned to make Cicero's orations, when translated, sound like "real orations" and Vergil's *Aeneid* sound like poetry.[5]

He was a shy, embarrassed youngster in high school "petrified with stage fright," when he was first called upon to participate in the activities of his debating society. But like it or not, he was expected to stand up and talk. Before long, despite persistent fear before an audience, he discovered that once in a while he "got something across and liked it." He was graduated in 1895 as valedictorian of the class and delivered an oration on the Armenian massacres.[6]

Fosdick was eighteen years old when he entered Colgate University at Hamilton, New York. Colgate was a denominational institution under the control of the Baptists. The president of the college was a Baptist minister, as were several of the professors, including Albert Brigham, the professor of geology and the college's lecturer on such subjects as "Science and the First Chapter of Genesis."[7] Young Fosdick at once found himself at home in the religious activities of the campus.

The professors were generally conservative, religiously, but not unfriendly to critical thinking. Eager and keen-minded, Harry found college a great experience, an intellectual-emotional revolution. For the first time he explored the doctrines of Charles Darwin and in them he found a new universe. He had had no thought of ever relinquishing the tenets of his religious faith, but before his freshman year was over, he had become an avowed evolutionist. Impressed by his own boldness, he prepared a letter, a bomb to drop into the peaceful circle of his family. With some interest and anxiety he awaited the explosion. His father wrote to

---

[5] Autobiography, pp.25, 26.
[6] *Ibid.*, pp.26, 28.
[7] *Madisonensis,* XXVIII (February 17, 1896), p.139.

him simply and directly: "Dear Harry: I believed in evolution before you were born."[8]

His course at Colgate, although considerably removed from the traditional language-centered program of an earlier period, consisted of first-year classes in Greek, Latin, and French, as well as mathematics, rhetoric, and public speaking. In the sophomore year Harry substituted German for French, took two more terms of rhetoric, elected English literature for two terms, and continued his courses in Latin, Greek, mathematics, and public speaking. As a lower classman he must take *systematic exercise* in the new and modern gymnasium which was "thoroughly equipped with the most approved apparatus."

In his junior and senior years he elected a great variety of courses: logic, ethics, history of philosophy, psychology, Anglo-Saxon, history of art, history of education, biology, zoology, geology, history of evolution, and every term, one to three courses in public speaking.[9]

Almost at once he impressed his classmates with his studiousness and his intellectual superiority. Quiet and serious, he seemed from the very beginning of his college career to be destined for the Phi Beta Kappa and *summa cum laude* which he eventually earned. Systematic in his study habits, he sat at his "big wide desk" in his fraternity room, "two unabridged dictionaries in their racks—one on each side of him" and pored over his books or composed his English projects and his speeches. He wrote his first drafts in a cheap, lined notebook on lines 1, 4, 8, and so forth, reserving the spaces between for revisions, new words plucked from the dictionaries, new sentences conjured up out of his thought.

Better mannered and better dressed than most of the "rather raw set" of Colgate students and "by no means a bookworm" despite his studious habits, he was rushed by three fraternities and pledged by Delta Upsilon. His attractive appearance, erect stature, and good bearing gave him more dignity than freshmen were

---

[8] Fosdick: Evolution and religion. *Ladies Home Journal*, XLII (September, 1925), p.12. Cf. Autobiography, p.30.

[9] Colgate University *Annual Catalogue*. Hamilton, New York, 1895, pp.14, 15, 26, 44; Records of the Registrar, Colgate University, 1895–1900.

supposed to have and led a few students to regard him as one who was not unaware of his superior abilitites. But most of his fellows thought him modest, cordial, and "genial enough." [10]

At the end of his first few weeks in school he earned his first honors when *Madisonensis,* the students' biweekly magazine, published his poem, "The Sirens," twenty-eight lines of iambic pentameter, a fable, in the Grecian mood, of the transformation of lovely sirens into the rocky islands off the coast of Sicily. He did not take part in sports, but he was an enthusiastic spectator and regular enough to write his class yell. He was regular enough, too —in a day when nicknames were a symbol of familiarity which contrasted with the formal address of the classroom and chapel— to be dubbed "Fuzzy" Fosdick, not simply because of his shock of dark, kinky hair but also because he and his fellows knew and loved Kipling's poem "Fuzzy-Wuzzy." In his junior year he was editor-in-chief of the school annual, *The Salmagundi,* and in his senior year he was associate editor of *Madisonensis,* as well as class poet and president of the student association.[11]

The dominant activity in Fosdick's life at Colgate, in classroom and out, was public speaking. He had weekly exercises in declamation during his freshmen and sophomore years. As a sophomore he also studied elocution and voice culture—breathing, *diaphragmatic action,* articulation, pronunciation, and *vocal expression.* In this third year he took up the principles of speech composition, writing, and delivering orations which were "freely criticized" prior to the required public presentation. He also elected courses in argumentation and debate, with parliamentary practice, legislative procedure, and debates on public questions.

His instructor in rhetoric and public speaking was Ralph Thomas, "a somewhat pompous and thick-set little fellow," who later resigned from his teaching position to practice law and to take his place as a member of the New York State Legislature.

---

[10] Letters to the writer from H. D. Gray, January 29, 1954; John M. Sayles, February 2, 1954; and others of Fosdick's classmates at Colgate, a few of whom prefer to remain anonymous.

[11] *Madisonensis,* XXVIII (November 11, 1895) ; letters to the writer from Norman F. S. Russell, February 1, 1954; John M. Sayles, February 2, 1954; Frank S. Squyer, February 10, 1954.

Fosdick remembers him as an elocutionist; he was "all for the old-time oratory" says a classmate: "right-hand gesture here, two steps to the left there." To some of his students he was "as empty of original ideas as a bass drum," but others recall that he emphasized organization and style more than gesture and vocal exercise. He taught his students "how to formulate a plan for debate," how to gather materials, weigh facts, search out and refute the opposing arguments. He put "much emphasis on writing speeches" and then insisted that the student "get the substance inside till it obsessed him." Whatever else may be said, he used Genung's *Practical Elements of Rhetoric*, with its emphasis on style and invention, as the textbook in his writing courses.[12]

Toward the end of his freshman year, Fosdick was chosen as one of six men in his Greek class to appear in a public debate in the Academy chapel on the question "Resolved, that the *Iliad* and *Odyssey* represent distinct periods of Greek civilization and cannot, therefore, be the composition of one author." In the same year, coached by a senior member of his fraternity, he took first prize in the Kingsford Declamation Contest. As a sophomore he won first prizes in Latin, Greek, and English essay contests. By the time he was a junior, he was eligible to compete in one of the numerous prize contests in public speaking and with an oration on "The Battle of Omdurman," won first place and sixty dollars.[13] A picture in *Madisonensis* showed him an eager, youngish-looking student, his chin held high above the stiff, straight collar and his dark, curly hair parted precisely down the middle.[14]

His senior year was a regular campaign of speeches, debates, and orations. As student-body president, in the Fall of 1899, he took the chapel platform, along with the college president and

---

[12] Colgate University *Annual Catalogue*, 1897. Letters to the writer from Charles W. Briggs, February 1, 1954; H. Loren Fassett, February 8, 1954; H. D. Gray, January 29, 1954; Burt G. Grenell, February 6, 1954; James H. Howlett, February 3, 1954; Charles M. Newton, February 1, 1954; William M. Parke, February 3, 1954; Norman F. S. Russell, February 1, 1954; John M. Sayles, February 2, 1954; Frank S. Squyer, February 10, 1954; Stuart R. Treat, February 4, 1954, and others of Fosdick's classmates. See also Roy C. McCall: Harry Emerson Fosdick, paradox or paragon. *Quarterly Journal of Speech*, XXXVIII (October, 1953), pp.284, 285. Cf.f.n.19.

[13] *Madisonensis*, XXXI (May 31, 1899), 251; H. D. Gray to the writer, January 29, 1954.

[14] *Ibid.*, XXXII (March 12, 1900), p.153.

dean, to make one of the addresses celebrating Dewey Day, in honor of Admiral George Dewey's victory over the Spanish at Manila Bay. The reporter for the *Madisonensis* thought that Mr. Fosdick "illustrated and amply sustained" his points in a "clear, forceful and polished manner." Speaking on "College Students and American Life," he carefully partitioned his subject, marking out the points in parallel construction. The man whom the American people "long inexpressibly to be," he said, "is fired with the spirit which should inspire America—*devotion to duty;* he is trained with the discipline which should control America—*self-control;* he is crowned with the victory which is America's destiny —*victorious ability.*" [15]

A few weeks later, he was the major hope of the seniors in the interclass debate with the juniors. The debate, planned weeks in advance and preceded by eliminations and long hours of study and practice, was one of the outstanding events of the fall term. The chapel was packed for the occasion. Each class had its cheering section; many townspeople, even ministerial candidates from the seminary, were present; and students from the Academy, unable to find seats, lined the walls. The question was, "Resolved: that industrial trusts are economically sound." Fosdick spoke first for the affirmative and gave the one rebuttal allotted to his team. His voice was pitched a little too high, the reporter thought, and he spoke at a "nervously rapid rate." But his argument was coherent, and he did not have "those hitches and halts in delivery which are sometimes—and wrongly—thought to be the invariable accompaniment of extemporaneous debate." The juniors put up a stiff battle, but the seniors, at the conclusion of the debate, were confident of victory, a confidence sustained a half-hour later when, after an intentionally torturous review of the issues, the chairman announced the decision.[16]

It was in oratory, however, that Fosdick particularly excelled. The formal composition, written and memorized, gave him opportunity to mold his thought into figurative language, to polish his phrases, and to smooth out the rhythm of his periods until the whole sounded like a peroration. Early in the spring of 1900 at

---
[15] *Ibid.,* XXXII (October 9, 1899), p.7.
[16] *Ibid.,* XXXII (December 18, 1899), pp.84–86.

the Sheldon Opera House, he won first prize in the Rowland Oratorical Contest with a speech on "The Rough Riders." He used a dramatic incident, Roosevelt's charge on San Juan Hill, to symbolize his concept of American democracy. Some there were who thought America hopelessly divided—the South against the North, labor against capital, the poor against the rich—some who thought patriotism itself was dead. But America had made reply "in the crowning representative of her life and character." The men at San Juan Hill were made of "that stuff that makes America." A cosmopolitan lot, they were rich, poor, ignorant and learned; they represented every race, occupation, and religion; in their number were Negroes, Indians, and Irishmen, and yet, "trained with the discipline that shall preserve America," they charged when the command came to charge, and intrepid in their courage, glorious in their self-sacrifice, they were at last "laureled with the victory which is America's destiny." [17] And so he learned the arts of oratory, but he learned also to confuse sentiment and insight, to stir the people, and to win prizes.

As commencement season approached he made a clean sweep of the honors, winning, in addition to the Rowland Contest, the first-place award of forty dollars in the annual senior class debate and the first prize of sixty dollars in the Lewis Oratorical Contest.[18] In the years after he had become one of the nation's most famous platform men, he remembered his college training in oratory as "one of the most useful disciplines" of his educational experience. "I cannot overestimate the value," he said, "[or] the time it saved me in developing technique as a public speaker. . . ." [19]

But while he grew more facile in speech, he became increasingly perplexed about what to say. The simple faith of his freshman days did not return. Darwin would not down, nor did Fosdick, once having accepted survival of the fittest, find it easy to harmonize the principles of natural selection with supernatural creation and the God of the Baptists.

---

[17] *Ibid.*, XXXII (March 12, 1900), pp.153–55.
[18] *Ibid.*, XXXII (June 21, 1900), pp.251–52.
[19] Lionel Crocker: The rhetorical theory of Harry Emerson Fosdick. *Quarterly Journal of Speech*, XXII (April, 1936), p.207. See Chapter 18.

For some two years he enjoyed a delightful rebellion. Friends who had known him as a devout Christian were astonished at the change in him. He could not be dragged into church, he scorned the prayer meeting, he taunted the young saints for their simple beliefs, and he noted with pride that a pious group at the Y.M.C.A. was praying for him.[20] He eagerly devoured Andrew D. White's two-volume *History of the Warfare of Science with Theology in Christendom*. White's relentless uncovering of the superstitions of the Bible and the church, his documentation of the consistent triumph of science against the opposition of the theologians finally "smashed" the whole idea of biblical inerrancy for Fosdick. "I shall have to clear God out of my universe," he told his mother as he left home to begin his junior year at Colgate.[21]

However, his rebellion soon ran full circle and he began to doubt his doubts. White's history, despite its criticism, was essentially sympathetic to the Christian faith; the professors at Colgate were religious men long accustomed to the rebellions of students. Chief among them, in Fosdick's mind, was William Newton Clarke, a professor in the theological seminary who, despite the fact that he was under fire for his liberal views, remained loyal to the church. Fosdick sought out the professor and found sympathy for his own criticial thinking, but the older man chided him, too, for his naïve rebellion.[22]

In his senior year, in a course in philosophy, he fell under the influence of Royce's concept of loyalty and Borden Parker Browne's insistence on the primacy and ultimacy of personality. These he tempered with the earthy, optimistic pragmatism of William James. Before he had completed the course, he had come to believe that "there really is a God." [23] He put God back into his thinking, but not, as he said, back into his life. His was an intellectual God, the kind about whom a man might speculate but not the kind on whom he could depend emotionally. Nonetheless, he elected to attend a theological seminary—to prepare himself to teach religion.

---

[20] *Autobiography*, p.33.
[21] *Loc. cit.*
[22] *Ibid.*, p.36.
[23] *Ibid.*, pp.39, 179.

The chief obstacle to Fosdick's continued study was financial. One year he had interrupted his course at Colgate to work and help out with the family income. When he was graduated he took the teacher's examinations in Buffalo and was offered a position teaching Latin in the high school. His younger brother and sister were in college and his family needed the additional financial support. But his father urged him to go on to seminary. "Harry, you know that you will never be satisfied outside the Christian ministry," his father had told him even before he had finished his undergraduate studies.[24]

He had a scholarship to cover his tuition at Hamilton Theological Seminary at Colgate and needed only money enough to meet his board and room and other expenses. Calling upon the skills he had learned in college, he entered an essay contest on the evils of vivisection. His argument was specious but persuasive. He won third prize of $250, enough to launch him on his ministerial career.[25]

At seminary he took all of the courses offered by William Newton Clarke, some of them intended only for advanced students. But he was not satisfied to remain at Hamilton. The scholarship of Clarke and of visiting lectures whetted his appetite for study with great teachers. He transferred, therefore, to Union Theological Seminary in New York, across the street from Columbia University.

Union offered him the kind of intellectual liberty and spiritual leadership that he had dreamed of at Colgate and Hamilton.[26] There were strong men on the staff: Charles Cuthbert Hall, president and professor of pastoral theology; Arthur Cushman McGiffert, who taught church history; Francis Browne, Hebrew and cognate languages; William Knox, ethics and philosophy of religion; and Charles A. Briggs. Briggs was past his prime, but his influence in the institution was marked. In 1892 he had been tried for heresy because he did not accept the ultimate authority

---

[24] *Ibid.*, p.38.
[25] *Ibid.* Years later, in his retirement, Fosdick was to write: "I have always felt guilty about my specious arguments against vivisection . . . but at least I believed them when I wrote them. . . ."
[26] *Ibid.*, p.53.

of the Scriptures. The Presbyterian Church suspended him from the ministry but lost control of the seminary. Briggs remained at the seminary but was transferred to the Chair of Biblical Theology, and the liberal tradition which he had tested at Union grew stronger with the years.[27]

Fosdick went down to New York in the summer of 1901 to work in the Vacation Daily Bible Schools. Admitted to Union on a scholarship, he was given a winter's job helping to run a mission in the Bowery. He was greatly keyed up by the prospect of at last entering a great university. Moreover, he had fallen in love and was beside himself with joy and wonder.[28]

At the opening of school his excitement reached a new pitch when he passed a special examination for advanced standing in Greek. He enrolled in classes in philosophy at Columbia, theology at the seminary, and assisted at the mission in the Bowery. He learned much, especially in the Bowery, where he helped to conduct as many as nine meetings on a single Sunday. Panhandlers, naïve as children in religious matters, clever as Wall Street merchants in driving a shrewd bargain for assistance, taught him lessons he could not learn in his textbooks.

Had it not been for his financial troubles, he might have handled his rigorous schedule and disciplined his nervous excitement. But his resources were so slender that he abused his body with overwork and improper diet. His most expensive meal of the week was a twenty-five cent dinner on Sunday.[29]

In November he broke down completely from nervous strain, overwork, and undernourishment. It was, he wrote later, "the most hideous experience of my life."[30] He went home, a victim of malancholia. After months of purposelessness and disintegration, he went to a sanitarium where, by tutoring his physician's son, he gained a modicum of self-confidence. His fiancée's father sent him to Europe, and slowly through the months he regained his health.

---

[27] George L. Prentiss: *The Union Theological Seminary in the City of New York: Its Design and Another Decade of Its History.* Asbury Park, N.J., J. M., W. & C. Pennypacker, 1899, pp.311-35.
[28] Autobiography, p.47.
[29] *Ibid.*, pp.48-49.
[30] *Ibid.*, p.49.

But his spirit did not revive. His religion was an intellectual exercise, not a faith. "I was in hell," he said afterwards, "and had to get a vital faith to climb out." [31] The faith came gradually, and with it the lifting of the clouds. When he returned to the seminary the next fall, struggling yet to find his way, he had learned a lesson of vital significance to his ministry, a lesson of faith that Union, with its splendid staff of professors, could not teach him.

At the end of his second year in the seminary, he took over his first pastoral charge, a tiny church in the Adirondacks where he preached during the summer months. In the fall, following an unusually successful speech which he gave at the Colgate banquet in New York and which attracted the attention of George C. Lorimer, minister of the Madison Avenue Baptist Church, Fosdick was appointed student assistant at the church. Upon his graduation from Union in 1904, he was called to the pastorate of the Montclair, New Jersey, Baptist Church.[32]

Fosdick served the Montclair church until 1915, a period of eleven years. A somewhat conventional preacher, he did not give much evidence of the intellectual struggle he had gone through, nor of the extent to which he had abandoned the faith of his fathers, nor yet of the shock which he was about to inflict upon all Protestant America.

He published his first book in 1908, *The Second Mile,* a slender volume which grew out of a sermon he had preached one Sunday morning. He followed it with *The Manhood of the Master* in 1913 and *The Meaning of Prayer* in 1915. All were exceptionally well received, and *The Meaning of Prayer,* subsequently republished, sold nearly a half-million copies of the American edition.[33]

By the time he was ready to leave Montclair, he had already arrived at the fundamental tenets of his later preaching: that personality is the supreme value; that religion is an experience, not an intellectual exercise, an intuitive knowledge of God, not an argument about Him; that its consequence is to be measured in conduct, not in rules, or creeds, or theologies; and that author-

---

[31] Edward Clary Root: The power of faith. *The American Magazine,* CI (May, 1926), p.156.
[32] Autobiography, p.53.
[33] *Ibid.,* p.66.

Harry Emerson Fosdick: The Growth of a Great Preacher 141

ity is to be found, not in the written word, even of the Bible, but in the experiences of men.

But if he was inclined to be conventional in his ministry, he was nonetheless effective. The skill in speaking he had learned at college gave a resonance to his message, an amplifying depth and intensity that excited the interest and commanded the respect of his people. He was already master of the point concisely stated and vividly illustrated, and he could look into the eyes of his congregation and speak directly, in an impassioned manner if need be, without the crippling aid of manuscript or notes. The membership of his church trebled in the eleven years he was at Montclair.[34]

Two things he learned, particularly, in these early years: he learned first to study: to set aside the morning hours to read, reflect, and prepare his sermons; to maintain his schedule against all hazards; he learned the advantage of an office away from his home and his church, the greatly increased efficiency in having a secretary copy and file the passages he had marked and classified; he learned the discipline of writing, of reducing his thoughts to paper and of studying what he had written in the light of questions or objections which particular members of his congregation might raise.[35]

He learned, secondly, to take his sermons from the personal problems of men and women, to regard all preaching as problem-solving, to make each problem so real that every man could recognize it as his own, to argue the alternative courses of action, and to plead the advantages of the way of Jesus.

In the fall of 1908, Fosdick began to lecture at Union Theological Seminary on Baptist principles and polity. Three years later he became an instructor in homiletics. In 1915 he resigned his pastorate at Montclair to accept an appointment at Union at the Morris K. Jesup Professor of Practical Theology. His task, he said in his inaugural address, was to teach the young ministers to use the Bible in their preachings. In recent years scholars had revealed the historic Bible, with all of its primitive concepts of

---

[34] *Current Biography.* New York, The H. W. Wilson Co., 1940, p.309.
[35] Autobiography, p.64.

science, ethics, and theology, and in consequence had shattered many a layman's faith in the present values of the Scriptures. His business was to teach the "real nature of God's revelation in the Bible"—that men must see meanings of the universe "in terms of personality and the meanings of personality in terms of Christ. . . ." [36]

II

Fosdick was finally dislodged from his essentially conservative preaching not by critical studies nor by liberal influences but by an event of world-shaking significance, the great war which broke out in Europe in 1914.

His analysis of the war was essentially rhetorical. He saw it in the stereotyped pattern of his preaching—a problem to be dramatized and resolved. He hated war because of its "persistent debauching and brutalizing of men's souls"; he hated it because it took hold of the finest qualities in human life—courage, devotion, sacrifice—and utilized them to kill and lay waste; he hated it because of the injustice it worked and the succeeding wars it spawned, until men came to believe that war itself was an integral part of the system of international relations.[37]

But while he hated war and preached his hatred, he saw in this one war the possibility, remote perhaps, that international anarchy would yield to law, that the resort to arms as a means of settling disputes would give way to the courts of world government. Indeed, the Christian, and only the Christian (who was first of all a citizen of the Kingdom of God on earth), could translate patriotism into world-wide loyalty.[38] For the moment war was terrifying and horrible, a barrier to human progress, but in the long perspective of history wars were but jutting rocks around which the advancing stream of humanity swirled and moved on.

For the present, action was necessary. He saw that clearly in alliterative terms—"the horrors of Verdun, the mutilated bodies

---

[36] Fosdick: *A Modern Preacher's Problem in His Use of the Scriptures.* An Inaugural Address as Morris K. Jesup Professor of Practical Theology, Union Theological Seminary, September 13, 1915, pp.18, 20–21, 27, 32.

[37] Fosdick: *The Challenge of the Present Crisis.* New York, Association Press, 1918, p.63.

[38] *Ibid.,* p.77.

Harry Emerson Fosdick: The Growth of a Great Preacher 143

of Belgian boys, the bleaching bones of countless children . . . and after sixty generations of Christian opportunity, some five million wounded men in the hospitals of Europe." How could America keep heart and stand aloof? [39]

The basic dilemma of his faith—how a Christian, believing in the absolute value of personality, could go to war and kill—he resolved, oddly enough, in the manner of his evangelical fathers. *"Personality and physical existence,"* he said, *"are not identical."* A man's personality was one thing, his physical existence another. If a bayonet reached a man's body, the problem of personality passed "far beyond an earthy battlefield." [40]

As the war progressed he grew "increasingly anxious" that the United States should get into it. He was impatient with Wilson, indignant when the President announced that he was "too proud to fight." In 1916 he condemned Charles Evans Hughes for not pledging to take America into the war. He wrote a volume on *The Challenge of the Present Crisis,* conservative and antimilitaristic in some respects, but on the whole strongly in support of the war. He preached prowar sermons at Stanford and at Harvard (the latter one of the "most moving" addresses he had ever delivered), and he stumped New York State with a team of speakers in a campaign for war and world federation.[41]

When at last war came, a crusade to make the world safe for democracy, nationalism and Christianity joined forces in one great religious impulse. While President Wilson demanded a peace without victory on the political front, the president of the Federal Council of Churches of Christ in America was declaring that "The war for righteousness will be won! Let the Church do her part." [42]

In the spring of 1918, Fosdick visited the war front. He talked to the boys of courage and sacrifice, of home and democracy, of

---
[39] *Ibid.,* p.31.
[40] Fosdick: *Challenge,* p.39.
[41] Autobiography, pp.81–83. He later repudiated these activities and said that *The Challenge* was the only one of his books he regretted having written.
[42] Ray H. Abrams: *Preachers Present Arms: A Study of the War-time Attitudes and Activities of the Churches and the Clergy in the United States, 1914–1918.* New York, Round Table Press, Inc., 1933, p.58, citing *Federal Council Bulletin* Vol. 1, No. 3 (March, 1918), p.12. Frank Mason North was then president of the Council.

victory and peace, of the use of force for moral ends. He praised them for their unstinted dedication, for their self-denial, for their faith which now and then flamed out like a flare in No-Man's Land, for the magnificent ways in which they were fundamentally religious.

But all the while he despised the pettiness of the Church—his brethren of the ministry who denounced the dance, the theater, cards, drink, smoke, and Sabbathbreaking, or solemnly warned the boys that more important than the work in France was "the preparation of your souls to meet the Lord who speedily will return!" [43] He was disgusted with the pettiness of the sectarian appeal. While the Church busied itself with denominational creeds, the Army preached a crusade. "I used to wonder at the Cross," a soldier said to him; "not now! I think that Jesus was a lucky man to have a chance to die for a great cause." Let the Church proclaim social aims worth fighting for, and her day of unprecedented opportunity was at hand; let her make "ethical negations only the shadows cast by the great light of positive ideals"; let her practice as well as preach fraternity, and she need not fear for her contribution, nor for her place in the lives of the men, either when they were in the army, or after they were out of it.[44]

Never before had he seen quite so closely that the old creed, with its shackling customs and dogmas, and its sectarian exclusiveness, must be shattered before the minister of God could preach the essential elements of a liberal faith.

III

Critical as he was of the Church's petty negativism, Fosdick did not regard himself as an iconoclast called of God to shatter the idols of orthodoxy. The pulpit of the First Presbyterian Church, offered to him in the fall of 1918, was a liberal pulpit, open to the liberal preachers of the New York Presbytery and the learned doctors of the Union Theological Seminary. The laymen who sat in the pews had already accommodated their Calvinistic doctrines

---

[43] Fosdick: The trenches and the Church at home. *Atlantic Monthly*, CXXIII (January, 1919), p.26.
[44] *Ibid.*, pp.26, 33.

to the higher criticism and the evolutionary hypothesis. They were no more shocked, therefore, when Fosdick challenged a docile acceptance of creeds than they were when he attacked a blind faith in progress.

For three and a half years Fosdick preached to the congregations of Old First Church without unusual incident. Sunday after Sunday the people crowded to hear him. On one occasion he caught the brief attention of the press when his congregation, for the first time in the history of the Old Presbyterian Church, openly applauded the remarks of a preacher—for his denunciation of the "narrow nationalism" of George Harvey, American ambassador to the Court of St. James. He was cited again for attacking the war spirit and for demanding that the United States end the warlike tension in the Far East.[45]

No unusual circumstance attended his preaching on Sunday morning, May 21, 1922. He had announced his sermon title, "Shall the Fundamentalists Win?" in advance, but no one, least of all Fosdick himself, anticipated that he was about to preach the most sensational and widely-publicized sermon of his generation.

Only a few Sundays earlier Dr. Clarence E. Macartney of Philadelphia had visited the First Presbyterian Church and heard Fosdick preach. An arch-conservative and a leader in the Philadelphia Presbytery, Macartney was soon to become Fosdick's major antagonist. But on the morning of his visit he was only an interested observer. Arriving at the church some twenty minutes before eleven o'clock, he was surprised to find long queues of people standing in front of the doors, such crowds as he had not seen since he had worshipped in the popular churches of Edinburgh.[46]

Escorted to a pew at eleven o'clock, he noted that in a short time the entire church was filled and "not a few" people were seated on chairs in the aisles and in the adjoining chapel. He found the church large and beautiful, the platform approached by long marble steps. At the left was the lectern for the reading of

---

[45] *New York Times,* June 6, November 9, 1921.
[46] Sermons here and there, II. Hunting for Christianity in New York. *The Presbyterian,* XCII (June 8, 1922), pp.8, 26.

the Bible, in the center the conducting desk, and on a pillar at the right, the pulpit.

The three ministers of the church made their appearance, the young assistant, Mr. Speers, in the lead, followed by the venerable pastor, Dr. Alexander, and at last Dr. Fosdick, "an earnest-looking man with a heavy shock of black hair, and from a distance with an Oriental cast of countenance." Mr. Speers made the announcements, Dr. Alexander prayed a "beautiful prayer," and Dr. Fosdick read the Scriptures. The stragglers who came in during the singing of the hymn were placed on the marble steps in front of the pulpit. When the venerable and distinguished-looking General Charles King (a writer of Civil War tales and the clerk at Plymouth Church in Brooklyn) was about to join the "bleacherites," Fosdick stepped down "graciously" and invited him to sit on the platform.

Although, as Macartney observed from his place in the pew, Fosdick did not take a text, he did base his sermon upon a biblical incident. He spoke in a pleasing voice, without gesticulation, but he made a "ringing and powerful appeal to men and women . . . to be true to the sanctity of life." "No one," he said, "could have mistaken it for anything but a notable discourse." There was, however, an ominous note in Macartney's reaction. The sermon could not have been improved upon, he thought, for "the territory which it covered." But something was missing: the great preacher did not touch upon the "hopes and warnings of the gospel." He spoke of the vain sacrifices of parents for a wayward boy, but he did not "tell his great congregation that Christ had died on the cross for them. . . ."

No Macartney sat in the congregation on May 21 to record his impressions for the press. Again, as on the earlier occasion, Dr. Fosdick took no text. He announced abruptly that he and the audience would think together on the fundamentalist controversy which threatened to divide the American churches, "as though already they were not sufficiently split and riven." [47] The funda-

---

[47] Fosdick: *Shall the Fundamentalists Win?* A sermon preached at the First Presbyterian Church, New York City, May 21, 1922, stenographically reported by Margaret Renton, p.1. See also *The New Knowledge and the Christian Faith,* Ivy Lee (ed.), reprinted from a sermon by Dr. Fosdick, preached at the First Presbyterian Church, New York, May 21, 1922.

Harry Emerson Fosdick: The Growth of a Great Preacher 147

mentalists, he said, were intent upon driving men and women of liberal views out of the evangelical churches, and no denominations were more affected than the Baptist and the Presbyterian.

He was concerned with the necessity for Christians to adjust their faith to the new knowledge, especially that derived from the critical studies of the Scriptures (the higher criticism) and the scientific findings of the biologists. Among the items of faith which needed reexamination, he singled out three: the literal transcription of the Scriptures, the virgin birth, and the second coming of Jesus.

He did not attack the doctrines directly but condemned, rather, the intolerant fanaticism with which the fundamentalists clung to them. They not only rejected the new knowledge but in the spirit of intolerance, were determined to shut the door of Christian fellowship against all moderns who sought to reconcile science and religion. There were great tasks before the church—men and women were on the rocks spiritually, crying for help; the world had not yet found a means to solve the problem of war, and the Turks were massacring Christians in Armenia. In the face of these colossal issues the Church could not afford to quarrel over creedal matters, to "play with the tiddledywinks and peccadilloes of religion." It was almost unforgivable that men "should tithe mint and anise and cummin, and quarrel over them" when the world was perishing "for the lack of the weightier matters of the law, justice, and mercy, and faith."

Fosdick's blunt sympathies with modernism were apparent, but his sermon was in some measure conciliatory. He recognized that there were many "beautiful and gracious souls" who clung to a belief in the virgin birth and the infallibility of the Scriptures. So he appealed to tolerance, he pleaded for a church broad enough to contain both groups.

The sermon might have passed unnoticed had not one of his parishioners, the head of a nationally known publicity agency, undertaken to distribute it. With a publicist's eye for easy reading, he cut the sermon into short paragraphs, used captions which brought the controversial sections into sharp focus, and deleted parts of it, including, unhappily, the conciliatory introduction and conclusion. He then inserted a small printed slip saying that Mr. Fosdick was preaching to the largest congregation in New

York and without indicating who was responsible for the printing of the sermon, mailed it to hundreds of preachers across the continent.[48]

The reaction among the fundamentalists was widespread and vocal. Macartney, who was soon to be elected moderator of the General Assembly of his church, was amazed to think that Fosdick, who was not a Presbyterian, should stand in a Presbyterian pulpit and take his bread from a Presbyterian congregation while he openly defied the Presbyterian creed. He was shocked by the "almost unpardonable flippancy" in Fosdick's comparison of the virgin birth, the inspiration of the Bible, and the second coming of Christ to mint, anise, and cummin. William Jennings Bryan, characterizing Fosdick as the "most altitudinous higher critic" of his acquaintance, denounced Darwinism and atheism to five thousand persons in the Moody church in New York.[49]

The warfare thus opened raged for more than three years, with the fundamentalists determined to drive the modernists from their strongholds within the Church. In the meantime, with the newspapers giving full play to the attack of the fundamentalists, Fosdick was preaching regularly to overflow congregations. But in the end, despite the warm support of his own congregation and of the New York Presbytery, he felt compelled to resign. His resignation, tendered in the fall of 1924, was to take effect the following spring.

Invitations for him to preach poured in from all over the country; he was offered a pulpit in Edinburgh for the summer of 1925, and he was invited to preach at the opening of the League of Nations—to occupy the pulpit of John Calvin, the great Geneva reformer and the founder of the Presbyterian faith. The conflict had proved but a sounding board for his preaching: where he had been heard by a few hundred in New York, he was now known across the continent, and his name had appeared in headlines from Christiania, Norway, to Istanbul, Turkey.[50]

---

[48] *The Presbyterian*, XCII (September , 1922) , p.24; Fosdick, Autobiography, p. 113.

[49] Clarence E. Macartney: Shall unbelief win? An answer to Dr. Fosdick. *The Presbyterian*, XCII (July 13, 1922) , p.26; *ibid.* (July 20, 1922) , pp.8–10; *New York Times*, January 9, 1923.

[50] Autobiography, p.150.

IV

Aside from the internecine battles on fundamentalism, the major problem facing the Church in the 1920's was that of its relation to war. Not long after the signing of the armistice, Sir Philip Gibbs exposed the fraud of the Belgian atrocity stories, and scholars began to challenge the thesis that Germany was responsible for the war. The treaty at Versailles, despite the pledges of Woodrow Wilson, had handed about subject peoples to meet the demands of the victors, and the League of Nations, for all its merit, guaranteed the new boundaries by armed force and the blood of the youth. It was the best that we could do, the President had said, and acceptable only because the terms of the League made possible a future peaceable adjustment of inequities. But his high-flung banner "Make the World Safe for Democracy"—a cloud by day and a pillar of fire by night to the Great Crusade— was soon to become a mockery on men's lips. The Church, particularly, was deeply penitent over its recent equating of God and patriotism.

Fosdick, taunted by the pacifists for having "prostituted Christ" and condemned by his own conscience for his participation in the war, sought expiation in energetic support of the League of Nations, the World Court, and other modes of international cooperation. The "most important single social problem" confronting humanity, he said, "is the provision of international substitutes for war." [51] In his opening sermon for the League of Nations in the Protestant Cathedral of St. Peter in Geneva, he warned: "If mankind does not end war, war will end mankind." His voice rang out, reaching every corner of the great edifice, in words both "courageous and brilliant." [52] He condemned not war alone but nationalism. Christians, he said, believing in God as the Father of all mankind, must learn that narrow nationalism is "the most explicit and thoroughgoing denial of Christianity, its thought of

---

[51] *New York Times,* March 12, 1923. For the most thoroughgoing attack on Fosdick, see Henry W. Pinkham: *Collective Homicide, Letters to Harry Emerson Fosdick.* Brookline, Mass., Association to Abolish War, 1923. The letters are dated 1919.

[52] Fosdick: *A Christian Conscience about War:* A Sermon delivered at the League of Nations Assembly Service at the Cathedral at Geneva, September 13, 1925, New York, 1925; *New York Times,* September 14, 1925.

God and its love of man that there is on earth." Only this year before, in London, his faith swept away in the high idealism of his rhetoric, he had prophesied that he would live to see the United States join the League of Nations.[53]

Not all of the peace groups concurred with Fosdick in his endorsement of the League of Nations, nor did all of them agree with him in eschewing nationalism, at least American nationalism. Confused as to their aims, the seekers after peace were by the mid-1920's marked out by their critics as prophets of Babel, a multitude of voices with no common tongue. The banner under which the diverse groups were finally able to unite was the outlawry of war. The idea, suggested by an American, was espoused by Charles Clayton Morrison, editor of the *Christian Century*, John Dewey, William E. Borah, and others. In 1926 Aristide Briand proposed it as the basis of a bilateral treaty between the United States and France; Secretary of State Frank B. Kellogg responded by suggesting that the treaty be extended to include other major powers. After some months of negotiation the great powers of the world met in Paris in August, 1928, and signed a pact which solemnly condemned "recourse to war for the solution of international controversies," and renounced war as "an instrument of national policy in their relations with one another." [54]

Fosdick approved of the renunciation of war, but he did not easily lose his perspective. He greeted the pact with the question: "magnificent or mad"? It would be magnificent, he said, if it were implemented by adequate substitutes for war, mad if people relied on the stroke of a pen to solve their international tensions.[55]

To the American people, however, and to the churches especially, and eventually to Fosdick himself, the appeal of renunciation of war (buttressed, paradoxically, by a sense of security derived from the apparent fact of geographical isolationism) was irresistible. The farther removed they were from the war, the

---

[53] *New York Times,* May 15, 1924.

[54] Selig Adler: The war-guilt question and American disillusionment, 1918–1928. *Journal of Modern History,* XXIII (March, 1951), pp.1–28; Charles Clayton Morrison: *The Outlawry of War; A Constructive Policy for World Peace.* Chicago, Willett, Clark & Colby, 1927; Allan Nevins: *The United States in a Chaotic World* (The Chronicles of America Series, Vol. 55 [New Haven, 1950]), Chap. iv.

[55] *New York Times,* April 16, November 12, 1928.

Harry Emerson Fosdick: The Growth of a Great Preacher 151

more they knew of its origins, and the more they reflected on its deceits and its brutality, the keener their sense of guilt and the greater their feeling of revulsion. Historically, pacifism had been only a tiny stream in American life, the confluence of a few devout and courageous Quakers, Mennonites, and Brethren, men who denounced war in times of war as well as in times of peace. Now a romanticized, peacetime pacifism, preached in the classroom, advocated by student groups, made the subject of youth gatherings and church conferences quickly swelled into a great flood. In increasing numbers men avowed their determination to go to jail rather than participate in war. There were waiting lines for martyrdom.

In 1934, in the second of two nationwide polls of Protestant ministers on the question of war, 67 percent of the twenty thousand ministers who replied said that they would refuse to sanction any future war.[56] At this point Fosdick, in the most dramatic speech of his career, was thrust into the leadership of the Protestant peace crusade. The results of the poll were announced and discussed at a mass meeting in New York on May 7, 1934, at the Broadway Tabernacle in the presence of some of the most prominent clergymen of the nation and with Fosdick as the principal speaker. The meeting had been well-publicized and reporters of both the religious and the secular press were present. Fosdick's subject was announced as "My Account with the Unknown Soldier." He had preached the same sermon to his own congregation six months earlier, on the Sunday preceding Armistice Day, but on that occasion important elements of the drama—the gathering of prominent clergymen, the mass meeting, the results of the poll, and the reporters—all were missing.

Dr. Fosdick spoke, said the *New York Times,* "as if he were making a confession to the Unknown Soldier." [57] His sermon was extraordinarily personal. It was a penance for past sins, a catharsis for the years of self-condemnation.

---

[56] What 20,000 clergymen think. *The Nation,* CXXXVIII (May 9, 1934), p.524; Dixon Wecter: *The Age of the Great Depression, 1982–1941.* New York, Macmillan Co., 1948, pp.306–7.
[57] May 8, 1934. The sermon is published in Fosdick's *The Secret of Victorious Living; Sermons of Christianity Today.* New York, Harper & Bros., 1934, pp.88–98.

He tried to picture the Unknown Soldier, a conscript, no doubt, coerced to fight. He had no doubt that he knew the Unknown Soldier, that he had met him somewhere on the battle front. He recalled the night in a ruined barn behind the trenches when he spoke to a company of hand-grenaders detailed to raid the German trenches. They said that on the average no more than half a company ever came back from such a raid. And he, "a minister of Christ, tried to nerve them for their suicidal and murderous endeavor." A "gullible fool," he had thought that modern wars could make the world safe for democracy. Was the Unknown Soldier in that barn that night?

Some there were who thought war a thrilling experience, the "most exciting episode of our time," but they were the ones who had never seen a battle. Some were thrilled to stand at Arlington before the tomb of the Unknown Soldier, where he lay in the full panoply of military glory, knowing that he was the symbol of the highest idealism and courage of America. No doubt about it. But it was these thoughts that made war "a blistering fury" on his lips and "a deep self-condemnation" in his heart, for war laid its hands on the "strongest, loveliest things" in men and used the "noblest attributes of the human spirit" for the ungodliest of deeds! Only war could recount with glee the tale of an infantryman, his ammunition exhausted, arming himself with a spade and splitting the skulls of enemy soldiers as one by one they rounded a traverse, and only war could produce in countless numbers the pictures painted by an officer, of "a pair of hands (nationality unknown) which protruded from the soaked ashen soil like the roots of a tree turned upside down. . . ."

Did they wonder that he, who had been sent into the camps to awaken idealism, had an account to settle between his soul and the Unknown Soldier?

As for himself, he would settle the war problem, not sentimentally but hard-headedly. He would plead with his country to stay our of war, to cooperate with every movement that had any hope for peace: to enter the World Court, to support the League of Nations, to demand disarmament, but above all to stay out of war. "We can have . . . this monstrous thing or we can have Christ, but we cannot have both."

As for his own account, he would settle that too, by the renunciation of war. "I renounce war," he said, in a final dramatic pledge, "I renounce war and never again, directly or indirectly, will I sanction or support another! O Unknown Soldier, in penitent reparation I make you that pledge."

The newspapers of the city caught up the story, featured it on the front page, and the wire services dispersed it across the country. *Christian Century* reprinted the sermon in full, *Scholastic* and *Scribner's Commentator* published extensive excerpts, and other magazines quoted the most dramatic passages. When he preached it again in substance at Yale University, he was startled for the first time in thirty years of speaking in college chapels to have the students break into the sermon with applause. Letters and telegrams poured in from all over the country.[58]

With his instinct for the dramatic, Fosdick had placed himself at the head of the pacifists and unwittingly in the vanguard of the isolationists. He had excited a dream for a world of peace which the people who heard him could never forget, but it was a dream which took little account of the realities of the international scene.

V

Fosdick had scarcely resigned from the First Presbyterian Church in 1925 before he was offered the pulpit of the Park Avenue Baptist Church where John D. Rockefeller and his son were prominent members. After some hesitation, he accepted the call, first having stipulated that his annual salary should not exceed $5,000 and that baptism by immersion should not be required of new members. The church accepted the conditions and agreed further, in anticipation of the large crowds he would attract, to replace its newly-constructed but small building with a much larger edifice which they would erect uptown, in the vicinity of Columbia University. Rockefeller, in order to reduce Fosdick's embarrassment as pastor of the "richest man in America," established and placed under control of the church a trust fund,

---

[58] *Christian Century*, LI (June 6, 1934), pp.754–756; *Scholastic*, XXVII (November 9, 1935), pp.9–10; *Scribner's Commentator*, XI (November 4, 1941), pp.97–100; Fosdick: *Secret*, p.102.

the interest of which was to constitute his annual contributions.[59]

Fosdick was installed on May 31, 1925, only two months after he had preached his farewell sermon at the First Presbyterian Church. He had, however, already arranged with the Union Theological Seminary for a sabbatical year in Europe and Palestine, and therefore did not begin his active ministry until the fall of 1926. In the meantime, Rockefeller purchased a site on Riverside Drive and 122nd Street and with Fosdick's approval began the construction of a mammoth edifice, popularly referred to as the "skyscraper" church.[60]

Ready for occupancy in 1930, the new building was a large neo-Gothic church, unmatched in American Protestantism save by the Cathedral of St. John the Divine, which was but a few blocks distant. Its gigantic tower, reaching four hundred feet above the level of the street, looked out over the Hudson River and housed the offices, educational plant, the smaller assembly rooms, and the recreational facilities. The nave, with seating for 2,400 people, was lined on the side walls with ten stained-glass windows which depicted the progress of man in learning, religion, and the arts. The pulpit was on the right of the chancel, the reading desk on the left, and between them a great stonework screen embellished with figures of Christ and the apostles. Some were impressed with the great beauty of the new structure, others only with its vastness and its cost.[61]

From the day Dr. Fosdick had accepted the call to the Park Avenue Baptist Church, all American Protestantism had experienced a feeling of tension over his new adventure. The fundamentalists were disturbed that such a master of "brilliant sophistries" and "graces of oratory" should have so prominent a pulpit from which to proclaim his heresies. Of one thing they were certain, however: the power of God would not be in the pile of cold stones erected by Mr. Rockefeller. The radicals were concerned lest

---

[59] Open-shop parson. *Time Magazine*, XLI (March 15, 1943), p.54; *New York Times*, May 29, 1925; Autobiography, p.147.
[60] *New York Times*, May 26, July 12, 25, August 8, 1925; January 29, 1926.
[61] John Hyde Preston: Dr. Fosdick's new church. *World's Work*, LVIII (July, 1929), pp.56–58; Dr. Fosdick accepts the challenge. *Christian Century*, XLVII (October 15, 1930), p.1239.

Fosdick, failing to accept his responsibilities of leadership, should give way to the forces of conservatism. Even his friends were not yet ready to say that he could escape the onus of wealth reflected in the very elegance and beauty of the new church. Was it possible for the pastor of such a church to avoid trimming his gospel or "suppressing an inconvenient segment of it?" [62]

Whatever the doubts of others, the people who heard him approved. Thirty-two hundred crowded into the nave and one of the assembly rooms on the opening Sunday, and hundreds were unable to find seats. On the following Sabbath the authorities placed loud-speakers in three assembly rooms and the small chapel. A line, four abreast, which began to form about 9 o'clock, had by 10:30 A.M. reached down Riverside Drive to the south end of the church grounds; by the time the services began, four thousand persons had pressed their way into the nave and the assembly rooms. Week after week, and year after year at periodical intervals, the press carried reports of such overflow crowds.[63]

If Fosdick preached to thousands in his congregation on Sunday morning, he preached to hundreds of thousands in his radio audience on Sunday afternoon. He had begun his radio preaching while he was still at the First Presbyterian Church and at Park Avenue had broadcast his Sunday morning services. In 1927 he initiated the nationwide broadcast of the National Vespers, a half-hour program sponsored by the National Broadcasting Company and devoted chiefly to his sermon. Always an attractive Sunday feature, the Vespers, at its interest peak, was rebroadcast by 125 stations and was heard by an estimated two-to-three million listeners. Fosdick received over 100,000 letters a year from members of his radio audience.[64]

His popularity in the pulpit and on the radio was reflected in his publications. When he accepted the call to the Park Avenue Church he had already published nine volumes, including the Lyman Beecher lectures at Yale, the Cole lectures at Vanderbilt, and his popular little devotional books on *The Meaning of*

---

[62] John Roach Straton in *New York Times*, May 20, 1925; Dr. Fosdick accepts the challenge. *Christian Century*, XLVII (October 15, 1930), p.1240.
[63] *New York Times*, October 6, 13, 1930.
[64] *Ibid.*, December 21, 1924; Autobiography, pp.171–73.

Prayer, The Meaning of Faith, and *The Meaning of Service.* He continued to write: two volumes on the modernists' religion, a book-length report on his pilgrimage to Palestine, a scholarly guide to the understanding of the Bible, and beginning in 1934, a half-dozen volumes of his sermons. In 1942 his three volumes on prayer, faith, and service, having sold an aggregate of over one-half million copies, were reissued as a single volume; one of his last books to be published was issued with an original printing of fifty thousand copies, their largest original print order for a religious book.[65]

What did this man preach, that he should command so large an audience, that he should become a prophet to the nation, that he should be heralded by his colleagues as the "greatest preacher in the English tongue"? [66]

He believed God to be an objective reality, revealed not in tablets of stone or in authoritarian Scriptures but in the progressive insights of men. He found the highest intuition of God in Jesus, the essential superiority of Christianity in its ethical code, the basis of which was its reverence for personality. In the tradition of Wesley and Schleiermacher he regarded the emotional state as the essential datum. Religious experience he defined as containing two attributes: (a) self-commitment, devotion to something greater than one's own personal interests—to truth, to beauty, or to goodness, not in the abstract but as embodied in particular causes; and (b) a transforming inward sense of peace and unity, of power and confidence, of harmonious relations with the vital forces of the universe.[67]

In a sense, his emphasis was not unlike that of the fundamentalists. Where the latter dramatized sin and its effect and called for

---

[65] Charles W. Ferguson: Who reads religious books? *Saturday Review of Literature,* XVI (July 10, 1937), p.14; Open-shop parson. *Time Magazine,* XLI (March 15, 1943) p.54.

[66] E. W. Powell in *New York Times,* June 12, 1925; Charles W. Gilkey: Dr. Fosdick preaches: review of *The Hope of the World. Christian Century,* LI (April 4, 1934), pp.459–460; Dr. Stephen S. Wise in *New York Times,* February 4, 1930. On his retirement the *Christian Century* characterized him, along with Henry Ward Beecher and Phillips Brooks as one of the three greatest names of the American pulpit. See Dr. Fosdick will retire next May. *Christian Century,* LXII (June 20, 1945), p.725.

[67] Fosdick: *As I See Religion* New York, Harper & Bros., 1932, pp.10–20.

repentance, Fosdick dwelt upon personal problems—tensions, maladjustments, purposelessness—and pointed the way to relief and power through the experience of religion. He not only recognized these identities in fundamentalism and modernism but on this basis justified his adherence to the Church even though he had sloughed off many of the traditional doctrines. He attacked the fundamentalists not simply on the basis that they denied the findings of science but that in an effort to defend an outworn creed, they had, like the Pharisees of Jesus' time, neglected the experience.

To Fosdick, religious experience, since it was not circumscribed by creed and doctrine, was not limited to the church or the synagogue. Sometimes a "downright unbelieving scientist," he said, who gave himself to his science and stood by it "through thick and thin" seemed "closer to New Testament Christianity than many of us in the churches." [68] "You are carried out of yourselves by something greater than yourselves, like the Fifth symphony of Beethoven," he said to the students of Columbia University, "are religious for me, no matter what terrible opinion you may have of yourselves." [69] Men and women who felt an inner sense of strength, of serenity and power in time of trouble, a power not *self-generated* but appropriated from some source beyond themselves, these people were religious whatever their creed.

In thus attacking doctrine and eulogizing experience, Fosdick faced a dilemma which his critics were quick to point out: if emphasis upon creeds made religion formal and barren, emphasis upon experience might well make it anarchistic. What excesses of emotion, what bizarre and irrational conduct had mankind indulged in, the name of religion! Recognizing the dilemma, he sought to delimit the experience of religion on empirical, pragmatic, not a priori grounds. Through generations of trial and error, progress and retreat, through the insights of the poets and prophets, mankind had learned the utility of belief in God, of faith, of devotion to social ideals, of placing the highest value on personality.

---
[68] Fosdick: *The Power to See It Through; Sermons on Christianity Today.* New York, Harper & Bros., 1935, p.7. See chapter 22.
[69] *New York Times,* December 10, 1929.

Although a man might find religious experience in music, or science, or social work, he would not realize its full significance, Fosdick preached, save through belief in God. Having said as much, he found it difficult to define God, who, as he put it, "had never sat for his photograph." [70] In a sense, God was a work of art, an objectifying of man's finest thoughts and highest ideals. Each man, having something of the artist within himself, created in his mind's eye his own image of God, but he was vastly aided by the great artists, the men of greater sensibilities and keener insights, the poets and the prophets. These were dependent, in turn, upon one another, the greater upon the lesser, the latter upon the crude imaginings and graven images of their predecessors, until Jesus himself had swept aside the clouds and revealed the very face of God.

Thus, faith in God had come to mean a faith in "an eternal moral purpose," which gave a man "wide horizons, long outlooks, steady hopes." [71] In their efforts to understand their experiences of such a God and to communicate to others, men had resorted to symbols. They thought of God as father, or mother; they recalled or intensified their religious emotions with a crucifix, a cross, candles and an altar, a hymn, or a prayer. The highest symbol of God was Jesus, who was neither omnipotent nor omnipresent, but who, more than any other man, partook of the essence of God. He was as the tiny inlet is to the ocean. A man might view the inlet, taste its waters, launch his boat upon it, and know that tiny as it was, it was yet of the essence of the mighty ocean—the near view of it.[72]

Fosdick was not satisfied in his mind, however, with this empirical, genetic approach to God. He was a theistic evolutionist. He could not think of the wonders of the universe, of a "cosmos infinite and infinitesimal, and as unified as it is vast," and of personality, the most amazing miracle of all, without seeking explanation in "the law of adequate causation." [73] So in concert

---

[70] Fosdick: *The Serect*, p.155.
[71] Fosdick: *Power*, p.9.
[72] Fosdick: *Secret*, pp.166–167.
[73] Fosdick: Religion's debt to science. *Good Housekeeping*, LXXXVI (March, 1928), p.21; *Secret*, p.135.

with many of the modernists, he posited the God of the philosophical idealists, the God who is the necessary cause for the otherwise inexplicable phenomena of the universe. Drawing freely upon the discoveries of science, from Copernicus and Newton to Darwin and Einstein and Freud, he preached the wonders of the universe and the marvel and sacredness of personality and eulogized the God of creative force.

He had no formula for getting religion or taking hold of God, but he believed that there was one indispensable element in the apprehension of Him: faith. Faith was a doctrine not easy to preach to the disillusioned, skeptical, debunking twenties. Fosdick, himself, in his attack on fundamentalism, was a part of the revolt against formalism and creeds, and thus far did he and his congregation both yield to the spirit of the times. But he would not yield the essential tenets, the reliance on God as the cosmic force, as the intellect and will which gave order and purpose to the universe. Attacking the skeptics of the twenties, he reaffirmed the wonders of the universe, the greatest of which was man himself. He ridiculed the believers in chance, the fortuitous falling-together of the stellar universe, the worshippers of dynamic dirt, the "little men," the mechanistic philosophers on college campuses who whipped out "final solutions of the eternal mysteries" with the same confidence that western Kentucky Baptists affirmed the superiority of their faith.[74]

His ultimate appeal, however, was not to the God of causation but to the pragmatic test. Forget your prayers, he said to his congregation, and in their stead some morning say to yourself, "I am an accident, a fortuitous by-product of the dust." And at night salute yourself with the same thoroughgoing honesty of the irreligious, as for example: "I am 'a parasite infesting the epidermis of a midge among the planets.'" "Do you really think," he asked, "that such words help to keep men on their feet?" [75]

So he preached faith, a quality which he did not so much define as illustrate. He praised the courage of Helen Keller who "out of the limitations of defeat . . . rose up to win one of the shining successes of human history"; he cited the determination of the

---
[74] Fosdick: *Secret,* p.132.
[75] Fosdick: *Hope,* p.81.

Wright brothers, who, despite the cynicism of their neighbors ("nobody's ever going to fly; and if anybody ever did fly it wouldn't be anybody from Dayton"), persisted in their attempts to fly. He told of Phillips Brooks and the bitterness of his despair when he failed at teaching, of the greatness of his success when he turned to the ministry. "Blessed be biography," he said, as he searched the pages of history for incidents of triumphant faith.[76]

When the fundamentalists attacked Fosdick on the grounds that in rejecting the Bible as divinely inspired he had no moral code to preach, he replied that the accumulated experience and wisdom of man, particularly as revealed in Jesus, was sufficient sanction. He based his preaching on social issues, on the proposition, which he credited to Jesus, that personality is the supreme value. That which is degrading to personality, therefore, is un-Christian, and conversely, that which is uplifting to personality is of the very essence of Christianity. On these grounds he condemned war for its destruction of human life, its debasing of conquered and conqueror alike; he lashed out against the corruption in Harding's Cabinet, demanded the removal of Mayor "Jimmy" Walker and the repudiation at the polls of that "highly organized plunderbund," Tammany Hall. If in 1927 he eulogized business for its "morality" in having shared the products of industry "more widely than has ever been done in modern times before," he at the same time warned against the swaggering arrogance of a prosperous nation.[77]

Those who feared that he had yielded to the charm of Rockefeller's wealth were somewhat reassured by his vigorous demands, following the crash of 1929, for fundamental reforms in the economic structure, for abandonment of the "crazy idea" that "competition is the life of the trade," for socialization of the basic industries. With some reservations politically, he even praised the New Deal for its efforts to codify competitive practices. He warned that capitalism was on trial with communism, that millions living under the shadow of economic insecurity were easy prey to the enemy. "Starvation does not call out devotion," he

---

[76] *Ibid.*, p.83; *Secret*, p.5.
[77] *New York Times*, November 22, 1926; April 25, 1927; July 4, 1932.

Harry Emerson Fosdick: The Growth of a Great Preacher

said. He joined eighteen thousand other Protestant ministers in a declaration against the "rugged individualism" of the capitalistic system, and he won for himself the distinction of a listing in Elizabeth Dilling's *The Red Network*. He lashed out at Lathrop Stoddard and the "cynical gospel" of the superiority of the Nordic race and denounced Hitler's anti-Semitic campaign. He was equally forthright in his condemnation of racial prejudice at work in America.[78]

He discussed issues of conduct, too: condemned the "lawlessness" and the devotion to "self-expression" of the twenties, the "freedom of flapperism and the hip flask"; he deplored the laxity in sex standards, the increasing divorce rate, and Judge Ben Lindsay's companionate marriage. He rebuked the novelists for their low tastes and censured the people themselves, the "wicked consumers," for their patronage of the New York theater. Conversely, he supported Margaret Sanger in her campaign for the dissemination of information on birth control. "God pity the children that come when they are not wanted," he said.[79]

When all of this is said, it must be admitted, however, that Fosdick was not primarily, nor even fundamentally, concerned with social issues. Aside from the subject of war, he rarely devoted an entire sermon to a social or economic question. He did not resort to the direct assault, the searching and withering fire of a prophet, but favored rather the incidental denunciation of the social problem as an illustration of the moral lack in individuals. Social and personal problems, he said, are like the two ends of the Holland tunnel: "if starting with personal religion we are constrained to go through to the problems of society, so starting with the problems of society, we are constrained to go through to personal religion." [80] "There is no social sin whose central responsibility is not inside individuals." The world ought to be transformed, he asserted, but in the meantime, while it is not trans-

---

[78] *Ibid.*, November 9, 1930; October 2, 1931; April 25, 1932; October 16, 1933; April 25, 1927; What 20,000 Clergymen Think, *op. cit.*, p.524.

[79] *New York Times*, June 15, 1925; January 16, 1928; December 17, 1928; Fosdick: What is happening to the American family. *American Magazine*, CVI (October, 1928), p.96.

[80] Fosdick: *Hope*, p. 30.

formed, ". . . we must transcend it, rise above it, be superior to it, and carry off a spiritual victory in the face of it." [81]

In view of the collapse of American prosperity and the rise in Europe of a new nationalism with the accompanying specter of war, Fosdick's emphasis on personal problems seemed to some Christians a retreat from the social and ethical issues of the day. For several years the modernists, and by reason of his preeminence, Dr. Fosdick in particular, had been under severe attack from the "New Realists," those "disenchanted liberals" of Marxian or Barthian influence, the neo-Orthodox.[82]

The neo-Orthodox charged that the modernists did not understand sin whether expressed in the individual or in society. Nor did the modernist understand the nature of man, his strange perversity, his inevitable sinfulness; the modernist could not comprehend the absolute distance between God and man and the necessity for a revelation which would simultaneously charge man with the tension of condemnation and forgiveness.

When, therefore, Fosdick preached a sermon in 1935 calling upon his congregation to go "Beyond Modernism," he produced a sensation. Long before the American followers of Kierkegaard and Barth had arisen to criticize the easy optimism of the modernists, Fosdick had warned, in his Yale lectures of 1922, against the "perils and delusions of progress." But in 1935 he had been sick and out of the pulpit for nine months; the press expected a story of perhaps sensational proportions and played it with the suggestion that the leader of the modernist forces, the great heretic himself, finding his liberal religion inadequate, was returning to the God of the fundamentalists. Even the reliable *Christian Century* saw great significance in the fact that the "most important, popular figure in the Protestant pulpit for two decades" was about to lead his people out of the barren wilderness of modernism.[83]

---

[81] *New York Times,* August 8, 1929.

[82] Dr. Fosdick shifts the emphasis. *Christian Century,* LII (November 20, 1935), p.1480.

[83] *Loc. cit.; Christian Century,* LII (November 20, 1935) p. 1480. Fosdick: *Successful Christian Living; Sermons on Christianity Today.* New York, Harper & Bros., 1937, pp.153–164; Fosdick: *The Modern Use of the Bible.* New York, Macmillan Co., 1924, pp.169–206; E. H. Abbot: Dr. Fosdick's religion. *Outlook,* CXXXIX (March 11, 1925), p.364.

Harry Emerson Fosdick: The Growth of a Great Preacher 163

Those who read the sermon, or heard it, knew full well that Fosdick gave small comfort to the fundamentalists, however much capital they made of his remarks. He appropriated rather than repudiated the gains of biblical criticism and the efforts to reconcile religion and science; these, he said, were the necessary starting point beyond which modernism must go.

Nor did he ally himself with the neo-Orthodox. He agreed with them that "inevitable progress" was a delusion, a sentimental softness induced by the rise of democracy, the improvement in economic conditions, the increase in humanitarianism, all sanctified by the doctrine of evolution. He insisted in the manner of the neo-Orthodox upon the reality of sin which "leads men and nations to damnation" and upon the reality of God as the "central message and distinctive truth of religion." He admitted, also, that modernism had too often lost its "ethical standing-ground and its power of moral attack." In its efforts to harmonize doctrines and science, it had too frequently accommodated religion to culture, adapted Christianity to nationalism, imperialism, and racism. The function of the Church, he said, was not to adjust itself to the prevailing culture but to "Stand out from it and challenge it!"

But he did not go along with the neo-Orthodox. He had appropriated their criticism but not their theology. "Beyond modernism" meant to him to go beyond biblical criticism, beyond the reconciling of religion and science to the fundamental religious experience. What application of his new modernism he would make was soon to be apparent in his dealing with the problem of World War II.

VI

The social revolution of the 1920's brought temporary disaster to a good many American churches. Although membership remained more or less constant, attendance figures skidded to new lows. Short skirts, bobbed hair, bathtub gin, and Freud seemed quite out of accord with the teachings of Sunday morning. The New Freedom mocked traditions of religion as blithely as it laughed at fashions of dress and codes of social conduct. Cartoonists standardized the caricature of the Protestant clergy: an elongated stern-faced puritan who saw and smelled evil in every pleasurable activity of his fellows. Sinclair Lewis, having with microscopic care uncovered the secrets of Main Street and Babbittry, put the clergy under his lens and revealed the ankle-gazing, pious-mouthed Elmer Gantry.

But Harry Emerson Fosdick was not easily mocked. Others might preach to empty pews but he had overflow crowds and waiting lines. Out-of-town visitors were advised to write in advance for special admission tickets. The First Presbyterian Church had ordered plush cushions so that late-comers might sit more comfortably on the marble steps leading to the platform. And even the new edifice on Riverside Drive, with its provisions for overflow crowds, was not able to accommodate the people who wanted to hear him.[84]

Some thought it was the gospel he preached and the publicity he received that attracted the crowds. But he was preaching to overflow congregations at the First Presbyterian Church long before he made the headlines with the quarrel over his sermon "Shall the Fundamentalists Win?" And he continued to attract the crowds despite his refusal to carry the quarrel into his pulpit.

Others thought that the source of his appeal lay not only in his modernist gospel but in the manner of his sermonizing. Fosdick thought so himself. The trouble with most preaching, he said, was that it was "uninteresting." It did not matter. "It could as well be left unsaid."[85] He condemned the expository approach. Who would seriously suppose that one-in-a-hundred in the average congregation was deeply concerned over the meaning of words which Moses, Isaiah, Paul, or John had spoken two thousand years ago? Within a moment or two after the preacher had begun to speak, wide areas of the congregation ought to recognize that he was "tackling something of vital concern to them." To prove his point, he appealed to the advertisers: Whether they sought to sell a five-foot shelf of books or an insurance policy, they plunged as directly as possible after contemporary wants, felt needs, actual interests, and concerns. It should be the same with a sermon. The

---

[84] *New York Times,* October 1, 1923; February 16, 1924; October 4, 1926; October 27, 1930.

[85] Fosdick: What is the matter with preaching? *Harper's Magazine,* CLVII (July, 1928), p.134. See Chapter 2.

essential element of sermonizing, he said, was "the solving of some problem—a vital, important problem, puzzling minds, burdening consciences, distracting lives. . . ."

A good divine, Fosdick practiced his own preaching. His whole process, not only of preaching but of sermon preparation, was geared to the problem-solving approach. He was primarily interested in persons, not in texts. He could never feel that a sermon was really under way, he said, until he had clearly in mind some difficulty that people were facing, some question that they were asking. The people had caught on to Darwin and his attractive doctrine that an organism, irritated by its environment, seeks constantly for a more satisfactory adjustment. They had embraced Spencer with his infinite hope for the progress of mankind. They had heard of Dewey and approved of his reduction of the thinking process to the solving of problems. They knew something of Freud, too, and his playing upon the eternal restlessness of man, his dipping down into the subconscious to find and conjure up the great disturber of man's peace.

Small wonder, then, that Fosdick should sermonize by problem-solving. The greater wonder is that more preachers of his era did not consciously use the same technique, that so few of them were able to throw off the homiletic tradition, the argument and exposition of the learned seminaries, the tradition of doctrinal preaching, the terminology, the incantations of an earlier century so completely divorced and yet so oddly present in the *scientific age*.

The approach was admirably designed to persuade. Once a preacher had wrought his congregation into a sufficiently high state of tension over a problem, he had rendered them suggestible and readily amenable to the solution he had to offer. The technique was familiar to generations of evangelical preachers who, having vividly portrayed the wrath to come, pointed to the mourner's bench or the sawdust trail as the sure way of salvation. Fosdick was thus in the evangelical tradition in his basic method of sermonizing as well as in his emphasis on experience, and he knew it. His approach was scarcely so exploitative, however. His problem-solving was closer to the classroom lecture than to the advertiser's poster or Billy Sunday's call to repentance.

He liked to think that the solutions he offered were reasoned discourses into which he introduced opposing personalities, conflicting hypotheses, arguments he must answer before his own solution could prevail. He thought this *Hegelian* approach not only more interesting to the audience but more useful in helping them to reach a logical conclusion.[86] Had his sermons fitted the pattern which he thus laid out, they would have, indeed, been remarkably parallel to Dewey's formula for scientific investigation. But Fosdick was a rhetorician, not a scientist. While it is true that in the years of his argumentative attacks on fundamentalism he sometimes introduced argument and refutation into his solution, he rarely treated the disparate views as hypotheses. As a matter of fact, he rarely formalized and presented opposing views. More often (and especially so in the later years of his affirmative emphasis on experience) he resorted to concession, or even to the taking over of his opponent's views. Did a critic attack the church? Fosdick not only conceded the point but appropriated the argument and directed it against the peccadilloes of fundamentalism or the negativism of the modernist-liberal tradition. Did a church member protest that events were overwhelming, that life was essentially disillusioning? Fosdick conceded the burden of his complaint, perhaps enlarged upon it, only to bring into sharper relief the magnificence of the Christian faith. When he set forth an opposing view, he did not always represent it in a favorable light. He could on occasion lay down a withering barrage against the faith of the skeptics in "dynamic dust" or the devotion of the fundamentalist to "Biblical literalisms." But whether he argued, or conceded, or attacked, he left no doubt with the audience where his sympathies lay. His business was persuasion.

With all of his emphasis upon problems and solutions, Fosdick did not fall into any simple rhetorical approach built upon the Dewey problem-solution pattern. Quite unconscious of the *motivated sequence* speech of the modern-day psychological rhetoricians, he constructed his sermons on the simple classical model which he had studied at college. Far from restricting the problem to the introduction, he sometimes used it like a minor chord, its

---

[86] *Ibid.,* pp.134–37.

Harry Emerson Fosdick: The Growth of a Great Preacher 167

disturbing melody rising again and again to heighten the effect of the triumphant major. If he opened his sermon psychologically with a problem, he treated it rhetorically as an introduction. He regularly focused all of his opening remarks upon a single question or proposition which he then proceeded to answer or develop in three or sometimes four and occasionally five or six topics, the "body" of his speech.[87]

What ingenuity he put into the phrasing of that central question or those topical divisions! With what verbal dexterity he could clothe the same recurring ideas or from what provoking and intriguing angles he could exhibit an old thought! His technique was exciting to the auditor. It was like the trick of the psychological perception test—one might look at a dull series of light and dark lines drawn at sharp angles and then blink his eyes and behold! a staircase. So one might look at the old ideas he held up and suddenly see them with a new insight.

Ordinarily, he clearly marked out the major steps of his sermons. Sometimes like a guide he stepped aside from the trail, the people gathered about him, for a moment's backward glance over the ground they had traversed, and a quick view of the road which lay ahead of them. More often he simply numbered his points: "let us say first"; "This first step alone, however, does not carry us out of our difficulty . . . So we must now face the fact . . ."; and "Finally and logically, then. . . ." Occasionally, without enumeration, he made his direction clear by a simple transitional phrase and the repetition of the key words of his central thought, as when he made "an excursion into remembrance, an endeavor to recall some of the old words which century after century, through stormy days, have kept men on their feet." "One such word," he said, "is that *life is an entrustment*"; "Here is another word that might help, that the *supreme successes of the world have been defeats*. . . ."[88]

---

[87] Gilbert S. MacVaugh: Structural analysis of the sermons of Harry Emerson Fosdick. *Quarterly Journal of Speech,* XVIII (November, 1932), pp.531–46. The analysis made by MacVaugh—showing that Fosdick's points are, from first to last, successively shorter in treatment—is not borne out with any degree of consistency in the sermons of the printed volumes. See Chapter 16.

[88] *Hope,* pp.78–82.

Now and then he drew upon some striking line from an illustration, a brief quotation perhaps, as a refrain which like a melodic theme recurred again and again and bound the whole together much more tightly than could any logical relation of main points. Consider, for example, his sermon on "Facing the Challenge of Change." In the introduction he told the story of Jeremiah who, distraught with the misfortunes of Israel, looked across the Jordan at placid Moab. Unlike Israel, Jeremiah cried out, "Moab hath been at ease from his youth . . . and hath not been emptied from vessel to vessel." Picking up the figure, Fosdick applied it conversely, praising the man who "never surrenders to sluggishness or stagnation—poured from vessel to vessel he makes change his friend." He praised the Christian ideal of the "maladjusted life," maladjusted to the war system, to economic injustice, race prejudice, and taunted his fellow-churchmen who would complacently permit non-Christians to beat them at what ought to be their own game, "pouring mankind from vessel to vessel." [89]

He could utilize for his refrain not only a verse of Scripture but such a commonplace phrase as Br'er Rabbit's taunt "Bred and bawn in a brierpatch," or a phrase from a contemporary incident, "they have sold something valuable very cheap." [90]

In structure, then, his sermons, in whatever manner they were bound together, were essentially arguments—"too intellectual," said one of his friendly critics, to constitute the best of sermonizing.[91] But while he argued in the framework, he was not argumentative in the details. He did not so much prove his points as illustrate them. Rather than pile up fact on fact or biblical citation upon biblical citation to buttress a theological dogma, he seized upon an illustration and used it like a lens to bring his proposition into sharp, clear focus, to magnify it, if need be, a hundredfold. Or, swinging an analogy into place like a floodlamp, he suddenly illumined his whole point with a full, bright light. Not infrequently he employed montage (a technique older to

---

[89] *Ibid.*, pp.107–16.

[90] *Ibid.*, pp.11–20, 79.

[91] Joseph Fort Newton (Ed.): *If I Had Only One Sermon to Prepare.* New York, Harper & Bros., 1932, p.108.

Harry Emerson Fosdick: The Growth of a Great Preacher 169

rhetoric than to the movies): the Wright brothers fighting derision and defeat in their own community of Dayton, Ohio; Helen Keller rising to victory against tremendous odds; *Cyrano de Bergerac*, crushed and dying but able to say, "One thing without stain . . . my white plume"; Socrates taking the cup; Jesus on Calvary; the supreme successes of history springing from defeats —all compressed into a single paragraph.[92]

The illustration—insight, argument from example rather than legal evidence—was especially suited to Fosdick because his propositions were drawn from experience rather than from dogma; they were psychological rather than theological. Yet he did not, on occasion, hesitate to argue like a lawyer to prove his psychological premises. He used the Bible for its poetic insights, but he turned to the psychologists and scientists for authoritative proof.

He ranged widely in his search for illustrative material and was unusually resourceful and imaginative in seeing relationships or in looking at an old event from a new angle. He drew freely and without apology from his personal experience. He remembered with vivid detail the bucket of raspberries his mother made him pick, the pool of water he and other boys made by damming a little stream. He remembered with equal vividness events of his adult life: the late afternoon at sunset in a ruined barn behind the trenches, when he spoke to a company of hand grenaders who were about to raid the German lines; the engineer, a friend of his, who vainly sought to explain relativity to him by comparing it to a shuffleboard game on a ship's deck.[93]

He pored over the biographies which crowded the booksellers' shelves of the twenties and thirties: the life stories of Phillips Brooks, Voltaire, Daniel Webster, Thomas Jefferson, George Arliss, Gladstone, Elizabeth Fry, Clarence Darrow, Henry Ward Beecher, and scores of others. He drew upon the novels he had read in his youth, Dickens, Eliot, Thackeray, and cited (more often to condemn than to praise) the despairing and cynical voices of his contemporaries, Lewis, Dreiser, Fitzgerald. He cited the professors of his day: MacIver, Beard, Whitehead, Fairchild, James, Royce, Haldane, and upon rare occasions, John Dewey.

---
[92] *Hope*, pp.83–84.
[93] *Secret*, pp.2, 89, 164.

Now and then he picked up a dramatic incident from the newspapers: the strange duality in human nature exhibited by two boys at a salacious show, giving their lives to rescue others when fire caused a panic; the leading and successful artist who killed himself and of whom the New York *Herald Tribune* said, "he was a successful artist, with editors eager to snatch the paper from beneath his pencil, but he found life emptier than do the hungry men on the breadlines"; the woman, who, in housecleaning, disposed of her old books to a ragman, only to remember, too late, that one of them contained four thousand dollars—she had "sold something very valuable very cheap." [94]

Of poetry, he knew the familiar passages from the standard poets and knew them well: Shakespeare in his many guises from Macbeth (a tale told by an idiot) to Polonius (to thine own self be true) and Romeo; Wordsworth, "I have felt a presence that disturbs me," Browning, Tennyson, Keats, Lanier. He knew Markham's "He drew a circle that shut me out," Kipling's "Something hidden. Go and find it," and the hymns of the church. He seemed not, however, to be a lover of poetry, a venturer among the muses, but a rhetorician who quoted it for the moral rather than for the beauty. Hence, he could cite Shelley's magnificent lines,

> Life, like a dome of many-coloured glass,
> Stains the white radiance of Eternity [95]

and in the next paragraph, save one, the uninspired doggerel,

> I am battered and broken and weary and out of heart,
> I will not listen to talk of heroic things . . .
> But be content to play some simple part,
> Freed from preposterous, wild imaginings. . . .

He loved music and drew upon it as he did upon poetry for illustrative purposes. He was not a musician, nor a critic, nor even a technically skilled listener, but a worshipper. He turned to music, therefore, for those indescribable emotional experiences which were akin to his religion: Toscanini and the Ninth Symphony, so conducted "that we came down from hearing it as from

---

[94] *Ibid.*, pp.4, 218–19; *Hope*, p.79.
[95] *Secret*, pp.174–175.

a Transfiguration mountain, trailing glory into the common street." Not infrequently he was as interested in the musician as in the music—Kreisler's early failure but ultimate triumph at the violin, Beethoven's struggle with the "darkening shadow of his inevitable deafness," and the divine afflatus of their music encompassing both of them.[96]

He was fond of odd facts, verbal twists, unexpected views of familiar scenes, sharp contrasts. There are a million notes in Wagner's opera, *Die Walküre,* he reported, "but what makes the opera great is the way the artist combined these isolated items into a community and cried, 'Say our!' " He was pleased with a cryptic remark of Whistler who, having failed at West Point and succeeded in art exclaimed, "If silicon had been a gas I should have been a major-general." He could even seize upon a bit of grammar and with a few deft twists have a finely wrought filigree to illustrate his point: we have learned in this nation, he said, as no other nation ever has how to conjugate the verb *to have* in all its moods and tenses, but "Progress consists in learning how to conjugate another verb altogether, *to be.*" [97]

Only rarely did his cleverness betray him into the analogical trick of the evangelicals—the figurative language and the double-talk of the dramatic incident with an obvious religious application. Such was his story of the man in the Welsh mountains, lost for two nights and a day in the fog, when suddenly, out of the unseen he heard a voice say, " 'I wonder if by any chance he could have come this way?' " So, said Fosdick, "May some such word come to someone here who thinks himself lost in the fog! May he hear a word out of the invisible that will put him on his feet!" [98] The illustration undoubtedly gained force through the suddenness of insight with which the audience perceived the point, but it lacked the Hallelujahs which would have given it resonance in an audience of fundamentalists.

The ability to look at a familiar incident from a different angle was of greatest value to Fosdick in his frequent use of biblical

---

[96] *Successful Christian Living,* p.76; *Secret,* pp.7, 221; *Living under Tension; Sermons on Christianity Today.* New York, Harper & Bros., 1941, p.205.
[97] *Living,* pp.83–84; *Hope,* p.69; *Secret,* p.44.
[98] *Hope,* p.86.

illustration. He could take a case like that of Demas, for example, mentioned only three times in the New Testament, unknown to most Christians, and read into it an instance of tragedy, the familiar story of a well-intentioned person who "lacked the power to see it through." Paul mentioned him first in a letter of Philemon: "Demas, Luke, my fellow-workers," and secondly to the Colossians, in inverted order, "Luke, the beloved physician, and Demas," and finally in one of the last letters Paul ever wrote, "Demas forsook me, having loved this present age." [99]

Fosdick's illustrations were nearly always short, occasionally a brief dramatic narrative, more often a quick setting forth, a summarization of difficult circumstances, and nearly always, whether incident or summary, brought to a climax by a well-selected quotation. It required infinite pains and untold industry to be specific instead of general, to cite an exact line from biography or history rather than to paraphrase vaguely, but it paid off in audience interest, and it made possible the repeated use of familiar incidents from popular figures: Lincoln, Helen Keller, Emerson, Beethoven.

He heightened interest in his illustrations not only by the use of the specific but by the use of contrast. He liked to throw into juxtaposition the atheist and the man of faith, the pretentiousness of a man like Sir John Bowring, who could write "In the cross of Christ I glory" even while he was forcing the opium trade upon China; Paul, lying in prison on Nero's order but towering above the tyrant in the course of history; Gutenberg, printing his Bible and revolutionizing Western civilization at the very time that the now-forgotten Tamerlane, the Tartar, was terrorizing Central Europe.[100]

Although he was not master of Emerson's incandescent phrase, Fosdick knew the economy of a metaphor or simile. His more vivid figures were products of his own imagination, sudden intuitive flashes that fused the experiences of his everyday world and the reflections of his study. He thought the conventionalized Jesus of the churches "as unlike the real one as the floral patterns on wallpaper are unlike the flowers of the field"; he thought modern

---

[99] *Power*, p.1.
[100] *Hope*, p.99; *Power*, pp.11–12; *Secret*, p.221.

industrial society a "good deal like the subway—it throws men together in physical proximity without uniting them in spiritual sympathy." He insisted upon restraint in human affairs—the result of letting everything go helter-skelter "would be like the corner of Broadway and Forty-Second Street without traffic regulations." Sobered by the catastrophes of war and depression, he was amused by his earlier confidence in progress, the temptation of his generation "to relegate God to an advisory capacity, as a kind of chairman of the board of sponsors of our highly successful human enterprise." [101]

His favorite source of figurative language was water—the streams and pools of his childhood, the turbulent Niagara, the restless seacoast in Maine where he had his summer cottage. He saw purpose in life as "an ever increasing central current, on which float the back eddies of our lesser loyalties," and he knew from the common emotion he had experienced in prayer and in looking out along the shoreline from his cottage that "Communion with God is a great sea fitting every bend in the shore of human need." He thought nothing more futile in religious history than the "outward forms from which the life has fled, like dry irrigation ditches with no water in them." [102]

Now and then he compressed his thought into a cryptic epigram: "You never can cleanse the water of a well by painting the pump," or "Calvary is only six miles from Bethlehem." More often, he adapted the familiar rhythms and anthitheses of the Bible: "unless we manage well in handling change, change will manage ill in handling us." [103] On rare occasions, when the tide of emotion was full, resorting to the ancient rhetorical device of apostrophe, he turned from his congregation to speak directly to the Herod of his sermon, the Christ Child, or the Unknown Soldier.

Whatever the details of his sermon, Fosdick always preached to persuade. Aside from his basic pattern of organization which was itself persuasive, his chief technique was to set forth the Christian ideals in a manner which would create a favorable climate of

---

[101] *Hope,* pp.36, 105, 205; *Successful,* p.160.
[102] *Successful,* pp.4, 59, 245.
[103] *Hope,* pp.107, 138, 144.

public opinion and effect a change in personal lives. He thought the imagination stronger than the will. "If we hang beautiful pictures on the walls of our souls," he said, "mental images that establish us in the habitual companionship of the highest we know, and live with them long enough, we cannot will evil." [104]

He was not, however, a sentimentalist. The readiness with which he admitted the shortcomings of the great men, the vigor with which he exposed the impostors, the men who intoned pious creeds to cover sharp practices, lent a sense of realism to the ideals he praised. Even at the height of his attack on fundamentalism, he was more evangelical than iconoclastic. He preached to fulfill the law, not to destroy it.

Another of his persuasive techniques was the use of the ancient language of the church to mean something quite different from what it meant to the fundamentalists. The intellectuals who sat in his congregation, who for all their rational approach to religion and science still found it difficult to sever the emotional ties of an old evangelicalism, responded most favorably to this pouring of the new wine into old bottles. Fosdick justified this tactic on the basis that the essential identity in the religion of Jesus and that of the twentieth century was in the psychological experience and not in the creed and that modernism, therefore, was the heir and bearer of the Christian tradition. Jesus, he said, *"did his best to adapt his new truth to the understanding of his people and to make it easy for them to accept it,"* and moreover, he "scrupulously worked within the boundaries of their synagogues," "used ancient and honored terms," and when he took a new position tried to mediate it "by arguments that the Jews could understand." [105] Even though he repeatedly pointed out the new significance which he gave to the old language, Fosdick's critics upbraided him sharply for his "subtle use of orthodox phrases." He is, said the Rev. I. M. Haldeman, the "most dangerous teacher in the professing Church. . . ." [106] However ungenerous the critics were on the matter of integrity, they were assuredly right on the question of persuasion.

---

[104] *Ibid.*, p.208.
[105] Fosdick: *Manhood of the Master*. New York, Association Press, 1913, pp.110–11.
[106] I. M. Haldeman: *Dr. Harry Emerson Fosdick's Book: "The Modern Use of the Bible," A Review*. Philadelphia, The Sunday School Times Co., 1925, pp.84, 86.

Quite as important as a technique of persuasion was Fosdick's use of concession. He rarely condemned without praising, he rarely eulogized without having first stated his reservation. He understood the temptation of a preacher to seek only the "sympathetic response," to give the people "what they want,"[107] but he also understood the effectiveness of his persuasive technique. He could damn flagrant patriotism, even of the American variety, after he had first conceded the incalculable value of nationalism in enlarging the human community; once he had praised the sacrifice, the courage, and the heroism of men in war, he could condemn war itself for its depredations, damn it for its prostitution of the noblest attributes of men; he could praise capitalism for the free play it gives to individual initiative and daring but arraign capitalists who made the country's economic life a "mere sordid, competitive struggle for wealth"; and he could disclaim his intention as a minister to speak for "special economic theories" but assert his responsibility to weigh business in the pulpit as "a matter of human relationships" and to condemn "every sordid and selfish policy which registers itself in broken homes, ruined childhood, and blasted opportunities."[108]

That he was in some degree equivocal on these issues is not to be denied, but he was also bold and persuasive. His apparent equivocation was intimately bound to his theory of salvation: he preached not to society but to men and women within society; he sought social reform through the reformation of individuals; he was more evangelical than prophetic.

Critics of public addresses commonly analyze the *motive appeals* of the speaker under categories borrowed from the psychologist: self-preservation, property, power, reputation, sentiments, and so forth. If the speaker throws the right switch, so the theory runs, he will close the circuit, deliver the charge, and activate the auditor. Certainly these appeals, regarded as value concepts, are motivating, but rarely, save in advertising and the crassest rabble-rousing, do they appear in undisguised forms. The analysis of motive appeals errs in its simple one-to-one, speaker-to-auditor relation. Aside from elementary physiological drives, values are motives only as they inhere in the structure of society, and even

---
[107] *New York Times,* June 4, 1923.
[108] *Ibid.,* January 4, October 5, 1931; *Secret,* p. 47.

the physiological drives are conditioned by the group. The speaker appeals not simply to motives abstractly stated but to the self-consciousness of the group and the standards by which group acceptance or rejection of the individual are determined. The more highly self-conscious the group, the more effectively can the speaker appeal to group norms and so actuate individuals.

Persuasion, then, calls not simply for the apotheosis of one or more of universally recognized values, the pressing of buttons to release springs of action, but the speaker's ability to intensify and utilize the group's self-consciousness. The agitator or the rabble-rouser knows his business well: stimulate discontent, malign the opponent, exalt the movement, deify the leader. A speaker of Fosdick's integrity, while disdaining any simple psychological formula for motivating men, while disdaining the techniques of the agitator, is nonetheless bound by the same laws of persuasion. The difference lies in the relative absence of distortion and the presence of the rational factor. Fosdick heightened group consciousness by criticizing the fundamentalists on the one hand and the materialists on the other; he charged the fundamentalists with ignorance, the skeptics with hopelessness; he condemned the fundamentalists for their worship of creeds, the materialists for bowing down to "agglutinated dust," and both of them for failing to solve the personal and social problems of men. In the growing intellectualism of his day, his appeal was tremendous. People were anxious to break the shackles with which fundamentalism bound their reason, but they were equally desirous of clinging to the emotional values attached to their old religion. So Fosdick and his colleagues in the liberal faith were able, between the extremes of fundamentalism and materialism, to wall off a somewhat self-conscious group, the modernists. These people, in part as a product of their times, in part as a result of the preaching of men like Fosdick, were committed to intellectualism and to the cardinal values of the liberal Christian faith: the worth of personality, the coming of the kingdom of God (social progress), the validity of the religious experience. These, then, were the values, the *motives* to which Fosdick appealed, and his rhetorical theory was admirably designed to induce persuasion, for in his problem-solution approach he first exploited the discontent of his auditors, gently upbraided them for failure to achieve the social justice or inner peace to which their group subscribed, and then exalted the values of their group faith as the chief means of solving the discontent. His persuasion lay not simply in appeal to motives but in the adaptation of his appeals to the complex social structure of his group.

VII

The entire period of Fosdick's preaching was characterized by intellectual ferment and social upheaval. He began his ministry at a time when the recalcitrant American church was just beginning to feel the impact of Darwin and the higher critics, and although he himself was nearly as conservative as the people to whom he preached, he was moved by circumstances to lead the fight of the modernists against the fundamentalists. He was reared in a martial age, schooled in patriotism and the glamor of war; he "conscripted Christ" for the glorious crusade of 1917, but when the war was over, repenting of his militarism, he campaigned for the League of Nations, the World Court, and the Kellogg-Briand pact; and then, as his personal remorse deepened and his hope for peace burned more brightly, he sought penance in the self-abnegating pacifism of the thirties. He was swept into national prominence in the prosperous twenties, called to the pulpit of a skyscraper church especially erected for him by the richest man in America, but he achieved his highest eminence in the age of the great depression, preaching his ablest sermons to men and women who, harassed by fear and financial disaster, sought comfort and faith and hope in his psychological gospel.

It was altogether fitting that such a ministry should encompass the final and most catastrophic event of the first half of the twentieth century, World War II. He had dreaded the coming of the war, he said, as "one might dread perdition." [109] In the last years of the decade he had repeatedly denounced the rising nationalistic spirt of Europe, and particularly the racism of the Nazis. He had been denounced in Hitler's papers for his "disgraceful agitation" in the pulpit and for his cooperation with the

---

[109] Fosdick: *A Great Time to Be Alive.* New York, Harper & Bros., 1944, p.3.

"notorious cabaret performer, Erika Mann." He had sharpened his understanding of democracy, had come to think of it as the political embodiment of the Christian values, the essence of which was "not the rule of the majority but the rights of the minorities." But he preached not simply to eulogize the American people but to judge and call them to repentance. "Stalin is not alone in making an economic class his god," he said. "A capitalist can do that as thoroughly as a Communist." [110]

When war broke out in Europe, he pleaded for neutrality and was vastly relieved to find that the overwhelming majority of Americans wished to stay out of the conflict. He warned his people against the siren call of the propagandists. "Only a delusive sense of mission," he said, "would betray America into fighting Europe's war." He took the stump for neutrality, testified before a congressional committee against peacetime conscription, and opposed the measure in public rallies at Cleveland and Detroit.[111]

He hated the war with his whole being, not only for the killing and the bombing, the laying waste of cities and the mass murders of civilians, the savagery of the concentration camp, and the paralyzing suddenness of the blitzkrieg but for the way it laid hold of and exploited the virtues of men and most of all, perhaps, for what it had done to the churches, for what it had done to him in 1917 when he had gone all-out for the war and had been proud after a speech when an officer told him he was "worth a battalion." "God damn the wars," he said, quoting Whitman and insisting he was not cursing but praying, "God damn every war: God damn 'em! God damn 'em." [112] If the United States were swept into war, he warned, he would remain true to his pacifist principles, he would become a conscientious objector.

When war finally came, he was surprised to learn that even with the shock of Pearl Harbor, the attitude of the people was vastly different from that of 1917. He was strongly sympathetic with the American cause, but he held it the responsibility of the church to stand aloof from the conflict, that it might hold to the

---
[110] *New York Times*, April 14, 1937; May 29, 1939.
[111] *Ibid.*, October 16, 1939; August 3, 1940; May 25, 1941.
[112] *Living*, pp.28, 29.

Harry Emerson Fosdick: The Growth of a Great Preacher 179

"eternal verities" and that it might better minister to the victims. His gospel and his ethic were strongly individualistic. When he preached world organization, he insisted upon its spiritual foundation. It cannot, he said, be built upon pride and complacency, nor upon vindictiveness and ill will, nor upon skepticism and cynicism, but it must be laid upon the solid foundation of humility and penitence, good will and magnanimity, faith and courage; he denounced the American sins of nationalism, Jim Crow segregation, and anti-Semitism, but he called for penitence, a change of heart, more than for new laws or group action. Righteousness, even among nations, he said, "is always, at bottom, a personal affair." He preached encouragement in the face of despair, faith in times of disillusionment, the inner calm of religious experience for those who suffered from personal strain. Difficult times, he said, call out the best in man. Confronted by disaster, some men merely endure, others are intellectually and spiritually stimulated, some are emotionally affected by the passions of bitterness and hatred, others become world-minded citizens, patriots for humanity. He held up to them the great men who had faced desperate times, Jefferson and the Revolutionary fathers, Whittier and the abolitionists, Jeremiah and the prophets of Israel, Jesus and his followers. These, he felt, were the greatest sermons of his career. Certainly they were preached to men and women at the time of their greatest need, and preached without a selling-out to the passions of war.[113]

Fosdick was, by contractual arrangement with his church, to have retired in 1943 when he had reached the age of sixty-five. Because of the war, however, his congregation prevailed upon him to continue. In the last years he frequently took stock of his ministry, looking back down the years to evaluate the issues for which he had stood.[114] He was still opposed to fundamentalism, although he had long since ceased to make it the focal point of his

---

[113] Elnora M. Drafahl: An Analysis of the Figures of Speech Used to Promote Clearness in the War Sermons of Dr. Fosdick. Master's thesis, University of South Dakota, 1946. Dr. Fosdick expressed his estimate of these sermons in a letter to Miss Drafahl. See pp.2-3.

[114] *A Great Time to Be Alive; Sermons on Christianity in Wartime.* New York, Harper & Bros., 1944, p.201; *On Being Fit to Live With, Sermons on Post-War Christianity.* New York, Harper & Bros., 1946, p.14.

preaching. He was an avowed pacifist and an ardent champion of world order, but these, along with his pleas for social justice, he subordinated to the personal religious experience. Throughout his ministry he had preached the God of the first cause, the premise of the philosophical idealist to explain the wonders of the universe, but to the congregations of his latter years the argument scarcely seemed necessary. It was enough that men and women, troubled and tense and disillusioned, could find satisfaction, and peace, and faith in the religious experience that he preached. Or almost enough. In his last years one new note crept in. He preached not only the God of causation and the God of personal experience but the God of history. The catastrophic events of his times had lessened his faith in progress. He had come to believe that there was not only Christ but Anti-Christ. The God of history, he believed, "sitteth above the circle of the earth, and the nations are accounted as a drop in the bucket." [115] He was a God to judge men and nations. And yet, for all of his warnings, Fosdick did not go the way of pessimism marked out by Karl Barth and Reinhold Niebuhr. Underlying his warning was a residuum of optimism, an assurance that the democracies were the chosen people and that God's word to the dictators had not "lost its power." Although somewhat more conservative, the faith of his latter days was strangely akin to that of his youth when he believed,

> . . . somehow good
> Will be the final goal of ill.

He was retired from the Riverside Church, as well as from Union Theological Seminary and the National Vespers radio program, in 1946, shortly after his sixty-eighth birthday. To the last, the crowds poured into Riverside Church or tuned their radio dials on Sunday afternoons to hear him. His voice still vibrant, his message still alive to the needs of his people, he was to thousands of men and women a symbol of their emancipation from worn-out creeds and the revitalization of their religious experience. Even in his retirement the people, demanding of him sermons, books, active participation in public affairs, could not let him rest.

---

[115] *Living*, p.115.

SELECTED BIBLIOGRAPHY
Books and Sermons

Abrams, Ray H.: *Preachers Present Arms; A Study of the War-time Attitudes and Activities of the Churches and the Clergy in the United States, 1914–1918.* New York, Round Table Press, Inc., 1933.

Atkins, Gaius Glenn: *The Making of the Christian Mind.* Garden City, New York, Doubleday, Doran & Co., Inc., 1928.

Bainton, Roland H.: *The Churches and War: Historical Attitudes toward Christian Participation, A Survey from Biblical Times to the Present Day.* Reprinted from *Social Action Magazine* (January 15, 1945).

Burtt, Edwin A.: *Types of Religious Philosophy.* New York, Harper & Bros., 1939.

Colgate University Annual Catalogue. Hamilton, New York, 1895, 1896, 1897, 1898, 1899.

Drafahl, Elnora M.: "An Analysis of the Figures of Speech Used to Promote Clearness in the War Sermons of Dr. Harry Emerson Fosdick." Unpublished Master's thesis, University of South Dakota, August, 1946.

Fay, Sidney B.: *The Origins of the World War.* (2nd ed.) 2 vols in 1. New York, Macmillan Co., 1930.

Gordon, Ernest: *An Ecclesiastical Octopus: A Factual Report on the Federal Council of the Churches of Christ in America.* Boston, Fellowship Press, 1948.

Haldeman, Isaac M.: *Dr. Harry Emerson Fosdick's Book: 'The Modern Use of the Bible,' A Review.* Philadelphia, The Sunday School Times Co., 1925.

Hofstadter, Richard: *Social Darwinism in American Thought, 1860–1915.* (American Historical Association: Albert J. Beveridge Memorial Fund) Philadelphia, University of Pennsylvania Press, 1945.

Fosdick, Harry Emerson: *Adventurous Religion, and Other Essays.* New York, Harper & Bros., 1926.

———: *A Great Time to Be Alive; Sermons on Christianity in Wartime.* New York, Harper & Bros., 1944.

———: *As I see Religion.* New York, Harper & Bros., 1932.

———: *The Assurance of Immortality.* New York, Macmillan Co., 1913.

———: *A Christian Conscience about War.* A Sermon delivered at the League of Nations Assembly Service at the Cathedral at Geneva, September 13, 1935. New York.

———: *The Challenge of the Present Crisis.* New York, Association Press, 1917.

———: *Christianity and Progress.* New York and Chicago, Fleming H. Revell Co., 1922.

———: *A Guide to Understanding the Bible; the Development of Ideas within the Old and New Testaments.* New York, Harper & Bros., 1938.

———: *The Hope of the World: Twenty-five Sermons on Christianity Today.* New York, Harper & Bros., 1933.

———: *Living under Tension; Sermons on Christianity Today.* New York, Harper & Bros., 1941.

———: *The Manhood of the Master.* New York, Association Press, 1913.

———: *The Meaning of Faith.* New York, Association Press, 1917.

———: *The Meaning of Prayer.* New York, Association Press, 1915.

———: *The Meaning of Service.* New York, Association Press, 1920.

———: *The Modern Use of the Bible.* New York, Macmillan Co., 1924.

———: *A Modern Preacher's Problem in His Use of the Scriptures.* Inaugural address as Morris K. Jesup Professor of Practical Theology, Union Theological Seminary, September 13, 1915.

———: *The New Knowledge and the Christian Faith.* Reprinted from a sermon preached at the First Presbyterian Church, New York, May 21, 1922.

———: *On Being Fit to Live With, Sermons on Post-war Christianity.* New York, Harper & Bros., 1946.

———: *The Power to See it Through; Sermons on Christianity Today.* New York, Harper & Bros., 1935.

———: *The Second Mile.* New York, Young Men's Christian Association Press, 1908.

———: *The Secret of Victorious Living; Sermons on Christianity Today.* New York, Harper & Bros., 1934.

———: *Shall the Fundamentalists Win?* A sermon preached at the First Presbyterian Church, May 21, 1922. Stenographically reported by Margaret Renton.

———: *Successful Christian Living; Sermons on Christianity Today.* New York, Harper & Bros., 1937.

———: *The Value of a Great Heritage.* A sermon preached before the Washington Association of New Jersey, Morristown, N. J., February 22, 1921.

Machen, J. Gresham: *Christianity and Liberalism.* New York, Macmillan Co., 1923.

McPherson, G. W.: *Radicalism Unmasked.* A sermon preached July 3, 1922, Old Tent Evangel, Yonkers, New York.
Morrison, Charles Clayton: *The Outlawry of War; A Constructive Policy for World Peace.* Chicago, Willett, Clark & Colby, 1927.
Newton, Joseph Fort (Ed.): *If I Had Only One Sermon to Prepare.* New York, Harper & Bros., 1932.
Niebuhr, Reinhold: *Moral Man and Immoral Society, A Study in Ethics and Politics.* New York, Charles Scribner's Sons, 1932.
Pinkham, Henry Winn: *Collective Homicide: Letters to Harry Emerson Fosdick.* Brookline, Mass., Association to Abolish War, 1923.
Prentiss, George L.: *The Union Theological Seminary in the City of New York: Its Design and Another Decade of Its History.* Asbury Park, N. J., J. M., W. & C. Pennypacker, 1899.
Rian, Edwin H.: *The Presbyterian Conflict.* Grand Rapids, Mich., William B. Eerdmans Publishing Co., 1940.
Schneider, Herbert Wallace. *Religion in 20th Century America.* Cambridge, Mass., Harvard University Press, 1952.
The Courses of Study . . . New York, Union Theological Seminary, 1901, 1902.

Periodicals

The correspondence between Dr. Fosdick and Dr. Macartney anent the Philadelphia overture, *The Presbyterian,* XCII (December 7, 1922), pp.6–8.
Craig, S. G.: Christianity according to Dr. Fosdick, *ibid.,* XCIII (February 22, 1923), pp.7–10; *ibid.,* (March 1, 1923), pp.7–10.
Crocker, Lionel: The rhetorical theory of Harry Emerson Fosdick. *The Quarterly Journal of Speech,* XXII (April, 1936), pp.107–13.
Dieffenbach, Albert C.: Religious liberty—the great American illusion; the Fundamentalists possess the land. *The Independent,* 118 (January 15, 1927), pp.64–66.
———: Lost leaders of Protestantism. *Ibid.,* 119 (September 17, 1927), pp.207–72 ff.
Dr. Fosdick accepts the challenge. *The Christian Century,* XLVII (October 15, 1930), pp.1239–1241.
Dr. Fosdick at Geneva. *The Review of Reviews,* 72 (November, 1925), p.538.
Dr. Fosdick shifts the emphasis; Modernism not enough. *The Christian Century,* LII (November 20, 1935), pp.1480–1482.
Dr. Fosdick will retire next May. *Ibid.,* LXII (June 20, 1945), p.725.
Epoch-making pact or futile gesture? *The World Tomorrow,* 11 (September, 1928), p.357.

Fosdick, Harry Emerson: Are religious people fooling themselves? *Harper's Magazine,* CLXI (June, 1930), pp.59–70.

———: Blessed be biography. *The Ladies' Home Journal,* XLI (April, 1924), p.18.

———: Heckling the Church. *The Atlantic Monthly,* CVIII (December, 1911), pp.735–742.

———: Putting Christ into uniform. *The Christian Century,* LVI (December 13, 1939), pp.1539–1542.

———: Science and mystery. *The Atlantic Monthly,* CXII (October, 1913), pp.520–530.

———: Then our men came! *The American Magazine,* LXXXVI (December, 1918), pp.30–31.

———: The trenches and the Church at home. *The Atlantic Monthly,* CXXIII (January, 1919), pp.22–33.

———: What Christian liberals are driving at. *The Ladies' Home Journal,* XLII (January, 1925), p.18.

———: What is the matter with preaching? *Harper's Magazine,* CLVII (July, 1928), pp.133–141.

———: What the war did to my mind. *The Christian Century,* XLV (January 5, 1928), pp.10–11.

The Fundamentalist controversy. *The Christian Work,* 115 (October 27, 1923), pp.487–488.

Gilkey, Charles W.: Dr. Fosdick preaches. Review of *The Hope of the World. The Christian Century,* LI (April 4, 1934), pp.459–460.

Macartney, Clarence E.: Sermons here and there, II. Hunting for Christianity in New York. *The Presbyterian,* XCII (June 8, 1922), pp.8, 26.

———: Shall unbelief win? An answer to Dr. Fosdick. *Ibid.,* (July 13, 1922), pp.8–10; *Ibid.,* (July 20, 1922), pp.8–10.

MacVaugh, Gilbert Stillman: Structural analysis of the sermons of Harry Emerson Fosdisk. *The Quarterly Journal of Speech,* XVIII (November, 1932), pp.531–546.

Madisonensis, 1895–1896; 1897–1900.

Modernism in confusion. *The New Republic,* 48 (September 1, 1926), pp.33–34.

Morrison, Charles Clayton: The treaty is signed. *The Christian Century,* XLV (September 6, 1928), pp.1070–1071.

The new Reformation. *Ibid.,* XL (February 15, 1923), pp. 198–199.

Niebuhr, Reinhold: What the war did to my mind." *Ibid.,* XLV (September 27, 1928), pp.1161–1162.

Open-shop parson. *Time Magazine,* XLI (March 15, 1943), p.54.

Root, Edward Clary: Power of faith: an interview with Dr. Harry Emerson Fosdick. *The American Magazine,* CI (May, 1926), pp. 18–19.
Smith, Helena Huntington: Respectable heretic. *Outlook and Independent,* CLIII (October 9, 1929), pp.208–210.
Van Dusen, Henry P.: The sickness of liberal religion. *The World Tomorrow,* 14 (August, 1931), pp.256–258.
Villard, O. G.: Dr. Fosdick renounces war. *The Nation,* CXXXVIII (May 23, 1934), p.581.
What 20,000 clergymen think. *The Nation,* CXXXVIII (May 9, 1934), p.524.

Newspapers

The Indianapolis News, May 15, 16, 21, 23, 24, 1923.
The Indianapolis Sun, May 18, 1923.
The New York Sun, April 10, 1923.
The New York World, March 2, 1925.
The New York Times, 1919–1950.
The Philadelphia Evening Bulletin, May 25, 1923.

Manuscripts

Fosdick, Harry Emerson: Autobiography (in typescript).

Chapter 15

Harry Emerson Fosdick and the Techniques of Organization

EDMUND H. LINN *

"I WOULD NEVER THINK of speaking," Harry Emerson Fosdick said on one occasion, "without in some way ordering my thoughts."[1] An examination of his published sermons shows that he consistently arranged his ideas with great care.

The primary basis of organization for Fosdick was the need of his congregation. Sermon materials were not to be ordered according to some preconceived plan but to meet some vital concern of the sermon's hearers. He thought first about people (objects) and then about ideas (subjects). The controlling purpose and the plan of a particular message grew out of his consideration of a specific listener's problem. The entire sermon was organized around a constructive attempt to meet a personal need.

After Fosdick had selected the definite problem that he proposed to deal with the following Sunday, he would then determine the precise goal at which he was going to aim. The general purpose of all preaching is to present a Christian truth and to persuade men to accept it, but any given sermon must go beyond that. Each sermon should have a specific purpose. It might be to

---
* Professor of Speech, Andover Newton Theological Seminary.
Note: From *Andover-Newton Quarterly*, Vol. 1, No. 4 (March, 1961), pp.19–40.
[1] This quotation, like many other ideas in this study, comes from personal interviews that the author had with Dr. Fosdick.

Techniques of Organization 187

teach a listener how to use fear constructively,[2] or what the divinity of Jesus means.[3] It might be to convince the hearer that nationalism is Christianity's supreme rival[4] or that the means determine the end.[5] It might be to persuade the auditor to abandon some popular sin[6] or to make a definite decision for Christ.[7] He could not begin a sermon until he saw clearly what he intended to accomplish on Sunday morning. Once his goal was plainly visualized, he thought of the sermon as well on its way. In his judgment, a primary cause of dull and harmless messages was the preacher's failure to have a target in sight before he began the construction of his sermon.[8]

Having decided upon the specific purpose of a sermon, Dr. Fosdick then looked for some concrete truth whose presentation would achieve that purpose. At this moment the Bible always came to mind. If a single passage presented the heart of the matter, it was explained, not for its own sake but to drop its relevant truth upon the purpose like a pile driver. If no single text contained the pertinent truth, he would start with his purpose and use several Scripture passages as they applied.

Dr. Fosdick said that no two of his sermons developed in exactly the same way. Every one of them was different. When all went well, he did not build the structure; it came emerging out of the thought material as though by spontaneous generation. Sometimes the entire organization emerged with striking clarity; sometimes he saw only where to begin, with but a vague notion of the succeeding steps. To put the matter another way, sometimes he started with the central idea, sometimes with the beginning, sometimes with an illustration, and sometimes with the ending. Once in a great while he saw the whole sermon before he began to

---

[2] *On Being Fit to Live With.* New York, Harper & Bros., 1946, p.125.
[3] *Living Under Tension.* New York, Harper & Bros., 1941, p.150.
[4] *The Hope of the World.* New York, Harper & Bros., 1933, p.156.
[5] *Living Under Tension*, p.102.
[6] *The Secret of Victorious Living.* New York, Harper & Bros., 1934, p.119.
[7] *What Is Vital in Religion.* New York, Harper & Bros., p.34.
[8] What is the matter with preaching? *Harper's* CXLII (July, 1928), pp.133–144 see Chapter 2. Also Animated Conversation, *If I Had Only One Sermon to Prepare.* Joseph Fort Newton (Ed.), New York, Harper & Bros., 1932, pp.109–113 see Chapter 4.

write, but generally it took shape slowly. Some sermons, therefore, were fully outlined before he started to write. On others, he began writing and felt his way, stage by stage, until the structure became clear. He said that he was never able, as was Phillips Brooks, to write an entire sermon in a single morning.

The organization of a sermon for Dr. Fosdick was part of the creative process. In spite of the fact that no two sermons were exactly alike in their development, certain steps can be distinguished: (a) He chose a particular listener with a specific problem. (b) He defined the precise purpose which focused on the problem. (c) He picked some truth, preferably biblical, relevant to the accomplishment of that purpose. (d) He practiced *free association* of ideas around his purpose (object) and subject (truth). At this stage, he did not consider the organization of the sermon, how it would begin or end. He gave his mind complete freedom to pick up anything that came within range of the matter before him. Any suggestion that came was accepted without regard for logical continuity. Vague notions were not labored. Precise thoughts were welcomed. Sometimes this process went on for hours, with one idea stimulating another and all of them appearing as a disorganized jumble. (e) He jotted down the thoughts collected in whatever order they happened to come. (f) He framed a tentative central theme. (g) He asked such vital questions of his central theme as the following:

1. What have I ever read in general literature—biography, history, novels, poetry—that throws light upon my theme?

2. What have I ever run upon in personal counseling that illustrates the human need with which I am dealing and the resources to meet it?

3. Where, beyond the passages I have already thought of, does the Bible—that vast storehouse of experience—illumine the sermon's problem and the way to treat it?

4. What in my own personal experience has this theme intimately meant to me, and what honest-to-goodness! does it really mean now in my own life? [9]

---

[9] How I prepare my sermons. *The Quarterly Journal of Speech*, XL (February, 1954), p.51. See Chapter 3.

At another period he asked the following questions of his theme:

1. Is the major idea true?
2. Is the major idea true according to human experience and history?
3. Is the major idea true according to the Bible and the best of religious experience?
4. What does the major idea mean to the contemporary world?
5. What does the major idea mean to this particular congregation?
6. What does the major idea mean to me? [10]

(h) He wrote the opening section. (i) He phrased the specific purpose and the central idea to achieve it. (j) He filled in the main points. (k) He wrote the sermon in full. (l) He revised the manuscript carefully. (The fact must be underscored that these steps overlapped and that Dr. Fosdick never held rigidly to them. His approach was always experimental.)

When organizing a sermon, Dr. Fosdick thought of the whole message rather than of the three divisions—introduction, body, and conclusion. Such divisions seemed artificial to him, and he rarely prepared each one individually. Even so, a beginning, a development, and an ending can be found in most of his sermons.

Since the ordinary introduction wasted the hearer's time, Dr. Fosdick believed that it should be eliminated. If a sermon had an introduction, he said that it ought to be relevant and brief. He tried, therefore, to construct sermons with short introductions or none at all.

In examining his sermons, however, a reader will usually find several pages of material before coming upon the customary cue to the body, "In the first place." Apparently Dr. Fosdick considered this material the opening section of the body of a sermon rather than an introduction. Because this section fulfilled the essential purposes of an effective introduction according to pres-

---
[10] Letter to the author, April 15, 1951.

ent-day speech authorities, that is what it will be called. It averaged about one-fourth of the total length of a sermon.

Assuming that the opening sections of his sermons are introductions, what significant purposes did Dr. Fosdick achieve by them?

First, the introduction stated real problems in the lives of his hearers. The means by which Dr. Fosdick expressed these problems were arresting and varied. He often started with a direct statement in his first sentence, such as, "One of the most disastrous evils that can befall religion is to have the best moral conscience of its generation get ahead of it." [11] Sometimes he opened the sermon with a brief story, which might be from a biography, a newspaper, the Bible, letters, or his counseling experiences. The following is an instance:

> Sometime since in a personal consultation I faced a young woman about to go over to the Roman Catholic Church. Reared in a liberal Protestant home, with a good mind and an excellent education, the reasons she gave for turning to the Roman communion were important. She had always had a religion, she said, which belonged to her—her private possession. Now, however, she needed a religion that possessed her.[12]

Frequently Dr. Fosdick introduced sermons and problems through the use of appropriate quotations. The quotations, like his stories, came from various sources. An indirect quotation from contemporary life with the problem implicit opened "The Hope of the World in Its Minorities": "One of the most arresting statements recently made by a public man was made by Mr. Einstein when he said that if 2 per cent of our population should take a personal stand against the sanction and support of another war, that would end war." [13]

Most of the time, however, the initial quotation was drawn from the Bible—the Psalmists, Prophets, Paul, or Jesus. A direct quotation from Jesus launched "Keeping Faith in Persuasion in a World of Coercion": "John's Gospel in its twelfth chapter reports that Jesus said about his crucifixion, 'I, if I be lifted up from the

---

[11] *Successful Christian Living.* New York, Harper & Bros., 1937, p.97.
[12] *What Is Vital in Religion,* p.55.
[13] *The Hope of the World,* p.1.

earth, will draw all men unto me.' The Master, that is, trusted his cause to the power of persuasion." [14]

There were also times when the beginning was varied by putting the problem in the form of a challenging question: "Jesus faced his disciples with a question which in these days of social unrest and reconstruction ought to disturb our consciences: 'What do ye more than others?' " [15] Occasionally the introductions contained references to special occasions, such as Memorial Day, Thanksgiving, Easter, Christmas, and World Communion Sunday: "This is World Communion Sunday and countless Christians around the planet will meet at the Lord's Table today to express their gratitude to Christ." [16] References by Fosdick to himself, as speaker, were infrequent.

When stating a problem, Dr. Fosdick always related it to his hearers. Most of the time he did this by direct references: "We may be sure that every one here, one way or another, faces the problem of fear." [17] He usually went beyond direct reference, however, and also tied the problem to the common experiences, beliefs, goals, interests, needs and perplexities of his listeners: "This sermon springs from endless inquiries sent me by radio listeners. They want to know what the 'divinity' or 'deity' of Jesus means." [18] From the outset he constantly tried to make his auditors think he was "bowling down their alley."

The second purpose which Dr. Fosdick accomplished by the introductions to his sermons was to stress the importance of the problem. Ordinarily the significance of the problem was evident as soon as it was stated. When it was not obvious, his customary means of emphasizing the importance of the problem was to show how it concerned nearly everyone and most of the major areas of life:

> But even a moment's serious reflection indicates that giving the Highest a hearing is about as important an event as ever happens in human life. The turning points in scientific progress have been associated with

---

[14] *A Great Time to Be Alive.* New York: Harper & Bros., 1944, p.181.
[15] *Successful Christian Living*, p.108.
[16] *On Being Fit to Live With*, p.108.
[17] *The Hope of the World*, p.59.
[18] *Living Under Tension*, p.150.

it. . . . Even more obviously is this experience associated with the turning points of man's spiritual progress. . . . Of all of us in this audience it is true sometime or other, in a way large or small, we have had a spiritual disaster. . . . we know that it need never have happened if we had listened to an inner voice.[19]

By the introductions to his sermons, Dr. Fosdick fulfilled a third purpose. They helped him to relate the problems to life as presented in the Bible. Many of his sermons began with a Biblical reference (an expository statement, a story, a question, or a text), which often stated the problem under consideration. When he did not begin with a reference from the Bible, he generally related the problem to the Bible later in the introduction with a "delayed" text. In his sermon "Starting with Trouble and Ending with Hope," the Biblical text appeared one page after the opening.[20]

The introductions of Dr. Fosdick's sermons usually achieved a fourth purpose. They clearly stated a major truth (central idea, controlling theme). The form of the major truth and the place where it was set forth varied considerably with each sermon. In his "The Church Must Go Beyond Modernism," the first sentence expressed the major truth: "If we are successfully to maintain the thesis that the church must go beyond modernism, we must start by seeing that the church had to go as far as modernism." [21] In "The Ethical Foundations of Prosperity" the big truth was presented near the middle of the introduction,[22] while in "The Field Is the World" it appeared at the end.[23] Occasionally the central idea was stated both at the beginning and the end of the sermon, as in "The Secret of Victorious Living." [24]

Once in a while Dr. Fosdick used part of the introduction to explain the nature and history of the problem, as in "The Contemporary Prevalence of Polytheism," [25] or to explain the theme. The more controversial the theme, the more material he seemed

---

[19] *Successful Christian Living*, pp.241-242.
[20] *A Great Time to Be Alive*, p.117.
[21] *Successful Christian Living*, p.153.
[22] *The Power to See It Through*. New York, Harper & Bros., 1935, p.106.
[23] *A Great Time to Be Alive*, p.32.
[24] *The Secret of Victorious Living*, pp.1 and 10.
[25] *Successful Christian Living*, p.56.

to use to establish it before developing his main points. For instance, in the message, "On Believing in Miracles," [26] the opening section was about four pages long, while in "The Free Spirit Confronts the World's Coercion" the remarks about the theme occupied less than half a page.[27]

Dr. Fosdick maintained that the primary objective of adequate organization was to make the ideas clear to the listeners. In what ways did he organize his sermons, especially their body, to achieve clarity?

1. He used a meaningful sermon title. The big truth, central idea, or controlling theme was often expressed in such titles as "Christ Himself Is Christianity," [28] and "Loyalty, the Basic Condition of Liberty." [29] If not the big truth, then the nature of the discussion was plainly indicated in the titles of many sermons, for example, "When Prayer Means Power," [30] "Six Ways to Tell Right from Wrong," [31] and "Christianity's Stake in the Social Situation." [32]

2. He presented only one big truth (central idea, theme). The big truth became the center around which all other material in the message was organized. The most common method of handling the major truth was to express it in the introduction and then to repeat it several times at crucial places throughout the message, either in the same words each time or rephrased in words that retained the basic theme. For example, the chief idea "The Means Determine the End" was reiterated eight times throughout a message with the same title.[33] In a large number of sermons the central idea was stated at the beginning, at the end or start of each major point, and near or within the conclusion, as well as at other less significant places. These well-placed repetitions contributed much, not only to the clarity of his sermons but also to their unity and forcefulness.

---
[26] *A Great Time to Be Alive*, pp.124–128.
[27] *Living Under Tension*, p.132.
[28] *A Great Time to Be Alive*, p.134.
[29] *On Being Fit to Live With*, p.185.
[30] *Living Under Tension*, p.71.
[31] *The Hope of the World*, p.126.
[32] *Ibid.*, p.21.
[33] *Living Under Tension*, pp.102–111.

3. He related the big truth of a sermon closely to the specific purpose. These two elements of organization were similar but not identical. The major truth was always expressed in terms of the sermon, while the specific purpose was stated in terms of the hearers. For instance, in the message "The Essential Elements in a Vital Christian Experience," the chief truth was plainly implied in the title. Here the specific purpose of the message is to teach the hearers the essential elements in a vital Christian experience.[34]

He clearly related the big truth or central idea to the main supporting points. Usually the relationship was obvious, as in "Making the Best of a Bad Mess." His implied big truth stood out: It is possible to make the best of a bad mess. The main supporting points were these: (a) by creating happiness in it; (b) by applying the spirit of Jesus to it; and (c) by trusting the power of God to see you through it.[35]

Ordinarily Dr. Fosdick related the big truth to the main supporting points by stating them together, as in "The Christian Outlook on Life." In this message he said, "Again, genuine Christianity changes a man's outlook [big truth] not simply on a detail like money but on the universe as a whole [36] [second main supporting point]."

5. He marked the main supporting points with signposts, for example, "in the first place," "for one thing," "consider again," "and still another." Observe the signposts in his sermon entitled "The Church Must Go Beyond Modernism":

> In the first place, modernism has been excessively preoccupied with intellectualism. . . . In the second place, not only has modernism been thus predominately intellectualistic and therefore, partial, but. . . . In the third place, modernism has even watered down and thinned out the central message and distinctive truth of religion, the reality of God. . . . Finally, modernism has too commonly lost its ethical standing ground and its power of moral attack.[37]

6. He usually stated the main supporting points in parallel form. Sometimes the form of the points was the same, except for

---

[34] *Ibid.*, p.181.
[35] *The Hope of the World*, p.117.
[36] *What Is Vital in Religion*, p.105.
[37] *Successful Christian Living*, pp.156–161.

the added thought. At other times the form of the points was only similar. In his sermon called "Six Ways to Tell Right from Wrong," the parallelism was exact:

> In the first place, if a man is perplexed about a question of right and wrong, he might well submit it to the test of common sense. . . . In the second place, if a man is perplexed about a question of right and wrong, he might well submit it to the test of sportsmanship. In the third place, if a man is perplexed about a question of right and wrong, he might well submit it to the test of his best self. . . . In the fourth place, if a man is perplexed about a question of right and wrong, he might well submit it to the test of publicity. . . . In the fifth place, if a man is perplexed about a question of right and wrong, he might well submit it to the test of his most admired personality. . . . In the sixth place, if a man is perplexed about a question of right and wrong, he might well submit it to the test of foresight.[38]

Such parallelism and repetition caused the main supporting points to stand out clearly, emphasized them, made them memorable, and added the quality of progression to the sermon.

It was not unusual for Dr. Fosdick to mark the minor as well as the main points in a sermon with signposts, but for the most part the former were much less conspicuous. Even so, they were often marked by a phrase such as "Here, then," or a word such as "further." Dr. Fosdick was usually careful not to confuse his listeners by using the same kind of signpost to mark a minor point as he had employed to designate a main one. In his message "When Life Goes All to Pieces," the main points were marked with the phrase "Carry this truth out . . . ," while the minor points were tagged with numbers, "First . . . Second . . . Third." [39]

7. He employed many clear transitions. Dr. Fosdick believed that transitions are as indispensable in building a sermon as directional signals are in driving a car. If a message is to be heard, understood, and remembered by the hearers, the development must be logical enough to make sense. He used careful transitions, therefore, to relate the big truth or central idea to the main points and the main points to the minor points. These transitions included signposts, but also more.

---
[38] *The Hope of the World*, pp.126–135.
[39] *The Power to See It Through*, pp.33–41.

There were transitional sentences. They usually united the major divisions of the message—the introduction, body (main points) and conclusion. Ordinarily the basic transitional sentences were placed at the end of the introduction or the beginning of the body, at the beginning of each main point, and at the start of the conclusion.

When a transitional sentence occurred at the end of an introduction, it seldom enumerated the main points which followed. To preview the main points in a message before developing them, according to Dr. Fosdick, often ruins interest and climax by giving the sermon away before it is preached.

When a transitional sentence began the body of one of Fosdick's sermons, it not only united the introduction and the body but it also plainly indicated the general direction of the sermon's development. In his "Righteousness First," he said: "On this Sunday, therefore, full of concern for, and loyalty to, our nation, I speak to you about some things we want that we will never get except by the route the Master pointed out: righteousness first." [40] The significance of such a transitional sentence was often increased by the fact that it included the big truth, as in this case: "We will never get what we want unless we seek righteousness first."

The transitional sentences, which commonly stated each main point and began its development, not only related the main points to each other by implication and the body to the introduction but also united the main points to the big truth or central idea. In his sermon entitled "A Religion to Support Democracy," for instance, the transitional sentence which connected the introduction and the body stated the big truth and indicated the direction the development would take as follows: "What kind of religion ought ours to be if it is to support a government of, by, and for the people?" The transitional sentences which stated each main point, began its treatment, related the main points to each other and the body to the introduction by implication, and united the main points to the big truth or central idea were expressed in this manner:

---

[40] *A Great Time to Be Alive*, p.23.

In the first place, obviously it must be a religion that dignifies personality. . . . In the second place, the kind of religion that will support government of, by, and for the people is one that recognizes a higher loyalty than the state. . . . In the third place, the kind of religion that will support the democratic faith and practice must genuinely care not only for the liberty but for the equality and fraternity of the people. . . . Finally, the kind of religion that will support government of, by and for the people must create responsible personal character in the individual citizens.[41]

Frequently the transitional sentences which followed the first or second main point of the body were internal summaries, containing both a review of the previous point or points and a preview of the point next to be developed. For instance, as Dr. Fosdick ended his third main point and began his fourth main point in "A Great Year for Easter," he said, "Come further now [signpost] and see that Easter is an affirmation [big truth] not only about the universe [Main Point I], and about God [Main Point II] and the meaning of man's spiritual life [Main Point III], but about every one of us [Main Point IV]." [42]

It was not unusual for Dr. Fosdick to increase the organizational clarity of his sermons still more by marking the heart and the conclusion of them with a variety of transitional sentences, such as "This, then, is the conclusion of the matter . . . ," "Here, then is the gist of the matter." [43]

Most of the time Fosdick made the structure of his messages clear by transitional phrases as well as by sentences. Ordinarily these phrases served as signposts, plainly marking the main supporting points and the chief movements in the development of a sermon. His transitional phrases, like his transitional sentences, were not only numerous but widely varied in kind and form. He used them to indicate addition: "consider again," "let us go further"; to point out contrast: "over against," "on the other side"; to mark exemplification: "to be sure," "of course"; to suggest alternation: "on the one hand," "not only"; to pinpoint result: "the consequence is," "the results are." Often Dr. Fosdick's transition was simply a word. Words such as "again" indicated

---

[41] *What Is Vital in Religion,* pp.200–208.
[42] *Living Under Tension,* p.251.
[43] *Ibid.,* p.212; *A Great Time to Be Alive,* p.83.

addition, "yet" suggested contrast, "or" pointed to alternation, "namely" marked exemplification, "since" labeled cause, and "thus" designated result. For the most part, the major sections of his sermons were connected by transitional sentences, while the minor divisions were united by a transitional phrase or a word.

8. He constructed *unit* paragraphs. Dr. Fosdick thought that each paragraph in a sermon should be complete in itself. It ought to have a beginning, a middle, and an end. It must be well-organized—coherent, unified, and finished so that it helped the hearers to understand and to remember the ideas. He attempted, therefore, to build a paragraph in such a way that it would be meaningful to the listener if he heard it and nothing else. Usually, his main points and minor points served both as subject heads and as the topic sentences upon which he constructed his paragraphs. Many examples could be given, but one from his sermon entitled "Spiritual Foundations for a Better World" will suffice:

> If the better world we want must be built on humility and penitence, on intelligent goodwill and magnanimity, it certainly must be built on faith and courage. Skepticism and cynicism will not sustain it. We naturally center our attention today on the political conditions of peace, but when a man like Professor MacIver of Columbia University writes a book about the matter, although politics lies within his specialty, he stresses what he calls the psychological conditions of peace. These are certainly in part the church's business, and how immeasurably important they are! They are the basis of the whole affair.[44]

Dr. Fosdick's overall approach to the development of his ideas was usually deductive. His thought moved from the general to the specific. Ordinarily he began, as we have seen, with a statement of his big truth (central idea, controlling theme). The big truth was always expressed within the introduction, usually near the end. This was followed by the presentation and elaboration of each one of his main supporting points, one at the beginning of the body of the sermon and the others distributed throughout it. The main points were expressed in the form of propositions which were more specific than his big truth. Each main point was frequently supported by minor points more specific than the main

---

[44] *A Great Time to Be Alive*, p.49.

point. Just as the main points undergirded the big truth, so the minor points held up the main points. Notice a part of this deductive development as it appears in his sermon called "The Christian Outlook on Life."[45]

> *Big Truth:* Christianity changes our outlook on life, because
> I. Christianity changes our outlook on money because
>   A. Christianity teaches us that our life does not consist of possessions.
>   B. Christianity teaches us that money is only a means to an end.
>   C. Christianity teaches us that money must not be our God.
> II. Christianity changes our outlook on the family.

According to Dr. Fosdick, there are at least three ways to organize a sermon: (a) As a box. Just as the boards are nailed on a box one by one, so the points of a sermon can be enumerated one by one. His message entitled "Six Ways in Which the Modern Man Can Pray" illustrates this type:

> Consider, then, six ways of praying that bring to life deepness of earth and strong rootage—all possible to an intelligent modern man who believes in God at all, and in this difficult time especially and desperately needed. First, the prayer of interior relaxation and serenity. . . . In the second place, the prayer of affirmation. . . . In the third place, the prayer of spiritual companionship. . . . In the fourth place, the prayer of moral conflict. . . . In the fifth place, the prayer of strong desire. . . . In the sixth place, the prayer of released power.[46]

(b) As a tree. Just as the smaller branches grow out of the trunk of a tree, so the main points of a sermon should develop out of the big truth. The "treelike" structure may be the form of his message "On Seeming as Christian as We Are":

> In this generation, then, with our reluctance and chariness about religious profession and pretension, there must be a lesson here for some of us—Let your light shine. For one thing there surely is something to be said for people who succeed in publishing their light rather than their darkness, their faith rather than fear, their courage

---
[45] *What Is Vital in Religion,* p.100.
[46] *Successful Christian Living,* pp.12-23.

> not their cowardice, their best not their worst. . . . Consider again that not only is this true in general but it applies particularly to religion. . . . Consider the force of this, when one stops thinking about what he ought to do and remembers what other folk have done to him. . . . Consider once more the essential importance, even from the standpoint of man himself, of this commonly neglected matter of expression—getting out what is in us, so that the world may know it is there. . . . Deeper than this, however, is a further matter which we are drilling for now, that what we do not express tends to die and what we do tends to live.[47]

(c) As a river. Just as a river impresses the sightseer with its one mighty movement and sweeping scenes, so a sermon should stir the listener with one great theme and broad views. The message with "riverlike" structure flows along without giving the hearers points sharply marked off from each other. It surges forward, opening up one new vista after another. The preacher's personality provides most of the continuity in the "river" sermon, which is usually less didactic, analytical, and logical but more autobiographical, meditative, profound, and emotional than other sermon types. Dr. Fosdick said that the "riverlike" sermon was the highest form of organization, even though the prevalent pattern of his own messages was either the "box" or the "tree" structure. His message "Every Man's Religion His Own" may exemplify the river pattern.

> Let us start by noting that something always does happen to Christianity when it comes into a new life. . . . With so much clear, let us pass to a further aspect of the matter. By its essential nature, religion is a kind of experience which, if we possess it at all, must be possessed by each man for himself. . . . Let us press on now from this to a matter immediately suggested by it. In a day of trial and strain it is only that much of the gospel which has become my gospel that can stand the storm of doubt and trouble.[48]

Whatever the external form, Dr. Fosdick always tried to arrange his thoughts in a psychological fashion. He said:

> I am not so interested to arrange my thoughts logically as I am to arrange them psychologically. To be sure, there need be no contradiction here: a sermon certainly ought not to be illogical. . . . A preacher

---

[47] *The Power to See It Through*, pp.163–168.
[48] *Ibid.*, pp.142–151.

is not a mere essayist illuminating a subject in a logical fashion. He is after his audience to create a change in them, and therefore, his primary endeavor must be to arrange his thought in a psychological fashion, so that he may start where they are in their thinking, and lead them on from one step to another along an inclined plane that is most natural for their feet to mount. . . . This contrast between a merely logical and a vitally psychological arrangement of thought can make or unmake an entire sermon.[49]

The means which Dr. Fosdick employed to give his sermons psychological order were several. As stated earlier, he related his messages to a vital concern of his listeners. In addition, he constantly related this personal problem and the big truth or theme of a message to the various attitudes of his listeners. Occasionally he expressed the main points of a sermon in the form of statements his listeners might make about his big truth:

> We shall have a revival of religion [big truth]. Of course, I can imagine objectors who will protest against this statement. Let us consider them. One person, for example, may say, There is going to be no revival of religion: no likelihood exists that this generation will ask searching questions about the spiritual ends of life, because we are too satisfied with the enjoyment of these new and fascinating means of living. To this I answer. . . . In the second place, I can imagine a man saying. . . .[50]

It was also Dr. Fosdick's common practice to express the minor points of a message in terms of individuals who supported the main points by their attitudes. Observe this in a short section from "A Kind of Penitence that Does Some Good":

> [Main Point III] If, however, this high use of the sense of shame is going to be effective in our public attitudes, we shall have to start with it in our individual lives, and to that end consider now how commonly this powerful emotion of self-reproach, personally experienced, serves no good purpose. Who has not met these people I shall now describe. [Minor Points set forth as examples] Here is one man. He has been guilty of moral failure. . . . Here is another man. . . . Here is another man. . . . Here is another man. . . .[51]

Another means by which Dr. Fosdick appears to have organized his messages psychologically was to associate the sermonic prob-

---

[49] "Animated Conversation," p.110.
[50] *The Hope of the World*, p.42.
[51] *A Great Time to Be Alive*, pp.85–86.

lem and big truth continually with the *basic wants* of his hearers. Occasionally his main points took their content and order from some of the fundamental desires of his listeners:

> On this Sunday . . . I speak to you of some things we want that we will never get except by the route the Master pointed out: righteousness first: For one thing, we want *a great nation* that will preserve unspoiled and carry to new meaning its heritage of *liberty* and *democracy*. . . . For another thing, we deeply want for ourselves and our children a world where the magnificent new powers that science gives us will be used to create a more *abundant life* and not destroy it. . . . Another thing we want is a world that will not disappoint the hopes of our youth who are pouring out their lives for us.[52]

At other times, he related his ideas to such deep motives as his listeners' longing for virtue, health, power, greatness, fellowship, prosperity, and happiness.

A further means by which Dr. Fosdick gave some of his sermons psychological structure was to present the main point with the greatest amount of emotional appeal last of all. The main ideas of his message "On Finding It Hard to Believe in God" were presented in the following order: (a) No one believes in all of God; (b) Psychologically, everyone has a god; (c) The way of disbelief in God has its difficulties; (d) You want a world where it is easy for children to believe in God.[53]

One other means increased the psychological form of Dr. Fosdick's messages. He often put an illustration with high *moving power* or emotional appeal near the end of the last point or in the conclusion, as in "Handicapped Lives":

> My friend at a midwestern university tells me that in all his years there he never heard such cheering, not even at a football victory, as greeted a crippled boy carried in the arms of his companions across the platform on Commencement Day. Four years before, that boy had answered "Present" at the first roll call of his class. "Stand up!" said the professor. "I should like to, sir, but I have not been able to stand since I was four years old." But, by being what he was in a difficult situation, that boy made such an impression on the university that when his companions carried him up for his diploma, the great assemblage broke forth into such cheers as that college generation had

---

[52] *Ibid.*, pp.23–28.
[53] *Successful Christian Living*, p.33.

not heard before. Never despise your handicaps. They are an opportunity for a kind of spiritual service that lusty Apollos cannot render.[54]

Although most of Dr. Fosdick's sermons were organized psychologically into what he called the "box" or "tree" patterns, many of them could be classified by other forms of structure: chronological, as in "Your Present Is the Past of Your Future"; [55] definitional, as in "What Does the Divinity of Jesus Mean?"; [56] classificational, developmental, or procedural, as in "Loyalty, the Basic Condition of Liberty"; [57] and logical, as in "Christianity's Stake in the Social Situation." [58] Nearly all Dr. Fosdick's sermons might be called problem-solution, topical, and combinational in structural arrangement. His method of organization cut across such traditional types as doctrinal, biblical, and ethical. In fact, as he tried to bring the hearers abundant life, he normally used all types at once.

Dr. Fosdick organized his sermons to give his listeners force as well as clarity and order in thought development. To emphasize his big truth or central idea, he stated it as soon as possible in the sermon—usually within the first two or three paragraphs. He said:

> Be like a mountain guide. Say, "There is Mt. Matterhorn." Then show them. Walk around the mountain two or three times making each view more impressive than the one before. Be sure that the progression becomes more dramatic as it moves along until at last, as though really seeing the mountain for the first time in all of its splendor, the sightseer cries, "My God, Mt. Matterhorn!" Never hold back the major truth to the end. State the case. Then show them. Build surprises, climaxes, and suspense into the sermon which grows as the theme develops. Make the first view slow and long; the second, less lengthy; and the third, the shortest of all." [59]

After expressing the big truth in the opening section or introduction, Dr. Fosdick developed it with the main points of the

---

[54] *The Power to See It Through*, p.51.
[55] "The Church Monthly," The Riverside Church, Summer, 1946.
[56] *Living Under Tension*, pp.151–158.
[57] *A Great Time to Be Alive*, p.134.
[58] *The Hope of the World*, pp.23–27.
[59] From an Interview with Dr. Fosdick at The Riverside Church, New York City, January 13, 1950.

body of a sermon. The principle of climax determined the order of these main points—climax of emotional appeal and moral impressiveness, rather than climax of idea. He always tried to place the least powerful point first in the body of a sermon and the most powerful point last. For example, in his "The Deathless Hope that Man Cannot Escape," after declaring that we cannot escape the deathless hope (big truth), he arranged his main points in the following climactic order: we cannot escape because of (a) the way we are made; (b) our love for other people; and (c) our fellowship with God.[60]

Although Dr. Fosdick emphasized a main point by placing it last, he never consciously stressed a point by assigning more space to it than to the others. He said that the body of a sermon usually should have between one and four major points; not more than four because too many points confuse the hearers. By assigning to the body all the material following a signpost such as "In the first place," the majority of his sermons have three main points plainly marked, although their number ranges from two to seven.

Of 180 published sermons examined, 22 seemed to have two points in the body: 90 had three points; 34 had four points; 10 had five points; 3 had six points; 2 had seven points, and 19 were developed so that the points were not discernible. Examples of each are as follows: a two-point sermon, "On Believing in Miracles"[61]; a three-point sermon, "On Being Strongly Tempted to be Christian"[62]; a four-point sermon, "the Impossibility of Being Irreligious"[63]; a five-point sermon, "How Much Do We Want Peace?"[64]; a six-point sermon, "Six Ways in Which Modern Man Can Pray"[65]; a seven-point sermon, "Christian Attitudes in Social Reconstruction"[66]; and "On Being Fit to Live With," a sermon in which the points are not evident.[67]

No consistency could be found in the amount of space given to

---
[60] *A Great Time to Be Alive*, p.226.
[61] *Ibid.*, p.124.
[62] *Ibid.*, p.107.
[63] *On Being Fit to Live With*, p.79.
[64] *The Power to See It Through*, p.115.
[65] *Successful Christian Living*, p.12.
[66] *Ibid.*, p.108.
[67] *On Being Fit to Live With*, p.1.

any one point. Sometimes Dr. Fosdick gave more space to the first point, as in "Life's Forced Decisions" [68]; sometimes more to the second, as in "Re-digging Old Wells" [69]; and sometimes more to the third, as in "TheTemptation of Maturity." [70] The space assigned to a point varied from as little as one page to as much as five. At times, without realizing it, Dr. Fosdick seems to have given the most space to the point which required the greatest amount of material to win its acceptance by his hearers, regardless of where that point might come in the body of the sermon—first, second, or third. If an average space allocation had to be estimated, however, it would be about three pages of space for the opening section, or introduction, in which the big truth was set forth, two pages for each of the three points, and one-fourth of a page for the conclusion, as in "Miracles of Character Possible for All." [71]

Ordinarily a main point in the structure of a sermon is emphasized by placement (putting it first or last in the body), by space (assigning more space to it than to the other points), or by significance (putting more material which touches the listeners directly into it than into the other points). Even though he was not aware of it, Dr. Fosdick appears often to have added force to a point, especially the third point of a message, by the method called significance. Look at how completely he engaged his listeners in the third point of "No Dry-As-Dust Religion Will Do Now":

> With this in mind, let us come to our own selves in these troublous days and emphasize the fact that no other kind of religion except this can meet our present need. So large a company could not be gathered without some here being tempted, as many in our day are tempted, to give up religion and get on without it. . . . Surely I am speaking to someone's personal condition here. You, too, are troubled because in this mysterious world so much is dark to you. Sometimes when you hear great faiths announced, great hymns sung, great Scriptures read, you say, I cannot believe that. My friend, on that account do not, I beg

---

[68] *What Is Vital in Religion,* p.113.
[69] *Ibid.,* p.160.
[70] *Ibid.,* p.216.
[71] *Ibid.,* p.46.

of you, shut yourself out of the Christian heritage. Start where you are, my friend, with what you do see: be true to that, and so go on to see more. . . .[72]

Dr. Fosdick used the short conclusions of his sermons to achieve several significant purposes. One purpose was to restate the big truth or central idea. Occasionally, the major truth served as a theme sentence that was repeated in the conclusion, as well as several times throughout the message. Here is such an instance from "The Means Determine the End," where the last part of the conclusion took the form of apostrophe with an address to the soul: "Ah, my soul, look to the road you are walking on! He who picks up one end of a stick picks up the other. He who chooses the beginning of a road chooses the place it leads to. It is the means that determine the end." [73]

In the conclusion of "Christianity's Stake in the Social Situation," the big truth came out rephrased.[74] In "When Great Events Make Common Tasks Seem Trivial," it was reflected in a poem.[75] In "Keeping One's Footing in a Slippery Time," it was mirrored in a short story.[76] In "Having a Faith That Really Works," it was suggested by a biblical quotation.[77]

A second purpose of his conclusions was to summarize the main points of the sermon. Many messages ended like "The Conquest of Fear": "Well, add up the sum and see what it comes to. Clean life, great faith, love that takes in enemies—the sum of that addition is a fearless soul." [78]

A third purpose was to appeal for the acceptance of his message. Sometimes such an appeal was related to the basic *wants* of his listeners, as in "A Religion That Really Gets Us," where the desire for freedom was a motive for acceptance:

> Indeed, I ask you, is the acceptance of these great affirmations of the Christian faith enslaving? Is it not, as Jesus said, the most liberating experience the soul of man can know? Look at what happens to the

---

[72] *A Great Time to Be Alive*, p.177.
[73] *Living Under Tension*, p.111.
[74] *The Hope of the World*, p.29.
[75] *Living Under Tension*, p.202.
[76] *The Hope of the World*, p.86.
[77] *What Is Vital in Religion*, p.23.
[78] *The Hope of the World*, p.63.

world when the opposite philosophy is accepted. It is anti-Christ, not Christ, who enslaves men. . . . So may the Christian faith come to some life here, saying, "Ye shall know the truth and the truth shall make you free." [79]

The appeal for acceptance was often given in the form of a challenge which urged the hearers to become part of a great and good cause. Dr. Fosdick used this form as the conclusion of his message "When God Becomes Real":

> This is the essence of the matter, that there is no religion which amounts to much except that which is to be found in people to whom the Divine is thus real. . . . From Gandhi in India and Kagawa in Japan to men like Phillips Brooks in our own tradition, these have been the flaming souls who amid the dust and ashes of religious conventionality have made religion a living fire. Give us enough people to whom in personal character and social relationships the Divine is real, and we can lift humanity yet out of its slough of despond. Well, what is real to us? For, my friends, nothing beside that can ever be any man's vital religion.[80]

Occasionally, the appeal for acceptance was presented as a visualization of a desirable future which would come to pass if the message was received and put into practice, as in "What About Our Social Pessimism?" [81] In his sermon "The Unknown Soldier," the appeal for acceptance took still another form—that of a strong declaration of his own personal intention and future course of action: "At any rate, I will do the best I can to settle my account with the Unknown Soldier. . . . I renounce war and never again, directly or indirectly, will I sanction or support another! O Unknown Soldier, in penitent reparation I make you that pledge." [82]

Dr. Fosdick appears to have employed the conclusions of his sermons to achieve at least one more purpose. He appealed for action. Ordinarily the action called for was intellectual rather than physical. Consider this ending from "Things That Money Cannot Buy":

---

[79] *What Is Vital in Religion*, p.64.
[80] *Ibid.*, p.77.
[81] *The Power to See It Through*, p.227.
[82] *The Secret of Victorious Living*, p.97.

Stand for a moment before the cross of Christ! We cannot pay for that, nor for the life that led up to it or the sacrifice that there was consummated. Such a free gift of life moves in the unpurchasable realm. We are the children of such living, its pensioners and beneficiaries, and all our finest benedictions have come thus from lives not for sale. So the whole weight of the gospel presses home our truth. It is a good thing to have money and the things that money can buy, but it is a good thing to check up once in a while and make sure that we have not lost the things that money cannot buy.[83]

Rarely was the action called for as overt as the plea to join the church in "Despise Ye the Church of God." Here an analogy enhanced the appeal:

And if you must confess that in that real sense you do not desire to live without the church, may I not invite some of you to come into closer cooperation with the Christian fellowship. There are great musical compositions which no artist, however fine, can play alone. No matter how well that first violinist can play, he cannot interpret them alone. It takes an orchestra—the oboes and violas and violins, the flutes and drums and horns—to interpret such great compositions. And Christianity is great. No soloist alone can render it. Ah, you solitary piccolo, trying to render the Overture to Tannhäuser! It cannot be done. But you might help. Even if nobody noticed you, you might help—in the orchestra.[84]

Occasionally the appeal for action was placed within a larger plea for acceptance, as in "Basic Conditions of Spiritual Well-Being." [85]

To achieve these four purposes, Dr. Fosdick used many types of conclusions. In addition to those already indicated, his endings frequently took the form of one or more questions, as in "The Hope of the World in Its Minorities": "As for being Christian, I suppose that, reduced to simplest terms, it means answering Christ's two-worded appeal "Follow me." Where do we think it takes a man when he does follow him? Never into a majority. I wonder where you and I are this morning—three measures of meal or leaven?" [86] "A Great Year for Easter" concluded with a

---

[83] *What Is Vital in Religion*, p.176.
[84] *Ibid.*, p.132.
[85] *The Power to See It Through*, p.141.
[86] *The Hope of the World*, p.10.

reference to the occasion.[87] A reference to the listeners finished "When Prayer Means Power." [88] "What Are You Standing For?" ended with a reference to Fosdick himself.[89] The conclusion of "What About God?" combined several kinds of material, a reference to the listeners, a quotation, a challenging statement, and a verse from the Bible:

> My friends, I have not painted a miniature of God for you to carry home with you today. God, as another said, never sat for his photograph. Distrust anybody who thinks he has a photograph of the Eternal. But the Universal Mind, the Unseen Friend, the Life in whom dwell goodness, beauty, and truth, the Purpose, mightier than man's purpose, that has laid hold on man—before the mountains were brought forth, or ever Thou hadst formed the earth and the world, even from everlasting to everlasting, Thou are God.[90]

What then does a detailed study of the organization of Dr. Fosdick's sermons teach the student of sermon-making? It shows him the supreme qualities of structural clarity, order, and emphasis. It familiarizes him with some of the skillful means which this great preacher employed to achieve those qualities and, through them, the desired response from his hearers. It gives him inspiring insights into the high art and awesome responsibility of preaching the unsearchable riches of Christ.

---

[87] *Living Under Tension*, p.253.
[88] *Ibid.*, p.81.
[89] *The Secret of Victorious Living*, p.223.
[90] *Ibid.*, p.157.

Chapter 16

Structural Analysis of the Sermons of Dr. Harry Emerson Fosdick

GILBERT STILLMAN MACVAUGH *

CAN IT BE that the pedagogics of public speaking have been all wrong? Modern writers on public speaking technique are commonly agreed that the most effective form of an introduction is one which is brief and one which is attention-getting.[1] "Lengthiness must be avoided at all costs,"[2] has become the conventional dictum of public speaking teachers. Furthermore, it is believed by some that "too lengthy an introduction destroys interest" in the speech long before the main ideas are reached.[3] Even Quintilian, in writing of the length of the *exordium*,[4] said, "It should propound rather than expound and should not describe how each thing occurred but simply indicate the points on which the orator proposes to speak." In speaking of arousing attention,

---

* Professor, The American University.

Note: Reprinted with permission from *The Quarterly Journal of Speech*, Volume XIX; pp.531–546.

[1] Sandford, W. P. and Yeager, W. H.: *Principles of Effective Speaking*. N. Y., Thomas Nelson and Son, 1930, p.175.

[2] Sanford, W. P. and Yeager, W. H.: *Business and Professional Speaking*. N. Y., McGraw-Hill Book Co., 1929, p.78.

[3] Sanford and Yeager: *Principles of Effective Speaking*, p.167.

[4] According to Quintilian, *Narration* was the remaining part of the introduction which stated the contents of the speech which were to be developed in the *Argument*. The Introduction, then, contains the *Exordium* and the *Narration*.

he continues, ". . . . We shall contribute still more to this effect if we give a brief and lucid summary of the case. . . ."[5] in the *exordium*. It was Cicero, after having discussed the amassing of material to be used in the speech, who said in reference to the content of the *exordium*, ". . . the judge should only receive a slight impulse at the outset."[6] He believed the function of the *exordium* was to gain for the orator favor in his hearers' minds. Having done this succinctly, he should state the facts in the case and proceed immediately into the argument. Elsewhere, while quoting Terence,[7] Cicero stresses the element of brevity in the *exordia* by remarking, they "should be like vestibules and approaches to houses and temples" and not as large as any major room within the house or the temple. Another conviction is that climax is best attained, usually, by placing the strongest ideas last, that is, the order of climax should be one of increasing vividness wherein the least vivid ideas are placed first, or wherein the most important is placed last, the next in importance first, and the least important in the middle.[8] All these are traditional dicta which have reverberated through the rhetorical centuries and which are still taught in our colleges today. Is it possible that these teachings are, after all, not the most effective methods of structuralizing a speech?

At any rate, these dicta seem to have dominated the speeches made in the recent past. An impartial and random selection of thirty speeches (made by prominent men during the period from Beecher to the present) which were surveyed to discover the practical validity of these rhetorical dicta seems to substantiate the fact that the above mentioned methods have been popularly accepted (cf Datum I and III).[9]

Now, when a man who is endowed with *die Rednergabe* and who is one of no meager prominence in the eyes of the public-

---

[5] Quintilian: *The Institutio Oratoria*. Vol. II, Book IV, 33 and 34. English translation by H. E. Butler, N. Y., Putnams' Sons, 1921.

[6] Cicero: *De Oratore*. Book II, CLXXIX, p.318. Translated by J. S. Watson, Geo. Bell & Sons, London, 1881.

[7] Cicero: *ibid*, p.318; also note 2.

[8] Sandford and Yeager: *Principles of Effective Speaking*, p.192.

[9] Data II and IV appear at the end of this paper; these are the calculations from which the graphs were made.

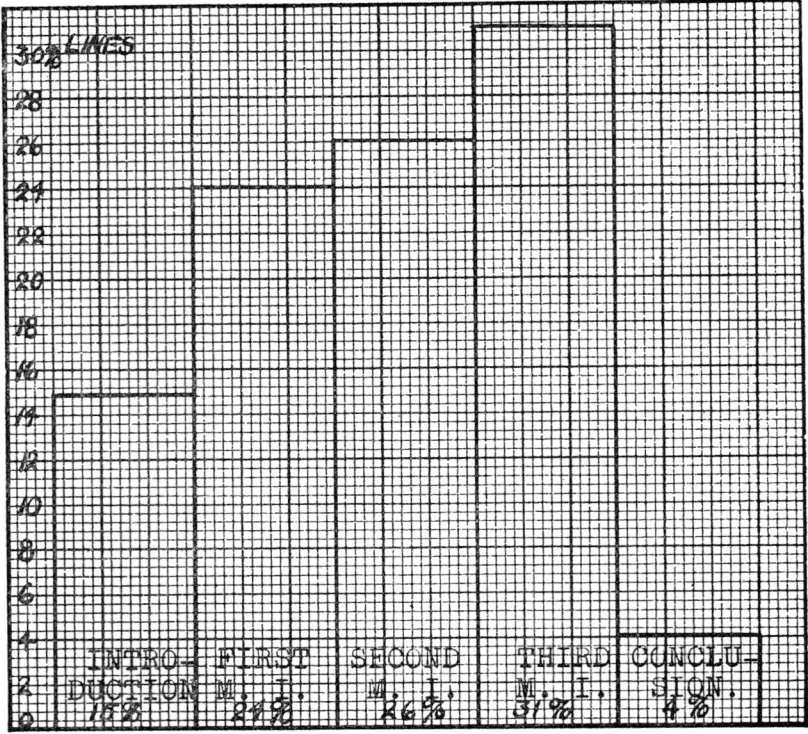

DATUM I. Speech Structure Parts. Percent of lines is speech structure parts from Beecher to present.

speaking world repudiates these rhetorical dicta, it is inevitable that the secret behind his innovations will be sought after and studied. In this instance one of the world's foremost ministers, Dr. Harry Emerson Fosdick, is the repudiator of these dicta, and this writing will be devoted to a presentation of the innovations found in his sermon structure.

His conception of good sermon development is to aim for climax, but the climax ought to be based on "a principle of emotional climax in appeal and of moral impressiveness rather than a climax of idea." It is a climax which is to be *felt* by the audience as a result of the total effect of the sermon instead of a climax which comes as a result of a cold, logical induction or as a

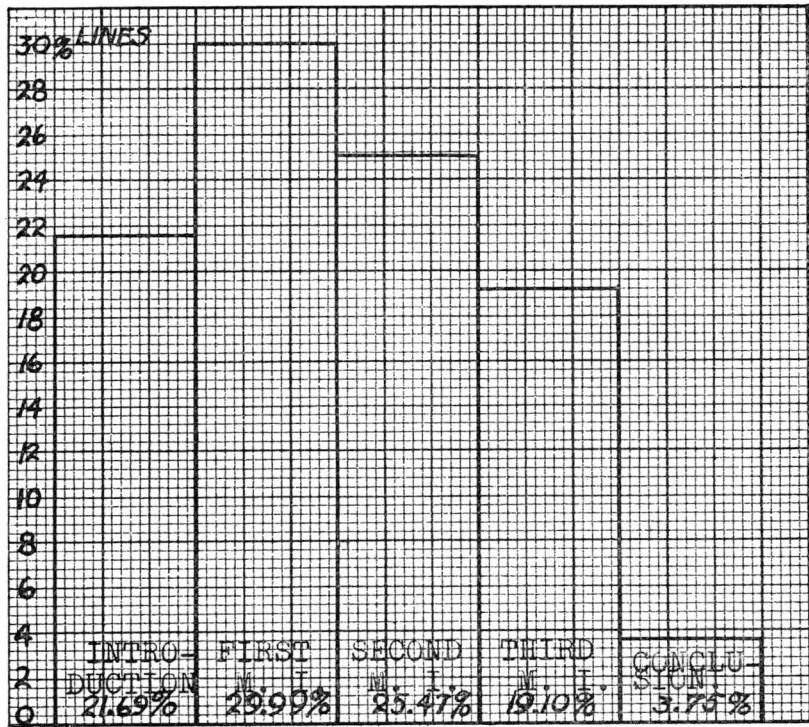

DATUM III. Speech Structure Parts. Line fatigue principle in Fosdick's sermons: percent of lines in speech structure parts of eighteen random sermons (period: four years).

result of a holding back of the best ideas for the final main point.[10] Therein lies a suggestion of the first innovation.

Before going further, it seems wise to explain how these innovations are dealt with graphically. The writer has in his possession many of Dr. Fosdick's printed sermons in which he uses consistently the transitions "In the first place," "In the second place," and "In the third place." His sermons, therefore, are so easy to outline that the reader perceives at once what his main ideas are.

---

[10] This information he furnishes to all students in his classes of Practical Theology at Union Theological Seminary, N. Y. Parenthetically, the writer was one of Dr. Fosdick's students.

All the material preceding "In the first place" is assumed to be the introduction. Now, taking one line of the printed manuscript as the standard of measurement, the writer counted in each sermon all the lines in the introduction, in the three main ideas, and in the conclusion. As can be seen by inspection of Datum IV, the percentage of lines of the whole sermon found in each of the five parts of the speech structure was computed and tabulated.[11] This procedure was followed for each sermon, and the results were arranged in columns to get the average percentages of the five parts in the "average" sermon. The "average" sermon is shown in Datum III.

Now, since an important idea is to be announced first in order to gain the audiences' attention and to begin the explication of the theme immediately, it is imperative that it be made concretely vivid. This necessity requires two things, namely, first, that the important idea be stated and expanded in the introduction, and second, that greater space be utilized in the development of the introduction.

Public speaking instructors advise the use of brief introductions, which, ordinarily, ought not to occupy more than twenty lines similar to those used in computation here. Students are advised to "get attention, get it quickly, and then pass to the discussion of your main ideas."[12] In the first place then, despite this convention of brief introductions, Dr. Fosdick's introductions average ninety-two lines per sermon or 21.69 percent of the total sermon manuscript. Under the requirements of his method, it would be difficult to develop the initial important idea with any degree of adequacy in fewer lines. The writer does not desire to mislead the reader by making any dogmatic assertion that length of space is always an index to the importance of an idea—not at all; but, assuming that his sermons in no place descend to superficialities and recalling that his advice is to start the sermon with a

---

[11] For those who find fractions difficult, these percentages were multiplied by 100.

[12] Sandford and Yeager: *Principles of Effective Speaking*, p.175. In the *Art of Debate* by W. C. Shaw, p.330, that writer would make the rule more general and thus agree with Fosdick's approach. Shaw says, the speaker ". . . may assign not more than one-third of the speech to the Introduction, at least one-half to the Discussion, and not more than one-sixth to the Conclusion."

very important idea, one immediately recognizes the logic of the system. If there are no superficial spots and if the beginning is of utmost importance, then it follows that one is justified in assuming that length is an indication of importance, because the first part of his sermons is unconventionally long. (By the first part is meant the introduction and the first main idea.) Not only are his introductions unusually long as compared with those shown on Datum I, but also they are, on the average, 2.59 percent longer than his own third main idea and almost as long as his second main idea. If space is assumed to be an indication of importance, then his introductions are, at least, more important than his third main idea.

In the second place, this principle of *space-importance* is found to be applicable in regard to the importance and the length of the *first main idea*. On the average, the first main idea occupies almost one-third of the space of the whole sermon manuscript. It is evident here, on the basis of the above assumption, that greater importance is attached to the first main idea than to the second and that the second idea is more important than the third because the second is more fully developed than the third. Parenthetically, by some, the third or last main idea is the place where emphasis is most effectively used.[13] The author personally knows from empirical data gathered in the psychological laboratory that this belief is very sound. The reader, however, must realize that Dr. Fosdick is not greatly concerned with the space-emphasis or the place-emphasis factors per se but primarily with the total effect and impressiveness which the whole sermon makes on the congregation. He allows himself much more freedom in trailing his theme through the bypaths of thought and experience in the beginning of the sermon than at the end. More space is needed for such

---

[13] Sandford and Yeager: *Principles of Effective Speaking*, p.204; attention is called, however, to the fact that circumstances might alter the arrangement so that the first idea might be the strongest and most vivid in order to catch attention. This method is frequently used in formal debate.

Prof. Phillips, in *Effective Speaking*, p.169, is more in harmony with Fosdick's method in saying, "The governing rule is: that arrangement is best which most effectively attains the desired result." It will be remembered that Dr. Fosdick had his students study *Effective Speaking* by Arthur Edward Phillips.

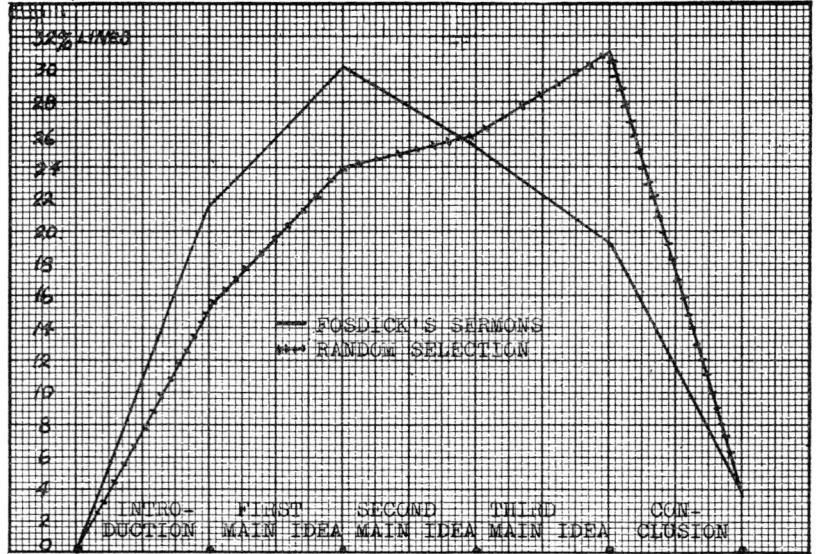

DATUM V. Comparison showing traditional method of speech structure and Fosdick's method of initial impressiveness by stressing the first part of speech.

ramification, and thus space again seems to be an index of importance. "Emphasis by space consists simply of giving more time to those ideas upon which you wish to lay stress."[14]

The remainder of the sermon development beyond the first main point is concerned with further explication of the important theme sited in the introduction. The important thing to note here is that his sermons are, according to Datum V, skewed to the left, showing that greater space for development is devoted to the first part, as compared to Datum I which on Datum V shows that greater space for development is devoted to the latter part of the speeches. After passing over the first main idea, the curve, in Datum V, over the remaining parts of the speech structure gradually descends and thus indicates that the second and third main ideas do not have as many lines devoted to their development as did the first main idea. This descensive tendency does not indicate any relative unimportance of the content materials found in the

---

[14] Sandford and Yeager: *Principles of Effective Speaking*, p.227, and Shaw: *ibid.*, p.260.

DATUM VI.
STRUCTURAL OUTLINE OF "HANDICAPPED LIVES"

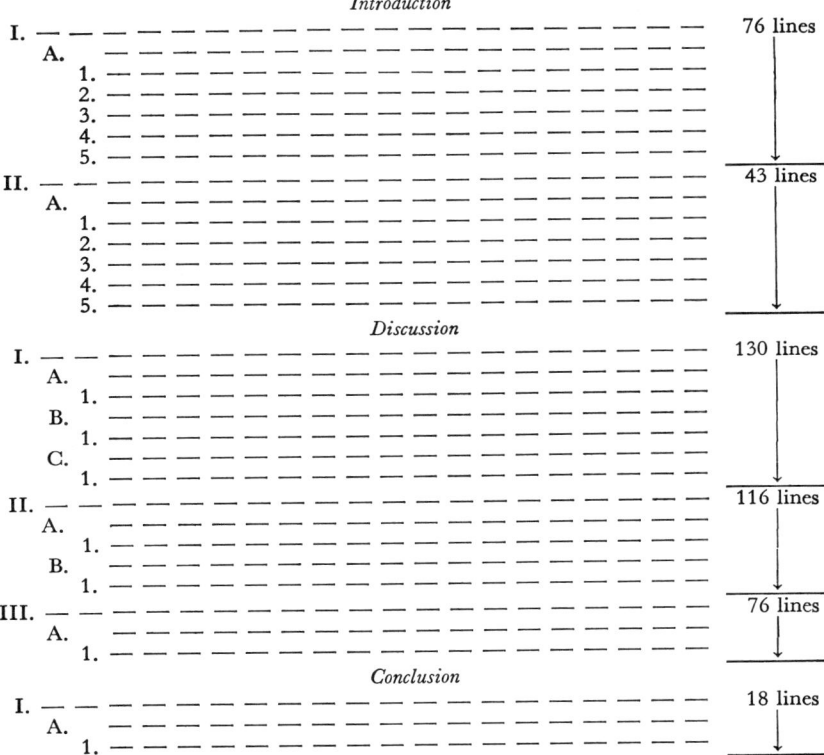

last two ideas but only that less space has been given to the explication of them. The descension of the curve is explained by another principle which the writer calls the *line-fatigue principle*. This too is an heretofore unheard of device among rhetoricians.

In the third place, after having seen the graphic representation of the importance Dr. Fosdick places on the first part of his sermons, the reader will be interested in another equally striking feature. This line-fatigue principle grows out of and is coexistent with the "space-importance" principle *q. v. supra* which is that more space is devoted to the development of the first part of the speech than to the second part, the last two main ideas, and the conclusion. Those who have listened to long sermons will recall that the intensity of one's concentration decreases with the prolongation of the strain of attending. If one sits attendingly through a ten-minute speech, obviously he is not as much fatigued at the end of this period as he would have been had the speech been twenty minutes or thirty minutes long. If the reader should set himself to outlining for example *Handicapped Lives* (Datum VI), which, to the writer, is one of Dr. Fosdick's best sermons, he will note that Dr. Fosdick recognizes this psychobiological fact of fatigue and constructs his sermons accordingly.

The reader will see that in this structural outline there are two main points in the introduction. The second of these has less linespace devoted to its development than has the first point. There is an important reason for this difference. At the beginning of the sermon it is assumed that the congregations' minds are fresh and receptive. (Dr. Fosdick, therefore, expects the hearers to be able to receive more ideas when their minds are fresh than if they were less receptive or tired.) Because the audience is receptive at the beginning, he uses in this introduction seventy-six lines for the development of the first point and only forty-three for the second point—a difference of thirty-three lines. Upon commencing the development of the second point in the introduction, he realizes that the ability of the audience to concentrate has been somewhat, though not appreciably, diminished. Recognizing this, he taxes the congregation much less mentally by requiring them to attend over a much shorter space of time for the second point. Put mathematically, it appears as though the *ratio of content to receptivity is kept at unity,* wherein the numerical values of receptivity at the outset are as great as the numerical values of content. That is, as the power to concentrate upon or to receive ideas diminishes, so too are the number of lines of printed manuscript decreased.

It will be noted that the same principle holds in the number of lines given to each main idea in the discussion proper. Each successive idea after the first has fewer lines devoted to its development than does its predecessor. That is, as the audiences' intensity of concentration upon each main idea lessens, they are required to attend to each succeeding main idea for a shorter period of time. In the discussion the first main idea contains 130 lines; the second, 116 lines; and the third, 76 lines. Each succeeding main idea indicates a decrease in the number of lines as the speech progresses toward the end.

In the fourth place, there exists in his sermons another interestingly novel method of dealing with the fatigue factor. In addition to finding a decrease in the number of lines utilized in the development of each consecutive main idea, the reader will also find a decrease in the number of subpoints supporting each consecutive main idea. As the sermon progresses, there is a decreasing degree of complexity of supporting material used in the explication of each subsequent main idea. This principle, for convenience, has been called the idea-fatigue principle.

Plainly, there are three main ideas. The first is "if we are to deal handsomely with our handicaps, we must at least have the grace to take not a negative but a positive attitude toward them." In developing this first idea fully, Dr. Fosdick uses 130 lines of printed manuscript. Moreover, these *130 lines* contain a further development of the idea through *three subideas*. The second main idea is "if we are thus to take a positive attitude toward our handicaps, some of us will have to throw off a sense of false responsibility." At the beginning of the second main idea, realizing that fatigue has already set in, and in order not to overtax the congregation mentally, he utilizes only *116 lines* and only *two subideas* for its development; that is, 14 lines and one subidea less than were used in the first main idea. The third idea is "if we are thus to take a positive and a hopeful attitude toward our limitations . . . . we always can make a spiritual contribution to the world." In addition to using only *76 lines* to develop this last main idea, he uses only *one subidea* in further support of it. And so, it becomes clear that as the sermon progresses and fatigue increases in the audience, Dr. Fosdick not only decreases the number of lines in each succeeding main idea but also he supports each subsequent main idea with one subpoint less. The hearers are thus required to remember less and to listen for a shorter period of time to each succeeding main idea.

Lines	Main Ideas	Subideas
130	I.	3
116	II.	2
76	III.	1

It is not to be opined that both of these principles appear together invariably in every sermon. When there is not absolute consistency in the line-fatigue principle, there frequently occurs the idea-fatigue principle alone. Reference, for example, to the speech structure outline of *Christianity and Unemployment* (Datum VII.) will clarify this fact. In this sermon, there are in the first main idea *three subideas* but *only 119 lines;* in the second main idea, there are *two* supporting *subideas* with *134 lines,* that is, 15 lines more and one subidea less than the first main idea; and

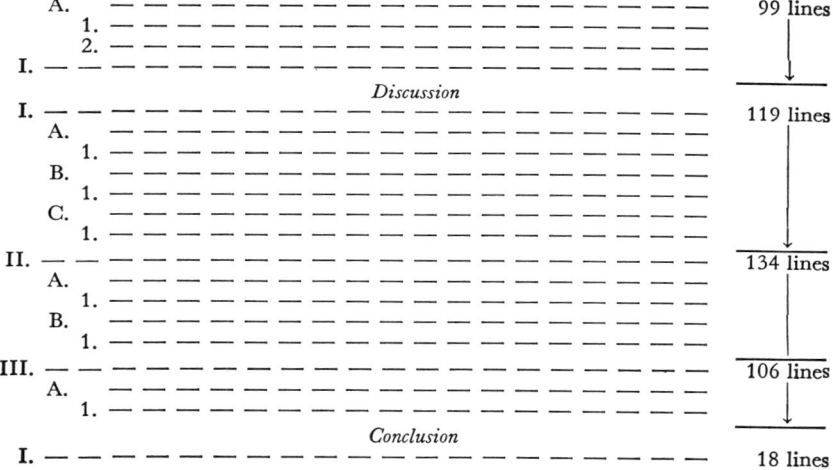

under the third main idea, there is only *one subidea* with 106 lines. It is thus clear that he manifests his ability to cope effectively with the problem of fatigue in the attending congregation.

The conclusions are invariably short—even shorter than those indicated in Datum I, and they comply with the conventional method of brief conclusion construction. (His sermons usually require about one-half hour for delivery.) Realizing that this is a long attending period, the conclusions are always brief—the average contains only 16 lines, or 3.75 percent of the entire manuscript.

Structural Analysis

DATUM II.†
THIRTY SPEECHES FROM BROOKS TO THE PRESENT, SHOWING PERCENTAGE OF LINES IN EACH STRUCTURAL PART

No.	Speaker	Int.	I.	II.	III.	C
1.	Brooks	13	23	19	42	3
2.	"	22	22	5	45	6
3.	"	15	19	20	43	3
4.	Beecher	11	25	16	43	5
5.	"	27	19	21	29	4
6.	Cadman	15	16	32	34	3
7.	McDowell	4	38	42	14	2
8.	"	11	14	31	42	2
9.	"	27	39	24	10	0
10.	"	9	16	32	38	5
11.	Borah	10	27	29	30	4
12.	Young, O. D.	13	13	20	50	4
13.	"	6	23	43	25	3
14.	Swope	11	19	47	18	5
15.	Wilson	35	26	24	10	5
16.	"	9	47	16	25	3
17.	"	18	18	32	24	8
18.	"	13	29	13	37	8
19.	Gibbons, J.	4	15	29	48	4
20.	"	6	21	25	45	3
21.	Abbott	12	32	22	30	4
22.	Hughes	18	22	30	28	2
23.	"	31	23	17	21	8
24.	Bliss	26	18	25	29	2
25.	Gifford	14	12	23	41	10
26.	"	6	28	37	24	5
27.	Sizoo, J. R.	17	38	14	30	1
28.	"	14	22	40	22	2
29.	"	18	36	25	20	1
30.	"	10	38	29	21	2
	Average	15	24	26	31	4

Percentage tables from which Datum I. was used.
Impartial and random selection: the first speech encountered which contained three main ideas was used herein.

Now, it is not to be supposed that the line-fatigue principle has not been dealt with in many other ways; it has. The use of the elements of interestingness, occasional humor, variation in rate and of emphasis in delivery, very intimate and personal appeals to the vital wants of the audience, and by the aid of the very numerous beneficial, external features of the building—not excluding the unusually comfortable pews—, and so forth, all these

DATUM IV.*

EIGHTEEN SERMONS PREACHED BY DR. FOSDICK OVER A PERIOD OF FOUR YEARS

(A).

No.	Title	Int.	1.	11.	111.	C.	Total
1.	Mystery of Life	116	104	118	73	18	429
2.	Handicapped Lives	119	130	116	76	18	459
3.	Pull Yourselves Together	89	149	86	66	26	416
4.	A Little Morality Is a Dangerous Thing	76	122	93	74	39	404
5.	Forgiveness of Sins	95	90	113	96	18	412
6.	Greatness of God	185	84	111	74	9	463
7.	The Wrong Way to Build a Church	62	140	91	71	18	382
8.	Christ and the Inferiority Complex	193	46	44	90	7	380
9.	Jesus' Appeal to the Irreligious	77	154	174	132	11	548
10.	Christianity and Unemployment	99	119	134	106	18	476
11.	Judas, Not Iscariot	21	117	120	160	14	492
12.	Christianity's Supreme Rival	158	82	129	91	18	478
13.	Making the Best of a Bad Mess	58	128	110	56	9	361
14.	Our Moral Muddle	103	130	117	43	0	393
15.	Overcoming the World	37	204	62	99	17	419
16.	Personal Responsibility in the Present Crisis	85	117	115	53	21	391
17.	What Are You Standing For?	18	138	137	66	28	387
18.	Handling Life's Second Bests	64	178	88	44	1	375
	Average	92	127	108	81	16	432

(B).
Percentage of Lines

No.	Int.	I.	II.	III.	C
1.	28	24	27	17	4
2.	27	28	25	16	4
3.	21	36	21	16	6
4.	19	30	23	18	10
5.	23	23	27	23	4
6.	39	19	24	16	2
7.	16	36	24	19	5
8.	51	12	12	23	2
9.	14	28	32	24	2
10.	21	25	28	22	4
11.	4	36	24	33	3
12.	33	17	27	19	4
13.	16	35	30	16	3
14.	26	33	30	11	0
15.	9	48	15	24	4
16.	22	30	29	14	5
17.	5	36	35	17	7
18.	17	47	23	12	1
Aver.	22	30	25	19	4

Note: (A). Number of lines in structural parts. (B). Tables showing the percentage of lines in each structural part.

* Impartial and random selection made from those sermons in print.

he has arranged and uses to hold the congregations' attention and to offset fatigue in order "to get his impressions across." *In toto,* apart from the exceptions which this writing expands, Dr. Fosdick, although he never used any textbook of public speaking in his training, utilizes in no small degree the basic principles contained in *Effective Speaking*[15] and *Principles of Effective Speaking*.[16]

The wonder of all this is (and it was as much a shock to the writer as it probably will be to the reader) that Dr. Fosdick was totally unaware of these specific details in his sermon structures. Upon learning of these findings he replied, "I am reminded of the poet who saw an analysis of his method in writing poetry and was astonished because he had never thought of it before." Both the surprise of the poet and of Dr. Fosdick are not unusual. All men have expressed a degree of surprise when they, for the first time, discover in nature the operation of new laws which had been, to them, theretofore unformulated. And so, it is natural for a man to express surprise when he sees, mathematically formulated, the rules of which he had been theretofore totally unaware and by which the orderly operation of his mind has been governed. The writer cannot withhold the inclusion of another statement. It is "most surprising . . . to read the schedule you have made out for my sermons. . . . I did not write them by schedule, and if I have worked out such a practical technique as you describe, I have rather blundered into it by wanting to get my business done with the congregation as effectively as possible and feeling my way toward that end rather than planning it." (What an effectual blunder! What an artistic feeling!)

The aim of this writing has been to stress (a) Dr. Fosdick's persistent and effective use of a seemingly overemphasized, unconventional, and lengthy introduction; (b) the fact that the skewness of the sermon structure toward the first part and that a gradual decrease in complexity in each succeeding main idea seems to indicate an apparent "instinctive" repudiation of the accepted methods used in traditional speech structures; and (c) his use of

---

[15] Phillips, A. E.: *Effective Speaking.* Chicago, Newton Co., 1908 and 1929.
[16] Sandford and Yeager: *Principles of Effective Speaking, supra.*

the line-fatigue and idea-fatigue principle wherein the first main idea has either more lines or ideas than the second—and the second has either more lines or ideas than the third, or wherein the first main idea has more subpoints than the second—and wherein the second main idea has more subpoints than the third main idea.

These three factors emphasize three things; first, the audience is not permitted to reach the fatigue line because of the excellent use he makes of the space element. Second, at the beginning of the sermon he is able to plunge more deeply into the details of the subject and to use more finesse when and because the hearers' minds are fresh and receptive than he could in the second half of the sermon because of the opposite reason. At the beginning of the sermon there is greater hope of his thoughts being followed much more closely than at the end of the sermon. To make an ineradicable impression—not to have the congregation remember a group of facts is his desideratum. Third, there is indicated a possibility that the ancient writers did not have a corner on the truths by which orators live. Theirs and later teachings may not all be wrong, but it is apparent that Dr. Fosdick's unique method is a contribution to the history of oratory and preaching.

The final result is that the speech critic perceives immediately the perfect sense of balance and design contained in the unique sermon structures of this Sir Christopher Wren sermonizer. If the popular acceptance of Dr. Fosdick's preaching is an index of the efficaciousness of his method, then here is a new psychological approach to effectiveness and to impressiveness which is destined to be placed alongside of or, in part, to supercede the other accepted and age-old traditional methods of the rhetoricians.

Chapter 17

Harry Emerson Fosdick: The Methods of a Master

CHARLES F. KEMP *

HARRY EMERSON FOSDICK is the master of life situation preaching. No one has done as much to influence the modern emphasis on life situation preaching as he has. In all the books that he has published, he has not published one on preaching as such; fortunately, however, there are some brief statements he has made which give an insight into his thought and his methods. We shall quote from three that come from rather widely separated points in his career.

The first is from an article in *Harper's Magazine* in 1928. Here he states the purpose of such preaching. We referred to it in the introductory chapter.

> Every sermon should have for its main business the solving of some problem—a vital, important problem, puzzling minds, burdening consciences, distracting lives. . . . This endeavor to help people solve their spiritual problems is a sermon's only justifiable aim. The point of departure and of constant reference, the reason for preaching the sermon in the first place, and the inspiration for its method of approach and the organization of its material should not be something outside the congregation but inside. Within a paragraph or two . . . wide areas of any congregation ought to begin recognizing that the preacher is tackling something of vital concern to them. He is handling

---

* Reprinted from Kemp, Charles F.: *Life Situation Preaching.* St. Louis, Mo., The Bethany Press, 1956, pp.88–91.

a subject they are puzzled about, or a way of living they have dangerously experimented with, or an experience that has bewildered them, or a sin that has come perilously near to wrecking them, or an ideal they have been trying to make real, or a need they have not known how to meet. One way or another they should see that he is engaged in a serious and practical endeavor to state fairly a problem which actually exists in their lives and then to throw what light on it he can.

Any preacher who even with moderate skill is thus helping folk to solve their real problems is functioning. . . .[1]

The second statement has to do with the preparation of a sermon. It appeared in 1932 as a chapter in a volume entitled *If I Had But One Sermon to Preach*. Here he gives us a view of the methods he follows in the preparation of his sermons.

Uniformly I am through with my manuscript on Friday noon. The next stage is one of the most important of all, for, fearful that in working out my subject I may occasionally have forgotten my object and may have got out of the center of focus the concrete personalities who will face me on Sunday, I sit down on Saturday morning and rethink the whole business as if my congregation were visibly before my eyes, often picking out individuals and characteristic groups of individuals and imaginatively trying my course of thought upon them, so as to be absolutely sure that I have not allowed any pride of discussion or lure of rhetoric to deflect me from my major purpose of doing something worthwhile with people. This process often means the elision of paragraphs that I liked very much when I first wrote them and the rearrangement of order of thought in the interest of psychological persuasiveness.[2]

The final statement is from an article written for the journal, *Pastoral Psychology*, after his retirement from the active pastorate. He emphasized the same central purpose that he had stressed twenty-four years earlier. In this article, "Pastoral Counseling and Preaching," there was more emphasis upon the possibilities and results of such preaching.

Every sermon should have for its main business the head-on, constructive meeting of some problem which is puzzling minds, burdening consciences, distracting lives, and no sermon which so meets real

---

[1] From What's the matter with preaching. See Chapter 2. *Harper's Magazine*, July, 1928. Used by permission.
[2] From Newton, Joseph Fort: *If I Had But One Sermon to Preach*. See Chapter 4. Copyrighted 1932 by Harper & Bros. Used by permission.

human difficulty, with light to throw on it and power to win victory over it, can possibly be futile.

He referred to one particular problem with which he had worked years before. A young man had fallen victim to alcoholism and sought his help. After months of effort with the boy ended in success, he said it did something to his preaching.

> From that day on the secret prayer which I have offered, as I stood up to preach, has run like this: "Somewhere in this congregation is one person who desperately needs what I am going to say; O God, help me to get at him!"

Again, speaking of the results that can take place in life, he said,

> It is a great day in a minister's life, when having seen what miracles can be wrought by Christ's truth and power brought to bear on individual souls, he mounts his pulpit sure that a sermon, too, can be thus a medium of creative and transforming effects.[3]

Through the years he has combined an effective counseling program with great preaching.[4] In both preaching and counseling he utilized the best of modern psychology and mental hygiene together with the resources of religion.

It was difficult to select one sermon from the eight different volumes of sermons he has published. We have selected one because it is a bit different in emphasis, but any one of many might have been included. A mere listing of some of the titles gives an indication of his approach to preaching:

>"Handling Life's Second Best"
>"Getting Out of Us the Best that Is in Us"
>"The High Uses of Trouble"
>"When Life Goes All to Pieces"
>"No Man Need Stay the Way He Is"
>"How to Stand up and Take It"
>"When Great Events Make Common Tasks Seem Trivial"
>"Finding Unfailing Resources"

Any one of these sermons might well be studied as an example of effective life situation preaching.

---

[3] Reprinted by permission from the March, 1952, issue of *Pastoral Psychology*. Copyright 1952 by Pastoral Psychology Press, Great Neck, N. Y.

[4] See Introduction, *On Being a Real Person*, Harper and Bros., 1943, for a brief statement of his attitudes and experiences in pastoral counseling.

Chapter 18

The Rhetorical Theory of Harry Emerson Fosdick

LIONEL CROCKER

TO TEACHERS of public speaking it should be a matter of satisfaction that such a pulpit orator as Harry Emerson Fosdick, called by Dean Charles W. Gilkey "the greatest living master of the craft of sermonizing," looks back upon his collegiate training in public speaking with a sense of gratitude. Especially are we encouraged to learn that he stresses the usefulness of the discipline when one recalls that Yale University recently dropped its course in public speaking because, it was said, it was too practical. In a letter to Professor John Marshman of Ohio Wesleyan University, Doctor Fosdick declared:

> In answer to your question, of what value has your college training in oratory been in your later life, I must content myself simply with saying that I regard my college training in oratory as one of the most useful disciplines that I ever received. I cannot overestimate the value that it has been to me, the time it saved me in developing technique as a public speaker, and the thankfulness that I feel for having attended a college where there was not only a strong department of public speaking but where high honors in student leadership were associated with success in that department. I sincerely trust that there may be a renaissance of interest among the colleges in the high art of public speech.

Note: Reprinted with permission from *The Quarterly Journal of Speech*, Volume XXII; pp.207–213.

I have used this quotation not only for its inspirational effect upon us as teachers of public speaking but for its use of the phrase "developing technique as a public speaker." Fosdick is technique conscious. In these days when there is not only talk about but evidence of the decline of the power of the pulpit, it is not an accident that Fosdick's church is always crowded. Indeed, strangers are advised to secure tickets early in the week to insure admittance on Sunday mornings. Shades of Henry Ward Beecher! And this is in New York City, sometimes called the graveyard of preachers. Such a phenomenon is partly explained by Fosdick in a few, altogether too few, articles. From these I want to dissect the heart of his rhetorical theory. His most valuable article is "What is the Matter with Preaching?" [1] Not quite so valuable is his essay "The Christian Ministry." [2] Statements by Fosdick on his theory of preaching are contained in two books, which every teacher of public speaking should have: *If I Had Only One Sermon to Prepare*,[3] compiled by Joseph Fort Newton, and *American Preachers of To-Day*,[4] written by Edgar DeWitt Jones. Besides the material found in these four sources, we have the article by G. S. Mac Vaugh, who was a student of Fosdick's at Union Theological Seminary. In his article "Structural Analysis of the Sermons of Dr. Harry Emerson Fosdick," [5] Mr. Mac Vaugh quotes directly from Fosdick's lectures, and I have drawn upon this material for one quotation.

At the outset the fundamental tenet of Fosdick's rhetorical theory is that of success. Successful preaching does not countenance empty pews. Rhetorical instruments which draw people are employed; others are discarded. The stress on success is seen in the following quotation: "There is nothing that people are so interested in as themselves, their own problems, and the way to solve them. That fact is basic. No preaching that neglects it can raise a ripple on a congregation. It is the primary starting point of all successful public speaking, and for once the requirements of

---

[1] *Harper's Magazine*, July 1928. This valuable essay may be secured from the Riverside Church.
[2] *The Atlantic Monthly*, January, 1929. See Chapter 6.
[3] Harper & Bros., 1932. See Chapter 4.
[4] The Bobbs-Merrill Co., Inc., Indianapolis, 1933. See Chapter 11.
[5] *Quarterly Journal of Speech*, November, 1932. See Chapter 16.

practical success and ideal helpfulness coincide." In demanding success of his preaching, Fosdick is in agreement with the principle set forth by George Henry Lewes in his *Principles of Success in Literature*.[6] It will be remembered that Lewes says success is the final criterion of worth in composition. "In how far is success a test of merit? Rigorously considered it is the absolute test."

The predominant quality of successful preaching is that of interestingness. "One obvious trouble," Fosdick says, "with the mediocre sermon even when harmless, is that it is uninteresting. It does not matter. It could as well be left unsaid." Let us proceed to discover what devices Fosdick advocates for making a sermon attractive.

Successful preaching is interesting because it employs the principle of contrast. Fosdick advises, "A wise preacher can so build his sermon that it will be not a dogmatic monologue but a cooperative dialogue, in which all sorts of things in the minds of the congregation—objections, questions, doubts, and confirmations—will be brought to the front and fairly dealt with. . . . He must see clearly and state fairly what people other than himself are thinking on the matter in hand. He may often make this so explicit as to begin paragraphs with such phrases as 'But some of you will say,' or 'Let us consider a few questions that inevitably arise,' or 'Some of you have had experiences that seem to contradict what we are saying.' " Is Fosdick successful with this instrument? Besides the evidence of a church full of attentive listeners, we have the testimony of a distinguished fellow-clergyman, Edgar DeWitt Jones.

> Fosdick can take a theme, say an appraisal of modern Protestantism, and in a series of pungent paragraphs bare to the bone every weakness, uncover and expose every blemish of organized Christianity, so that when he finishes there seems nothing left worth preserving. As you listen, you become alarmed, apprehensive, indignant. You say to yourself, "This man has gone too far; he has given his case away." You are humiliated and chagrined, when lo! Fosdick begins an assessment of the world's debt to Protestantism and what remains is of priceless value and marshals brilliantly the reasons for conserving the same; the man speaks with the fire of the crusader. Your heart beats faster, your cheeks are warm, something stirs within you in response to the

---

[6] *Principles of Success in Literature*. F. N. Scott (Ed.), Boston, Allyn & Bacon.

preacher, and you feel that a real discipleship of Jesus Christ in these modern days is the mightiest challenge and the grandest thing in the world.

Clayton Hamilton has written of the value of the principle of contrast in composition in his recent book.[7] After considering many other instruments which seem essential to dramatic composition and putting them to one side, he discusses contrast as the one fundamental principle necessary to any and all dramatic situations.

> I figured out that there cannot be a really dramatic scene that does not contain some element of contrast, between one mood and another, between one set of ideas and another, etc. . . . Although I have never regarded this theory as a matter of importance in the long and leisurely progress of dramatic criticism, it is a fact that I have never yet been able to find an undeniably dramatic passage which did not contain this apparently essential element of contrast.

Fosdick, as we have seen, employs the contrast of one set of ideas with another for his effect. To be sure, he uses other interest devices, but the one he chooses to discuss as the most valuable to him is this principle of contrast.

A sermon may be begun in any one of three different ways: according to Fosdick, two of these ways are wrong. If the sermon begins with a text, or the exposition of an idea, dullness and futility result.

> Many preachers indulge habitually in what they call expository sermons. They take passage from Scripture, and proceeding on the assumption that the people attending church that morning are deeply concerned about what the passage means, they spend their half hour or more on historical exposition of the verse or chapter, ending with some appended practical application to the auditors. Could any procedure be more surely predestined to dullness and futility?

The other way to failure is for the preacher to have the genesis of the sermon in his own interests. Of this kind of preaching, Fosdick says, "One type of minister plays 'Sir Oracle.' He is dogmatic, assertive, uncompromising. He flings out his dicta as though to say to all hearers, 'Take it or leave it.' He has settled

---

[7] Hamilton, Clayton, *So You're Writing a Play*. Boston, Little, Brown & Co., 1935, p.69.

the matter concerning which he is speaking and he is telling us."

The third and successful way to begin a sermon is what Fosdick calls a cooperative enterprise. Of this kind of preaching, he says: "It makes a sermon a cooperative enterprise between the preacher and his congregation. When a man has got hold of a real difficulty in the life and thinking of his people and is trying to meet it, he finds himself not so much dogmatically thinking for them as cooperatively thinking with them."

This third and successful way of sermon composition is a formula that is used in other fields of literary endeavor. For example, the drama and the sermon have much in common. Both deal with a particular audience at a particular time and place. The preacher must succeed with his congregation or he faces empty pews; the dramatist must succeed with his audience or he faces bankruptcy. Maxwell Anderson [8] has recently reiterated this principle of collaboration for the theatre. The parallel between his remarks and those of Fosdick will be immediately apparent.

> It follows that the playwright must pluck from the air about him a fable which will be of immediate interest to his time and hour and relate it in a fashion acceptable to his neighbors. That is the job for which he is paid. But he will also try to make that fable coincide with something in himself that he wants to put in words. A certain cleverness in striking a compromise between the world about him and the world within has characterized the work of the greatest as well as the least of successful playwrights, for they must take an audience with them if they are to continue to function. Some may consider it blasphemy to state that this compromise must be a considered and conscious act—will believe that the writer should look in his heart and write—but in the theatre such an attitude leaves the achievements to chance, and a purely chance achievement is not an artistic one.

Fosdick believes that successful preachers as well as successful dramatists collaborate with their audiences in producing their effects. It is significant that Fosdick speaks of the "Sir Oracle" type of preaching in which the preacher looks within himself and speaks, as uncompromising, thus using the same word that Maxwell Anderson employs. The sermon, as well as the drama, is a

---

[8] *The New York Times.* October 6, 1935.

compromise between the thought of the author and the audience. Otherwise, it is a failure.

Henry Ward Beecher, a successful preacher, preferred to collaborate with his congregation as he stood in their presence. Fosdick achieves his collaboration through the period of careful meditation in his study. His practice is interesting enough to quote at length. In the following, notice those parts of the quotation which deal with his conscious attempts at collaboration with the thought of his congregation.

> The big business is the selection of the definite problem that I propose to discuss the next Sunday, the determination of the goal that I am going to drive at; when that is clearly visualized, I count the sermon well on its way. . . . I should be wretchedly unhappy not to have this whole matter clearly in mind and the initial stages of it stated by Tuesday noon at the latest. On Wednesday, Thursday, and Friday morning I work on the development of my strategy in achieving the goal that I have in mind with the congregation. Uniformly I am through with my manuscript on Friday noon. The next stage is one of the most important of all, for fearful that in working out my subject I may occasionally have forgotten my object and may have got out of the center of focus the concrete personalities who will face me Sunday morning, I sit down on Saturday morning and rethink the whole business as if my congregation were visibly before my eyes, often picking out individuals, and characteristic groups of individuals, and imaginatively trying my course of thought upon them so as to be absolutely sure that I have not allowed my pride of discussion or lure of rhetoric to deflect me from my major purpose of doing something worthwhile with people. This process often means the elision of paragraphs that I liked very much when I first wrote them and the rearrangement of order of thought in the interest of psychological persuasiveness. My sermon is always ready for the pulpit Saturday noon.

No discussion of this paragraph is needed, but perhaps it would be worthwhile to point out that Fosdick is stating in his own way that principle of literary composition set forth by Edgar Allan Poe, "I prefer commencing with the consideration of an effect." At the conclusion of the above quotation, Fosdick calls attention to the arrangement of his thought when he keeps his mind on his effect.

On the matter of psychological arrangement, Fosdick gives a few suggestions. If the preacher is more interested in satisfying the spiritual needs of his people than he is in explaining a text, he will not tack on a few practical applications to his exposition. Instead, he will begin with his practical applications. So important is arrangement in his theory of preaching that Fosdick states: "He need not have used any other text or any different materials in his sermon, but if he had defined his object rightly he would have arranged and massed the material differently. He would have gone into his sermon via real interest in his congregation." The importance of psychological arrangement is further emphasized, "I often find that this contrast between a merely logical and a vitally psychological arrangement of thought can make or unmake a sermon." Can anyone find in the entire field of rhetoric and oratory a more direct statement as to the effect of arrangement upon the success of a platform production. Having something to say is not enough!

It is too bad that Fosdick has not done more than enunciate this principle of psychological arrangement. He has not shown how it works out. That he has contemplated the effect of psychological persuasion upon arrangement is evinced in a remark reported by Mr. MacVaugh * from one of Fosdick's lectures at Union Theological Seminary. The culmination of a sermon should be based on "a principle of emotional climax in appeal and of moral impressiveness rather than a climax of ideas." Would that there was more of this sort of insight expressed!

Successful preaching is interesting because it is persuasive. Fosdick's preaching is aimed at a transformation of personality. His definition of preaching emphasizes the personal relationship. "Preaching is wrestling with individuals over questions of life and death, and until that idea of it commands a preacher's mind and method, eloquence will avail him little and theology not at all." Fosdick believes his technique works. "People have habitually come up after the sermon," he tells us, "not to offer some bland compliment but to say, 'How did you know I was facing that problem only this week?' or 'We were discussing that very matter at dinner last night,' or best of all, 'I think you would understand my case—may I have a personal interview with you?' This is I

---

* See Chapter 16.

take it the final test of a sermon's worth: how many individuals wish to see the preacher alone?"

In the passage of Edgar DeWitt Jones quoted above, the persuasive effect of Fosdick's sermon was recorded in his sentence, "You feel that a real discipleship of Jesus Christ in these modern days is the mightiest challenge in the world." What is this but persuasion! To secure persuasion, Fosdick aims at the springs of human conduct. He declares:

> One often reads modern sermons with amazement. How do the preachers expect to get anything done in human life with such discourses? They do not come within reaching distance of any powerful motives in man's conduct. They are keyed to argumentation rather than creation. They produce essays, which means that they are chiefly concerned with the transformation of personality. . . . The old preachers at their best did know where the major motives were. Fear, love, gratitude, self-preservation, altruism—such springs of human action the old sermons often used with consummate power. . . . I often think that we modern preachers talk about psychology a great deal more than our predecessors but use it a great deal less."

One concludes from Fosdick's brief remarks that he is but returning to the thesis of Aristotle that rhetorical theory must be determined by its effect upon the individual soul.

Chapter 19

Henry Ward Beecher and Harry Emerson Fosdick

LIONEL CROCKER

Beecher was the greatest preacher of the nineteenth century as Fosdick is of the twentieth. Beecher broke with Calvinism, and Fosdick continued the cleavage. Both men were not ashamed to admit the part formal training in public speaking played in their pulpit success. It is stimulating to point out the likenesses and unlikenesses in these two great preachers. For example, Beecher preached to the common people whereas Fosdick preached to the intelligentsia.

HARRY EMERSON FOSDICK is often called the Henry Ward Beecher of the twentieth century. Such a comparison is suggestive, and it might be worthwhile to point out some of the similarities and dissimilarities in their careers as top flight Protestant preachers.

To orient Beecher in time and place, let us remember that he was born four years after Abraham Lincoln, in 1813, and died in 1887. Thus, his life is part and parcel of the stream of events in the nineteenth century. In 1830 he went to Amherst College, and, on his graduation in 1834, joined his father, Lyman Beecher, the President of Lane Seminary in Cincinnati. On completing his

---

Note: Reprinted with permission from the *Central States Speech Journal.* Volume XII, Number 2.

theological course in 1837, he spent three years at Lawrenceburg, Indiana, where, he said, he learned how to preach. Then from 1839 to 1846, he was preaching in the capitol of a pioneer state, Indianapolis. He was called to Brooklyn, N Y., where he remained for forty years, preaching to three thousand people morning and night. Just as Fosdick was a tourist attraction on Morningside Heights at Riverside Church, Beecher was a tourist attraction at Plymouth Church on Brooklyn Heights. For example, Lincoln took the ferry from Manhattan to Brooklyn, when he was there to deliver the Cooper Institute Address, on February 26, 1860. And Matthew Arnold asked Andrew Carnegie to take him to Plymouth Church when he visited America in 1883 on his lecture tour.

Both Beecher and Fosdick employed the printed word to promote their Gospel message. In Indianapolis, Beecher preached and published a series of *Sermons to Young Men,* which had a wide sale. In Montclair, Fosdick wrote and published *The Meaning of Prayer, The Manhood of the Master,* and *The Second Mile.* The printed word made both preachers nationally known. No man was more widely reported and thoroughly covered in the nineteenth century America than Beecher. Historians have found his publications a fertile source of quotation. The faithful Ellinwood, the reporter, was always on hand to take down Beecher's words as they fell from his lips, for they had monetary value. Beecher's sermons sold thousands of copies each week from the newsstands. Lyman Abbott suggests that it was Beecher's refusal to permit his sermons to be published in Henry C. Bowen's newspaper, which Theodore Tilton, a free lover, edited, that caused him to be framed by Bowen and Tilton. The circulation of Bowen's paper declined when Beecher's sermons were withdrawn. In the twentieth century, no preacher has had a wider reading public than Fosdick. For example, no *Yale Lectures on Preaching* has been as popular in sales as his *Modern Use of the Bible,* which sold more than eighty thousand copies.

Both preachers were always in the midst of controversy. Beecher's life and thought were inextricably bound up with slavery and the civil war and later with the theory of evolution. His congregation put up $100,000 to defray the expense of his tour of propaganda in Great Britain in the fall of 1863. His speeches at Liverpool, Manchester, Glasgow, Edinburgh, and London so impressed President Lincoln that he was invited to give the address at the raising of the flag at Fort Sumter on April 14, 1865. Fosdick's battles were with theology and biblical criticism. His sermon *Shall the Fundamentalists Win?* preached in 1924 made him a leader of the modernists. He spent his life trying to get the results of biblical scholarship accepted.

We must remember that Lyman Beecher, one of the great preachers of his day, was the father of Henry Ward Beecher. Thus, Henry Ward's training for the pulpit began in the home. Fosdick's father was an educator. Harry Emerson was brought up with a respect for learning. Beecher, unlike Phillips Brooks, who discounted training in elocution, but like Fosdick, praised the instruction he received in platform speaking. In *Yale Lectures* (1st Series), there is an entire lecture devoted to "Rhetorical Drill and General Training."

> It was my good fortune in early academic life to fall into the hands of your estimable fellow citizen Professor John E. Lovell, now of New Haven, and for a period of three years I was drilled incessantly (you might not suspect it, but I was) in posturing, gesture, and voice culture. His manner, however, he very properly did not communicate to me. And manner is a thing which, let me remark, should never be communicated or imitated. It was the skill of that gentleman that he never left a manner with anybody. He simply gave his pupils the knowledge of what they had in themselves. Afterward, when going to the seminary, I carried the method of his instruction as did others. We practiced a great deal on what was called Dr. Barber's system which was then in vogue, and particularly in developing the voice in his lower register and also upon the explosive tones. There was a large grove lying between the seminary and my father's house, and it was the habit of my brother Charles and myself, and one or two others, to make the night, and even the day, hideous with our voices, as we passed backward and forward through the wood, exploding all the vowels, from the bottom to the very top of our voices. I found it to be a very manifest benefit, and one that has remained with me all my life long. The drill that I underwent produced not a rhetorical manner but a flexible instrument that accommodated itself readily to every kind of thought and every shape of feeling, and obeyed the inward will in the outward realization of the results of rules and regulations.[1]

---

[1] *Yale Lectures*, First Series, p.134.

Harry Emerson Fosdick in a personal letter to me, dated May 10, 1938, wrote:

> I thank you for your letter and for the accompanying copy of *The Speaker*. It is encouraging to know that there is revival of interest in public speaking on our college campuses. In recent years there has been a distinct decline in the interest of students in public speech as a fine art, and I am sure that this is greatly to be regretted.
>
> Despite the importance of the printed word I think that the influence of public speech is likely to increase rather than decrease, particularly in view of the unprecedented opportunities now presented through the radio for influencing public opinion through the spoken word.
>
> I can never be sufficiently grateful for the fact that in my undergraduate days public speaking was regarded as one of the most important enterprises on the campus, and we were rigorously disciplined and drilled in it.

Henry Ward Beecher preached to the masses while Harry Emerson Fosdick preached to the intelligentsia. But this broad generalization does not mean that thoughtful men and women did not attend Beecher's Plymouth Church. Henry W. Sage was one of the merchant princes of his day. It was Sage who endowed the Lyman Beecher *Yale Lectures on Preaching,* for he wanted an opportunity for his pastor to tell young preachers how to preach extemporaneously. And when Herbert Spencer visited this country, Beecher was invited to speak at the farewell banquet in 1882. Let me quote from his protege Lyman Abbott who describes beautifully an audience situation that would try the skill of any speaker.

> A remarkable illustration of charm and power combined was furnished by his speech delivered at the testimonial dinner given in New York City to Herbert Spencer, on the eve of the latter's return to England. The dinner was a long and elaborate one. The diners were with few exceptions scientific men of eminence. There were very few who were known as active in the Christian church or in the religious world. Mr. William M. Evarts presided and lightened an otherwise heavy series of speeches with occasional sallies of wit. But there had been no humor, and no emotion, and little of literary charm in the speeches. The last two speakers were Mr. Fiske and Mr. Beecher: their theme Science and Religion. Mr. Fiske read an essay, clear, crystalline, coldly intellectual; he dealt with theology, not with religion. It was

nearing midnight when Mr. Beecher rose to make the last address. The room was filled with tobacco smoke. The auditors were weary and ready to go home. Not a vibrating note had been struck throughout the evening. It seemed to me as Mr. Beecher rose that all he could do was to apologize for not speaking at that late hour and dismiss the audience. By some jest he won a laugh; caught the momentary attention of his audience; seemed about to lose it; caught it again; again saw it escaping, and again captured it. In five minutes the more distant auditors had moved their chairs forward, the French waiters, who had paid no attention to any one else, straightened themselves up against the walls to listen; Herbert Spencer on one side of him and Mr. Evarts on the other were looking up into his face to catch the utterance of his speaking countenance as of his words. And then he preached as evangelical a sermon as I have heard from any minister's lips. He claimed Paul as an evolutionist; he read or quoted from the seventh chapter of Romans in support of the claim; he declared that man is an animal and has ascended from an animal but is more than animal, has in him a conscience, a reason, a faith, a hope, a love, which are divine in nature and in origin; he appealed to the experience of his audience to confirm his analysis; he evoked cries of "That's so! That's so!" like Methodist amens from all over the room; and when he ended in what was, in all but its form, a prayer that God would convey Herbert Spencer across that broader and deeper sea which flows between these shores and the unknown world beyond and that there the two might meet to understand better the life which is so truly a mystery and the God who is so much to us the Unknown here, the whole audience rose by a common impulse to their feet, as if to make prayer their own, cheering, clapping their hands, and waving their handkerchiefs. I can see the critic smiling with amused contempt at this paragraph, if he deigns to read it. None the less, he is shallow in his perceptions, as well as wrong in his judgments, if he is not able to recognize both the charm and the power of the orator who can win such a response, at such a time, from such an audience.

And, in discussing the types of audiences Beecher and Fosdick addressed, we must not forget the lecture audiences Beecher commanded throughout the country. His lectures "The Reign of the Common People" and "The Wastes and Burdens of Society" were in great demand. One lecture manager said he could always charge 25 cents extra per course ticket when Beecher was scheduled to appear. And Fosdick's radio audiences ran into the millions. There has never been a more popular preacher to college audiences than Fosdick. Both names were magic in the lecture

Henry Ward Beecher and Harry Emerson Fosdick

halls of America, although Fosdick lectured almost exclusively under religious auspices.

Beecher and Fosdick were different in regard to the preparation of a specific sermon. In his early years Beecher did write out his sermons, but at the height of his career his method was that of the genius, which would spell the ruin of a lesser man. He tells us that during the week he had several themes germinating in his mind, and when Sunday came, he used to feel among the themes as a farmer feels among his fruit to discover which is the ripest. Sometimes he would discard this chosen theme when he got into the pulpit and proceed to preach upon another more timely and appropriate theme.

After breakfast on a Sunday morning, at the height of his career, Beecher would shut himself up in his study and work out the introduction and conclusion of his sermon, to set up the main lines of thought, and when he heard the church bells toll he would slip on his coat and grab his hat and hurry over to the church. There he would develop the theme in the presence of his congregation. Too much detailed preparation would kill inspiration in the pulpit. It was this method of preaching that Henry W. Sage wanted young preachers to hear about at Yale Divinity School.

In contrast to this method Harry Emerson Fosdick was meticulous in the preparation of his manuscripts for his public appearances. It is of interest to compare and contrast the method of Henry Ward Beecher and Harry Emerson Fosdick in the preparation of the *Yale Lectures on Preaching*. Beecher says that the outline of his Yale Lectures came to him while shaving in his hotel prior to giving them. Harry Emerson Fosdick wrote Edgar DeWitt Jones that his Yale Lectures were the product of years of thought and study. In *The Royalty of the Pulpit,* p.103,* we read:

> I have no idea, either, how much time I spent in immediate preparation. For years I had been giving at Union Theological Seminary a year long course on the same subject I used at Yale. What I did, therefore, was to take advantage of the lectureship at Yale to arrange,

---
* See Chapter 12.

condense, write out carefully and prepare for publication the material I had been working on for a long time.

In another connection in commenting on the preparation of his sermons, Fosdick said he would be desperately unhappy if he did not have his sermon written out by Friday noon.

Both preachers had a memorable way of stating their thoughts. Many compilations of Beecher's sayings have been made. William Norwood Brigance in his *Speech Composition* employs ten quotations from Beecher. This same book has three quotations from Fosdick. Beecher said, "Some people pray cream and live skimmed milk." Fosdick said, "Are you a part of the problem or a part of the solution?"

The two men differed in their delivery. Beecher, when he had the opportunity to build his church, built an auditorium. He told the architect that he wanted the congregation to surround him. "I want them to surround me, so that they will come up on every side, and behind me, so that I shall be in the center of the crowd, and have the people surge around me." When Fosdick had the opportunity to build his church he built a Gothic structure, which would not have suited Beecher at all. Beecher said he could not abide what he called a "swallow's nest on the wall," where the preacher was hidden from the congregation. He wanted to be seen. He said, "Sometimes the foot is emphasis." He employed a reading stand for a pulpit.

Beecher in his delivery was not afraid to be dramatic. One time he came into the pulpit of the Broadway Tabernacle rattling a chain and cried out, "This once bound a slave." At another time, he had a Negro slave girl in his pulpit and he pleaded for contributions to set her free. More than three thousand dollars was poured into the baskets. Spurgeon said this was the most dramatic illustration recorded in pulpit history.

Beecher was excellent at pantomime. One time when he was dramatizing a conversation with a ditch digger, he pantomimed the ditch digger removing the quid of tobacco from his mouth. To complete the action, he wiped his hand upon his trousers.

Beecher was a master of audience psychology when there were no courses in persuasion or in social psychology. Listen to this advice:

People often say, "Do you not think it is more inspiring to speak to a large audience than a small one?" No I say; I can speak just as well to twelve persons as to a thousand, provided those twelve are crowded around me and close together, so that they touch each other. But even a thousand people with four feet space between every two of them would be just the same as an empty room. Crowd your audience together, and you will set them off with not half the effort. (*Yale Lectures,* First Series, p.72)

Charles Dickens, after he had given one of his lecture-recitals in Plymouth Church, sent back word to Beecher not to build another hall for speaking because Plymouth Church was perfect in all respects.

On the other hand, the Gothic structure fitted Fosdick's delivery. The years at Riverside called for a less emotional and dramatic delivery and a more carefully reasoned discourse from Fosdick than the years at Plymouth demanded of Beecher. Critics of Fosdick's delivery never fail to mention the unpleasant voice, harsh, high pitched, inflexible, as compared with the mellow voice of his contemporary Ralph Sockman. Beecher looked the orator, whereas—but let Fosdick tell it. In his autobiography, *The Living of These Days,* p.91, he uses these words to describe himself: "When Fred Harris introduced us, Gulick looked at me with my nonmonastic, nonascetic, 'prosperous butcher-boy' appearance— as one newspaper reporter once described me—and said: 'You certainly do not look like the author of *The Meaning of Prayer.*'"

Lyman Abbott stated that Beecher did more to change directly the religious life and indirectly the theological thought of America than any preacher since Jonathan Edwards. This gives a clue to his themes. Beecher preached the God of love rather than the God of vengeance. In his sermon "Preventive Religion," Fosdick quotes a passage from Beecher which gives an insight into the nature of Beecher's thought.

Alongside this historic emphasis in the New Testament one must put the medieval conceptions of heaven and hell as a reason for stress upon the religion of rescue. Hell was a desperate reality to the whole Western World, whether Christian or non-Christian, and as far down in time as 1877 Henry Ward Beecher was thundering against this belief in Plymouth pulpit, saying, "To tell me that back of Christ there is a God who for unnumbered centuries has gone on creating men and sweeping them like dead flies—nay, like living ones—into hell, is to ask me to worship a being as much worse than the conception of any medieval devil as can be imagined; but I will not worship the devil, though he should come dressed in royal robes and sit on the throne of Jehovah."

When Henry Ward Beecher gave the first *Yale Lectures* in 1872, the large part of the battle over Biblical criticism was still ahead. The preacher was still speaking in what was in many evident ways still an "age of faith," the break up of which Matthew Arnold was to sing in his "Dover Beach." But the theory of evolution was making itself heard. Beecher gave a series of sermons on this theory. His sermons were telegraphed verbatim to Chicago and printed in newspapers there. One of his volumes of sermons is called *Evolution and Religion*.

Beecher was well known to Fosdick. In Fosdick's publications quotations from Beecher are sprinkled over many pages. Did Fosdick learn his theory of objective preaching from Beecher or did he derive it, as Beecher did, from study and practice? The parallel is so interesting that it is worth-while to quote the statement of both great preachers on the method.

In his essay on "What's the Matter with Preaching?" (*Harper's*, 1928), Fosdick states:

> The text was good and the truth undeniable. The subject was well chosen and well developed, but for all that, nothing happened. The effect was flat. So far as the sermon was concerned, the congregation might as well have stayed home. It may have been a "beautiful effort," as some kindly woman doubtless told the preacher, but it did no business in human lives. The reason for this can commonly be traced to one cause: the preacher started his sermon at the wrong end. He made it the exposition of a text or the elucidation of a subject instead of a well planned endeavor to help solve some concrete problem in individual lives before him. He need not have used any other text or any different materials in his sermon, but if he had defined his object rightly he would have arranged and massed the material differently. He would have gone into his sermon via real interest in his congregation and would have found the whole procedure kindling to himself and to them.*

---

* See Chapter 2.

In another way, Henry Ward Beecher said the same thing (*Yale Lecturers,* 1st Series, p.11)

> There was a reason why when the apostles preached they succeeded, and I will find it out if it is to be found out. I took every single instance in the Record where I could find one of their sermons and analyzed it and asked myself: "What were the circumstances? Who were the people? What did he do," and I studied the sermons until I got this idea: That the apostles were accustomed first to feel for a ground on which the people and they stood together; a common ground where they could meet. Then they heaped up a large number of particulars of knowledge that belonged to everybody; and when they got that knowledge which everybody would admit, placed in a proper form before their minds, then they brought it to bear upon them with all their excited heart and feeling. That was the first definite idea of taking aim that I had in mind.

To the student of rhetoric it is worthwhile to compare the theory and practice of two pulpit geniuses such as Beecher and Fosdick. Beecher took time out to deliver his *Yale Lectures on Preaching* (1872) which have so greatly enriched our knowledge of extemporaneous speaking. How wonderful it would be if Fosdick could be persuaded to write a book on preaching or at least gather together his chapters and essays that deal with the problem of preaching. I think of three contributions that should be in such a book: "Animated Conversation" from Joseph Fort Newton's *If I Had Only One Sermon to Preach* (1932); *The Harper's Magazine* article on "What's the Matter with Preaching" (1928); and the chapter, "Learning to Preach" from his autobiography, *The Living of These Days* (1956). So much of rhetorical theory has been developed by preachers, such as Blair, Campbell, and Whately.

Chapter 20

Phillips Brooks and Harry Emerson Fosdick

LIONEL CROCKER

Harry Emerson Fosdick during his years in the pulpit at Riverside Church, New York City, was often referred to as the greatest preacher in the English tongue. On his retirement in 1946 *The Christian Century* characterized him, along with Henry Ward Beecher and Phillips Brooks, as one of the three greatest names in the history of American preaching.

Phillips Brooks is mentioned many times by Harry Emerson Fosdick as one of his respected predecessors and mentors. For example, we have the following insight from him on how he studied the old masters for homiletic methods.

> So I went through project preaching and beyond it, and began to see how much the old preachers had to teach us. At their best they did achieve results. Their sermons were appeals to the jury, and they got decisions. They knew where the great motives were and appealed to them with conclusive power. I began to study the sermons of men like Phillips Brooks—not merely reading them but analyzing them sentence by sentence to discover the steps they took toward working in their auditors the miracles they often did achieve—and I concluded that while we moderns talk about psychology much more than our predecessors, we commonly use it a good deal less.[1]

Phillips Brooks used a process called analytic discrimination. The entire development, not infrequently, consists in an analysis

---

[1] Harry Emerson Fosdick: *The Living of These Days.* New York, Harper & Bros., 1956, p.100. See Chapter 1.

of those traits and those motives by which human character is disclosed. His humanistic interests and his study of human character and life are constantly manifest. He takes hold of a principle and carries it strongly and steadily through, so that it appears pervasively in every part of the sermon. Analysis contributes to the central idea of the sermon. This is what Harry Emerson Fosdick found in his study of Phillips Brooks.

Harry Emerson Fosdick also remembered the materials of Phillips Brooks. In his sermon "Six Ways to Tell Right from Wrong" he no doubt felt that he could not put the point better than his teacher.

> How often in politics, in church life, in business, in personal character we see things that remind us of a claque at the theatre hired to applaud a play! They can get away with it as long as the public does not know it is a claque. It depends on secrecy for its success. What a test publicity is!
> Do you remember how Phillips Brooks put it,
> To keep clear of concealment, to keep clear of the need of concealment, to do nothing which he might not do out on the middle of Boston Common at noonday—I cannot say how more and more that seems to me to be the glory of a young man's life. It is an awful hour when the first necessity of hiding anything comes. The whole life is different thenceforth. When there are questions to be feared and eyes to be avoided and subjects which must not be touched, then the bloom of life is gone. Put that day off as long as possible. Put it off forever if you can.

As another example of his sitting at the feet of his tutor, consider the following use of the same text by the two preachers: "Demas hath forsaken me, having loved this Present World." II Timothy iv:10. A Bible text always precedes the printed sermons of Phillips Brooks. One never finds this practice in the sermons of Harry Emerson Fosdick. Let us take a look at the introductory paragraph of each sermon on these words. Phillips Brooks preached on this text November 18, 1888. He entitled his sermon "Higher and Lower Standards."

> Of Demas we know almost nothing except what is suggested in these words. Once in the Epistle to the Colossians, and once in the Epistle to Philemon, St. Paul alludes to him as one of his own fellow-workers, in tones of sympathy and love. Then in the Epistle to Timothy there comes this statement of his follower's defection.

And following is the opening of "The Power to See It Through" * by Harry Emerson Fosdick:

> There is one character in the New Testament, mentioned only three times, concerning whom one suspects that many Christians have not even heard. His name was Demas, and, alas, some of us are much more like him than like the Great New Testament figures we know so well. First, in Paul's letter to Philemon, we read, "Demas, Luke, my fellow workers." So Demas along with Luke, and named first at that, was standing by Paul in his Roman imprisonment, a devoted and promising disciple. Second, in Paul's letter to the Colossians, we read, "Luke, the beloved physician, and Demas." Reading that one wonders why Demas and Luke, who were praised together at the first, were separated in this passage as though Luke indeed retained Paul's confidence as "the beloved physician" but Demas had become merely "Demas." Third, in the Second Letter to Timothy, incorporating, we suppose, one of the last messages Paul ever wrote, we read, "Demas forsook me, having loved this present age." Three points on a curve, that enable us to plot its graph! For here is the story of a man who made a fine beginning and a poor ending; Demas, my fellow worker; Demas; Demas forsook me.

In both these sermons we see a fundamental tenet of their preaching: they wanted to change individual lives. Frequently in Harry Emerson Fosdick's sermons we find the sentence, "I wish this message could come home now to someone here who needs it." A radio sermon of his did affect the life of young Samuel H. Miller, who testified to this:

> It is twilight and Sunday. I have been sitting in my home listening to a voice—a voice of prophecy in a land of much preaching. The service is over, the radio is turned off, and I want a little time for meditation, for I am convinced that somehow that voice left me different. I have untangled a snarl in the many skeins of life. I have crossed a barrier into a vaster land. Pent-up energies have been released that were log-jammed by confusion.**

Samuel H. Miller later became Dean of the Harvard University Divinity School.

In his classic *Yale Lectures on Preaching* Phillips Brooks declared: "All successful preaching, I more and more believe, talks to individuals." The same thought by Harry Emerson Fosdick is

---

* For a rhetorical analysis of this sermon see Chapter 21.
** See Chapter 8.

found in "Animated Conversation." "My ideal of a sermon is one that carries up this interest and directness of attack on real problems into the pulpit, and discusses real questions with real people in a real way." * His preaching was often referred to as personal counseling. Sometimes this type of preaching is called situational preaching. A sampling of sermon titles will show how the preaching of both dealt with life problems:

Phillips Brooks	*Harry Emerson Fosdick*
The Battle of Life	Handicapped Lives
Is it I?	What are you Standing For?
Whole Views of Life	The Inescapable Judgment
The Purpose and Use of Comfort	The Mystery of Life
Unspotted from the World	Handling Life's Second Bests

The life of Phillips Brooks must have made a deep impression on Harry Emerson Fosdick, for we find him using his struggle to be somebody in the chapter "Shouldering Responsibility for Ourselves" in his best seller *On Being a Real Person*. It tells the story of Phillips Brooks recovery from failure.

> Did Phillips Brooks, well born and fortunately bestead, have to be the man he was? Graduating from college he turned to his chosen profession, teaching, and made a complete failure of it. By Christmas of the first year the situation was desperate, by January hopeless. He was compelled to resign; "I don't know what will become of me," he wrote, "and I don't care much." "I shall not study a profession. I wish I were fifteen years old again. I believe I might make a stunning man; but somehow or other I don't seem in the way to come to much now." Was his recovery from despair, his comeback, his personal response to his life's problems, and the "stunning" consequence, an inevitable effect, foreordained by his genes and his environment? Did he have nothing creative and self-determining to do with it?

Both preachers stress how much the personality, the character of the preacher affects his life work. Listen to Phillips Brooks: "Whatever is in the sermon must be in the preacher first; logicalness, vivacity, earnestness, sweetness, and light must be personal qualities in him before they are qualities of thought and language in what he utters to his people."

And this is what Harry Emerson Fosdick says about the necess-

---
* See Chapter 4.

ity of personality and character in the preacher. "Of course, there is no process by which wise and useful discourses can be distilled from unwise and useless personalities, and the ultimate necessity in the ministry, as everywhere else, is sound and intelligent character."

The personalities and character of both were shaped by their homes. Phillips Brooks had on both sides of his house a most distinguished ancestry. The Cotton-Phillips-Brooks lines are his. His father, his mother and their forbears inherited Puritan traditions. The Brooks family left the Unitarian church when Phillips was four years old and joined St. Paul's Episcopal Church. He attended Miss Capen's Private School, public grammar school, Boston Latin School, Harvard (A.B., 1855) and the Virginia Theological Seminary.

Harry Emerson Fosdick was brought up in a Baptist home. He decided on his own to be baptized when he was seven years old. Secretly, after hearing a sermon on foreign missions he decided to be a missionary. His family, deeply Christian, believed in the church and were always active in its service. His father was principal of the Masten Park High School. To thousands of boys and girls in Buffalo he was affectionately known as "Pop." He received his formal education from the Buffalo Public Schools, from Colgate University (A.B., 1900), Union Theological Seminary (B.S., 1904) and Columbia University (M.A., 1908).

The attitudes of these men toward the denominations they served is similar. Harry Emerson Fosdick was raised a Baptist but was never bound by any ritualism or theology of that or any other denomination. In his essay on "The Christian Ministry" * he declared the future is for the church without hard and fast lines of dogma. Phillips Brooks was baptized a Unitarian and he may have been influenced by the intellectual freedom and moral earnestness of that persuasion. But he was not a Unitarian. As an Episcopalian he was nurtured in the evangelical piety of this branch of the Christian church, but he felt free from any forms of that church. He was a broad Church man but he was not a product of the Episcopal church. He was not an ecclesiastic. He

---

* See Chapter 6.

was loyal to his church but he was free from many of its limitations. For him the Kingdom of God was broader than any church. He was called a Christian humanist.

How similar was the attitude of Harry Emerson Fosdick. Early in his career he denounced all dogma. His belief was in man and his redemption. Like Phillips Brooks his impulses were humanistic rather than ecclesiastical. Both were assailed for their liberality, and their orthodoxy was questioned.

Both men were deeply committed to the Christian ministry. They could not conceive of themselves doing anything else. In his *Yale Lectures on Preaching*, Phillips Brooks told the students: "The real power of your oratory must be your own intelligent delight in what you are doing. Let your pulpit be to you what the studio is to the artist, or his court to the lawyer."

And in one of his sermons he described the Christian ministry in an unforgettable figure of speech: "It is no dead brake on the wheels of time. It is no burnt-out cinder among the glowing coals of life. It is the very wheel itself. It is the livest coal in all the furnace, making the other coals seem cold beside it." In the same enthusiastic manner Harry Emerson Fosdick described his life as a minister of Jesus Christ. "Looking back on my twenty years as a minister at the Riverside Church I often wonder how I got through them. The opportunities were always greater than I could compass, the demands heavier than I could carry. Whether my nerves would much longer stand the strain at times seemed questionable. Being a minister can seem 'a heartbreaking way of making a living' but always I knew that I 'would not give it up for all the world.' "

The careers of both preachers were partly shaped by the beautiful sanctuaries occupied by them. By 1869 Phillips Brooks had become a national figure and was called to the Trinity Church, Boston. Thereafter, until his death, Trinity pulpit was his throne and eventually America and England became his parish. Richardson presently built for him and Trinity a noble Romanesque church whose interior John LaFarge decorated. That type of architecture and interior decoration were then new to America. Harry Emerson Fosdick served his apprenticeship at Montclair, New Jersey (1904–1915) and at the First Presbyterian Church,

New York City, (1918–1928). After leaving the Presbyterian fold he became pastor of the Park Avenue Baptist Church of which John D. Rockefeller II was a parishioner, who built the ten million dollar cathedral, complete to the smallest detail, for his pastor. This Protestant Cathedral occupies a commanding site on a magnificent boulevard in the academic complex of Union Theological Seminary and Columbia University.

Such edifices in such locations caught both preachers in preaching situations they did not relish. In many of his writings we find Harry Emerson Fosdick lamenting the fact that the Protestant church tended to become a class church. Surely, his Riverside church, attracting the intelligentsia of New York City and environs and visitors to New York, constituted a definite class. And Phillips Brooks Sunday after Sunday preached to the wealthiest and most fashionable Episcopal congregation in America.

The physical appearance of both preachers in their pulpits is an interesting contrast. Henry Pitney Van Dusen describes Harry Emerson Fosdick in this manner:

> Sunday after Sunday, following an uplifting service of worship, a short, stocky, dynamic figure, ruddy cheeks crowned by bushy graying hair, mounted that pulpit and a clear, strong, resonant voice with an arresting metallic ring and almost mesmeric command launched forth on the discourse for which all had been eagerly waiting and which held every listener in alert attention until its end.

Of Phillips Brooks's appearance in his pulpit, it has been said:

> Six feet four inches in height, weighing over two hundred pounds, clad in the robes of his church, he hurries into the pulpit. His hair is brown and beginning to gray; his head superbly shaped; his eyes dark and deep-set. As he moves into his sermon, his voice, at the rate of 215 words a minute, increases in volume and tempo, and now and then he stumbles or has to extricate himself from grammatical difficulty. There is little gesture other than a majestic dilation of the whole body as his feeling rises in intensity.

Commentators on the two preachers point out that Harry Emerson Fosdick lacked the warmth and glow and poetic temperament of Phillips Brooks. Joseph Fort Newton says that Harry Emerson Fosdick's sermons lose much of the winsomeness of his personality unless one heard him and then reads. He also said

Phillips Brooks and Harry Emerson Fosdick

that one wonders at times whether he has not overintellectualized religion and why one misses the haunting notes of the poet and mystic. On the other hand, Phillips Brooks shows the poetic touch in such sermon titles as "The Candles of the Lord," "The Egyptians Dead upon the Seashore," "The Sea of Glass Mingled with Fire," and "The Wings of the Seraphim." One of his memorable analogies is "A sermon should be like the leaping of a fountain not the pumping of a pump." He possessed to a marked degree the capacity to perceive the similarities in things dissimilar; the noise of the busy streets, the images of light and the scudding clouds, the sparkling sea, the lofty mountains, and the fruitful earth occur to him as natural figures for spiritual and moral truths. Consider the poetic touch in this passage.

> There is a new tranquility which is not stagnation but assurance, when a life thus enters into Christ. It is like the hushing of a million babbling, chattering streams as they approach the sea and fill themselves with its deep purposes. It is like the steadying of a lost bird's quivering wings when it at last sees the nest and quiets itself with the certainty of reaching it and settles smoothly down on level pinions to sweep unswervingly towards it. It is like these to see the calm of a restless soul that discovers Christ and rests its tired wings upon the atmosphere of His truth and so abides in Him as it goes on towards Him.

The reputation of Harry Emerson Fosdick was greatly increased by his radio pulpit. And the reputation of both spread through the English speaking world through their published works that were always in great demand. Early in his ministry he began writing such handbooks on religion as *The Second Mile*. This series sold more than a million copies. A friend wrote him that he had seen Gandhi reading one of them. And he said that that was as close as he ever got to being a foreign missionary. Harper & Brothers yearly issued a volume of his sermons that found a ready market. His *Yale Lectures on Preaching, The Modern Use of the Bible*, sold eighty thousand copies, the only one of the Yale series to become a best seller. His hymn "God of Grace and God of Glory" was written by him for use at the dedication of Riverside Church. It has since become one of the most popular hymns by a modern author. More requests were received by the hymnal committee for his hymn to be included in the new Pilgrim Hymnal than for any other twentieth-century hymn. In 1924 he was one of the exchange preachers to Britain. He spoke at the Liberal Club in London, to a congregation of "Free St. George's" in Edinburgh, to Queen's College, London, and to the congregation of the Church of England at St. Martin's-in-the-Fields, London. The University of Glasgow gave him an honorary D.D.

Similarly, the sermons and books of Phillips Brooks made him widely known not only in America but abroad. His *Yale Lectures on Preaching* has been called the most valuable of the recent contributions to homiletic literature. In 1891 the edition of his sermons sold more than thirteen thousand copies. His Christmas Carol "O Little Town of Bethlehem" is imbedded in the English language. On a triumphal tour of England he preached before the Queen in Westminster Abbey. He was personally invited by the Bishop of London to preach in St. Paul's Cathedral. And the cathedral towns outside of London invited him also. He preached at City Temple, the nonconformist church, where later Harry Emerson Fosdick was to preach. The 215 word-a-minute rate of utterance caused Phillips Brooks trouble where English reporters were unable to follow him. He was asked to slow down but that was impossible. Perhaps it was this tumultous flow of words that prompted one American critic to speak of his sermons as monologues.

Thus, we have tried to show why Harry Emerson Fosdick of the twentieth century is the inheritor of the mantle of Phillips Brooks of the nineteenth century. Both believed in the homiletic theory that preaching must be directed to individuals for personal salvation. Wherever they preached their gospel attracted great crowds. Both became household words. Harry Emerson Fosdick gladly admitted that he was a student of Phillips Brooks. He discovered and put into practice the lessons of how to work miracles in a congregation. Both preachers were products of homes where there was a strong religious heritage. Both preachers believed in humaneness rather than in ecclesiasticism. Their influence was nationwide and international. Both men left a written record that will stand the test of time.

Chapter 21

A Rhetorical Analysis of Harry Emerson Fosdick's Sermon, "The Power to See It Through"[1]

LIONEL CROCKER

1. Dr. Fosdick is a master of the word, the phrase, and the sentence. The opening sentence ends with the important Demas. This sentence gives the outline of the paragraph "three times." This paragraph could well be used as a model in a text on paragraph writing. Demas is to be the symbol of one who did not have the "power to see it through." The second sentence suggests one of the themes of the sermon—"a fine beginning." The third sentence repeats the title and the main theme of the sermon. Dr. Fosdick is a master of repetition in all its variations. The principle of embodying a truth in a personality is employed: Demas is to be the antithesis of what the preacher is to proclaim. The title is used as the refrain of the sermon, a device often employed by Dr. Fosdick. The

1. There is one character in the New Testament, mentioned only three times, concerning whom one suspects that many Christians have not even heard. His name was Demas and, alas, some of us are much more like him than like the great New Testament figures we know so well. First, in Paul's letter to Philemon, we read, "Demas, Luke, my fellow-workers." So Demas, along with Luke, and named first at that, was standing by Paul in his Roman imprisonment, a devoted and promising disciple. Second, in Paul's letter to the Colossians, we read, "Luke, the beloved physician, and Demas." Reading that, one wonders why Demas and Luke, who

---

[1] Reprinted by permission of the publishers, Harper and Bros., New York.

remainder of the paragraph gives the three instances when Demas lacked the power to see it through. Demas is repeated eleven times in this opening paragraph. Demas and Luke are contrasted. Contrast is an elemental rhetorical device. The dramatic disintegration of the character of Demas is portrayed in this paragraph. The climax of the paragraph comes in the third mention of Demas. Dr. Fosdick speaks in a figure the twentieth century can understand, "plotting a curve." The final sentence is a recapitulation of the entire paragraph. If a listener left the church after the opening paragraph, he would have the gist of the entire sermon. This is a good example of Dr. Fosdick's preaching psychology. Any future reference to Demas will bring back this careful delineation.

2. The transition words "Luke and Demas" keep the listener on the mental track. "Demas" is the keyword of the sermon. "Staying power" is the key phrase. The preacher knows his Bible and sees beneath the surface the significance of Luke's being the only one who records the story about the man who started the tower and did not finish it. Note the dramatic power of introducing conversation, "Which of you, desiring to build a tower," and so forth. This is an overtone to Dr. Fosdick's preaching. His preaching is symbolic. This quotation might well be the text. By putting it here, he makes the text take on a vitality which it would not have if he had introduced it earlier. The refrain is employed at the conclusion of the second paragraph.

were praised together at the first, were separated in this passage as though Luke indeed retained Paul's confidence as "the beloved physician" but Demas had become merely "Demas." Third, in the Second letter to Timothy incorporating, we suppose, one of the last messages Paul ever wrote, we read, "Demas forsook me, having loved this present age." Three points on a curve, that enable us to plot its graph! For here is the story of a man who made a fine beginning and a poor ending: Demas, my fellow-worker; Demas; Demas forsook me.

2. One's imagination plays about this condensed biography, especially the relationships between Demas and Luke. Intimate companions of Paul in the Roman circle, they must have known each other very well. Now, Luke is the only narrator of Jesus' life whose gospel records the parable about the man who started to build a tower and was not able to finish. Matthew did not remember that, nor Mark, nor John; only Luke recalled it. One wonders if he remembered it because of Demas. Demas was slipping, let us say. Through Paul's little group in the Roman prison, anxious apprehension ran that Demas was not holding out, and one imagines Luke

Analysis of Sermon, "The Power to See It Through"

pleading with his friend. The Master himself, he might have said, warned his first disciples about the peril which is besetting you. For once he said, "Which of you, desiring to build a tower, doth not first sit down and count the cost, whether he hath herewith to complete it? Lest haply, when he hath laid a foundation and is not able to finish, all that behold begin to mock him, saying, This man began to build, and was not able to finish." So one thinks of Luke pleading with his friend, and at least Luke, alone among the evangelists, put the parable into his gospel. He had seen its truth too vividly illustrated in the life of a friend ever to forget it. Demas, my fellow-worker; Demas; Demas forsook me.

3. *Starting power and staying power are contrasted. The next three paragraphs are concerned with this contrast. The analogy of the ship is used several times in the sermon, showing the pictorial ability of the preacher. In paragraph 7 one sees an echo of this analogy, "romantic launchings." In this paragraph one finds the use of four members in succession—a rhetorical device much employed by Dr. Fosdick, "fine impulses, generous responses, idealistic loyalties, and eager loves." See paragraphs 21 and 27. The repetition of Demas keeps alive the central idea.*

3. As one considers this familiar experience of a fine beginning and a poor ending, it is obvious, for one thing, that the qualities which make a good start possible are not identical with the qualities that see life through to the end. Starting power and staying power are not the same thing in any realm. A ship can make a grand getaway at the launching only to make a poor stand later against the fury of the waves and winds when the northeasters are unleashed. So one sees in Demas a character—how familiar!—capable of fine impulses, generous responses, idealistic loyalties, and

4. *The preacher's ability to phrase is seen in "festival of fresh beginnings." Note the alliteration. In speaking of a good beginning, Dr. Fosdick is treating the antithesis of his theme, which is staying power, or a good ending. We may consider all the material up to paragraph 9 as an introduction. At the beginning of a new year the congregation would expect the preacher to speak on a good start; therefore, Dr. Fosdick uses psychology by disposing of this phrase of the subject first. He terms preaching "animated conversation." Note the personal pronouns* you, I, and we. *The one who makes a poor ending is identified with Demas. Never again will the congregation think of Demas without being reminded of this sermon. Familiar analogies are used: "Over what thin ice have we skated!" Note the exclamatory sentences and the short sentences. The desired, oral style is apparent. The refrain is repeated.*

eager loves; only he lacked staying power.

4. One thinks of this not simply because of the New Year season, which is naturally a festival of fresh beginnings, but because our generation, above every other generation in history, has stressed the gospel of a good start. How we have emphasized the importance of childhood and of the influences that play on childhood! To give a child a good start, we have said, is the most essential benediction that can be bestowed upon a human life. So we have thought and accordingly have labored. Now, that gospel of a good start is profoundly important, and it tells the truth, only not the whole truth. For many of us here had a good start. We have no complaints about that. In family and church, in school and early Christian training, we had a fine beginning. But for all that, some of us are Demas and all of us know we could have been. Over what thin ice have we skated! How easily we could have broken through! How many of us here have already fallen far from a faith that once was strong and a character that once was clean. We know Demas. The mirror shows him to us. Introspection reveals the process of his downfall. Nearly two thousand years ago he lived and died, his very name barely preserved, as though by accident, and yet how

Analysis of Sermon, "The Power to See It Through"

vivid he is in our imaginations! Demas, my fellow-worker; Demas; Demas forsook me, having loved this present age.

5. *Note the use of definition. What is a good end? "Staying power" is repeated. Again Dr. Fosdick employs a Biblical illustration. Jesus in the Garden is the best illustration he could have found. It is familiar to his audience. "Could have spoiled everything" is in the vernacular. Watch the use of the word "indispensable." When Dr. Fosdick gets the word he wants, he does not hunt for synonyms. Again, he uses the familiar analogy of chopping a tree. The climax of this paragraph is powerful.*

5. Another general truth concerns our thought: namely, that however beautiful one's start, nothing matters much in human life without a good ending. Of course one does not mean that we may demand an outwardly successful and fortunate conclusion, as in old sentimental novels where everything had to come out all right. But without a *good* end, without morale and staying power and steady character to see a man through to a worthy conclusion, what else in human life can be much worth while? Jesus could have spoiled everything in the Garden of Gethsemane and, had he done that, all for nothing would have gone his unremembered Sermon on the Mount and his unselfish months of ministry. The career of Jesus was like splitting a log. Every previous blow of the ax is indispensable but it is the last blow that splits it. So we know there was a Christ, and the rich meanings of his ministry have come to us because he had staying power to go through to the end, where he could say, "It is finished."

6. *In this paragraph note the use of well-chosen adjectives: "lamentable," "tragedy" and "disheveled."*

6. What would you consider the most lamentable tragedy in human life? To face suffering, to

The oral style is illustrated in the use of rhetorical questions. The theme phrase "staying power" is used. One can cut this sermon at any point and it bleeds with the central idea. Coherence is achieved not only by the thought but by the use of key words and key phrases. "All their flags flying when they came into port" is another instance of the analogy of ships, familiar to people who live at a great port. This paragraph seems to be built out of the preacher's experience. He speaks with authority. It is like the synopsis of a life which he has witnessed. Note the metaphor "shining metal." The major theme, Demas, forms the climactic sentence of this paragraph.

be cruelly handicapped? Surely not! For we have seen some terribly handicapped people who had moral staying power so that they came through to a great conclusion, all their flags flying when they came into port. But there is a tragedy so appalling that when one has seen it in the circle of one's friends the very reminiscence of it makes one's blood run cold—to be so fortunately born, to have so glorious a boyhood, to rise to such responsible position, to be so loved, so trusted, and then to crack as though all the time the shining metal had had a flaw in it, to betray one's trust, deceive one's friends, blow out one's brains! You see, whether it be in dramatic fashion like that or in homelier wise, where a fine beginning lapses by slow degrees into a disheveled ending, Demas is the tragedy.

7. "Marriage" is one of the great common denominators of life. It touches the experience of most of his hearers. "Romantic launchings" reverts to the figure of the ship. In the previous paragraph and in this, consider the declamatory sentences. Another minor theme, "loyalty," is introduced. The word "tragic" is associated with a poor ending. In the final sentence "a good beginning" and "an unhappy end" are contrasted. This paragraph seems to close the introductory part of the sermon, if it can be called that. Dr. Fosdick does not use the traditional textbook introduction.

7. In this regard life is like marriage. How beautifully love begins! With what romantic launchings can it get its start! But we elders, who watch the young folks at their lovemaking and their weddings, habitually ask a deeper question. They have qualities that can start a home; have they the qualities that can keep one—the deep fidelity, the long-term loyalty, the steady and abiding love that can keep a home? For in marriage, as in all life, a good beginning only makes more tragic an unhappy end.

Analysis of Sermon, "The Power to See It Through"

8. *Note the paragraph of transition. Dr. Fosdick never leaves his congregation in doubt as to where he is in the development of his theme. The minor theme of a good beginning which the congregation might expect on the first Sunday of the year is now temporarily put aside for the development of the unusual topic "staying power." Note the Walt Whitman style, "I celebrate the qualities of faith and character that enable a man to see life through." This sentence pattern is repeated in paragraphs 25 and 26. The preacher is about to explore two words, "faith and character." He permits no lost motions in his preaching. The first two points taken up in regard to staying power have to do with character, the third has to do with faith.*

9. *Note the use of "For one thing," and in the 13th paragraph "In the second place" and in the 21st "Finally." These are definite landmarks in the development of the theme which the listener cannot escape. "Staying power" is repeated. The preacher is telling the congregation how they may obtain "staying power." He not only tells about it but he shows the congregation how to get it. The congregation, being cultured, is interested in music. This interest is reflected in the illustration of Chopin. The conclusion, the 21st paragraph, employs music again. The words "indispensable" and "absolutely indispensable" are repeated many times. The preacher's insight into the spiritual life is very evident here, "live on high terms with him-*

8. On this first Sunday of the New Year, therefore, let us talk together not about starting power —there is no soul here that has not more than once made a fine beginning—but about staying power. I celebrate the qualities of faith and character that enable a man to see life through.

9. For one thing, staying power is always associated with a certain central integrity of conscience. Whatever else life may give or may deny, one thing is absolutely indispensable to a man—that he should not break faith with himself, that he should not inwardly be a failure. Such quality of conscience, making it indispensable that a man live on high terms with himself, whatever happens, is of the essence of staying power, and it is the glory of great artists that so commonly in their art they have exhibited it. Elsner was a teacher of music in Warsaw to whom came, one day, a young man for music lessons, and at the end of the first term one finds this self." Note the use of alliteration—"career cost conscience." The conclusion is an echo of this thought. The weaving and interweaving of ideas help make Dr. Fosdick's preaching very effective. "So Chopin became Chopin." This emphasis is suited to oral presentation. This use of the maxim is suited to public speaking, for it gives the audience something easy to remember.

in Elsner's record: "Lessons in musical composition: Chopin, Fryderyk, third-year student—amazing capabilities, muscial genius." That was a fine start. But to finish that career was costly. It cost hard work—one would take that for granted. It cost discouraged hours—one would expect that. Once Chopin was so disheartened he talked of turning to interior decorating instead of music. But, deeper yet, Chopin's career cost conscience. He would not, for popularity's sake, write music that violated his own interior standards. One thing was absolutely indispensable, no matter what happened: he must not break faith musically with himself. So Chopin became "Chopin." As another put it, "the artist's conscience is a fearful thing."

10. *The transition sentence discusses Paul's experience in Rome. Paul is held up as the ideal. "Having loved this present age" is a new theme which will be used more and more as the sermon progresses. It is the reason why Demas slipped. The comparison of Roman civilization with our own makes the sermon pertinent. Note the alliteration, "Paul's poor prison house" and the echo, "no Chopin in his character." The preacher's imagination is evident in "Christ had never dug so deep as that into Demas." "To be loyal to the royal" is a sentence that pleases the ear. The use of assonance can be used by the speaker as well as*

10. Now, as we see Paul and Demas in Rome, it is obvious Paul had "that." He would have liked outward good fortune and success could he have had them on honorable terms—of course he would! But whether fortune or misfortune befell, one thing was absolutely indispensable—he must not break faith with himself and the Christ within him. Not simply as a matter of duty but as a matter of happiness—that was indispensable. Demas, however, was of another sort. He soon found something else that was indispensable. "Demas forsook me," wrote

Analysis of Sermon, "The Power to See It Through" 263

the poet. *This phrase comes from Tennyson. Again, note the concluding sentence of this paragraph.*

Paul, "having loved this present age." So that was it! Roman civilization was brilliant like our own. It had ugly aspects, but for agile minds and grasping hands there were prizes to be gained. All around Paul's poor prison house was Rome. So Demas, no Chopin in his character, wrote his music down. He did not have an artist's conscience, Christ had never dug so deep as that into Demas. To be loyal to the royal in himself was not absolutely indispensable. He loved this present age.

11. *We have a good example of the preacher's direct style: "You see . . . Listen!" In thought, too, the preacher is direct, "I am talking about us." Echo of the cost of conscience should be noted. Here is help for man in trouble. Again, note the use of the maxim: an audience can remember this. The succeeding illustrations follow each other in rapid succession, each forming a complete picture. The audience can understand these concise, familiar illustrations. Dr. Fosdick uses illustrations with which his congregation is familiar. A less skillful speaker would go into greater detail. The preacher is careful to point out how his hearers can avoid being failures. The repetition of "loyal to the royal" with the slight difference in phrasing is pleasing and is a characteristic of good composition. The ear is pleased with the old and the new. The image of the ship should be noted. This is one of the minor repetitive themes.*

11. You see, I am not really talking about Demas now but about us. One would not minimize the sacrifices that such a conscience as we are speaking of often costs in a world like this, but the great souls who have most possessed such conscience have commonly thought of it not as a burden of duty but as a gospel of liberty. Listen! No man ever needs to be a failure. Trouble, outward breakdown of hopes, may come, but a man who cares most that he should not be a failure can capitalize trouble. "All sunshine," say the Arabs, "makes Sahara." Men may give the hemlock to Socrates, nail Jesus to the cross, behead Paul outside the gates of Rome. Livingstone may die in the heart of Africa, his work unfinished, and Lincoln may be shot by a crazy man. All such souls have known an inner liberty. Whatever

12. Dr. Fosdick is careful to use internal summaries. The point must be driven home. Nothing must be left to chance. Those who have not listened must be made to see the point. The contrast between Paul and Demas is drawn again. Note the picture painted of Demas. The imagination pictures Demas tending the idols of the pagan temple. The distinction between facing failure and being a failure is personified.

13. The structure of the sermon is bared. "In the second place . . ." Dr. Fosdick uses this device of enumeration with no apology. He wants to be sure that the congregation is following. The alliteration "captured by a cause" shows the care with which the sermon is composed. The minor theme of loyalty is repeated. Note the enumeration of the specific types of causes one can be devoted to. The preacher economizes the attention of his listeners by reverting to the illustrations already employed. Dr. Fosdick makes his point with the least mental effort on the part of his congregation. He is immediately intelligible. Note the vernacular "They stood the gaff." The major theme, "staying power," is repeated.

happened, they did not need to *be* failures. That was within their control. Still they could be loyal to the royal in themselves and come to their last port with their flags a flying.

12. That is the final difference between people. Paul faced many kinds of failure, but he himself was no failure. If, however, the old legend is correct, Demas went back to Thessalonica and became a priest of idols in a pagan temple. He himself was a failure.

13. In the second place, staying power is always associated with the experience of being captured by a cause, laid hold on by something greater than oneself to which one gives one's loyalty—an art, a science, a vocation, a social reform, an object of devotion which one conceives to be more important than oneself. This was the common property of those to whom we have turned as illustrations of persistent character—Chopin in music, Socrates in philosophy, Livingstone as a missionary, Lincoln as a statesman with a cause. They all cared for something so much superior to themselves to which they gave their long-term loyalty, that they stood the gaff, as we say, so far as their individual fortunes were con-

14. *In paragraph 10 we had the thought of digging deep into Demas. Here, then, is an echo of that thought. Notice the balanced sentences. There is an echo here of the thought in paragraph 2, that of building a tower. The theme of this section is repeated in different words. There is a clever distinction in this paragraph of being possessed by some of the detail but not by the cause itself.*

15. *The word "fascinating" reveals Dr. Fosdick's enthusiasm for his craft of preaching. While he uses repetition he does it skillfully. Here a new light is thrown on the theme. A new facet of the truth is shown. The idea which he has planted in the mind of his audience is compared with a new aspect of the theme. Again the truth comes from the Bible. Note the development of the theme by definition.*

16. *The preacher's knowledge of the thinking process of his audience*

cerned, and followed through to a strong conclusion for their cause's sake. All staying power in character is associated with that.

14. Christ had never gotten so deep as that into Demas. Demas had laid hold on some of the more comfortable aspects of the Christian gospel, but the Christian gospel had never laid hold on Demas. Demas had possessed himself of this or that detail of Christ's message, but Christ had not possessed himself of Demas. So the man's Christianity was a superstructure easily put up, easily taken down—jerry-building on slim foundations. For the foundation of enduring character is always laid in something greater than oneself which one will serve through life and death.

15. There is a fascinating contrast between two phrases in the New Testament: the first, Paul's description of a true Christian in the Epistle to the Hebrews as one who has "tasted the . . . powers of the age to come." So, *that* is the difference, as the New Testament sees it. An apostate is a man who loves the *status quo*, this present age; a Christian is a man who has tasted the powers, been laid hold on by the hopes, of the age to come.

16. When someone tries to tell you that the Christian social gos-

is apparent. Here is the debater overcoming objections. Note the direct address, the new application, the new turn of the theme of having a cause to live for: the Kingdom of God. Note the repetition in the form of a balanced sentence. The preacher is the teacher; he instructs his audience.

pel is a modern innovation not in the New Testament, face him with that. The Christian social gospel is in the very heart of the New Testament—set, to be sure, in mental frameworks appropriate to the first century and different from ours but indubitably there. The primary emphasis in Jesus' teaching on the Kingdom of God and in the first church was so dominant that they tested Christian discipleship by it. A man who loved this present age was an apostate; a man who had tasted the powers of the age to come was a Christian. Whenever we see a New Testament Christian carrying through to the finish, one fact is always apparent: he had set his devotion on a coming Kingdom of God on earth for which he was willing to live or die.

17. *In the next three paragraphs we find three illustrations of men who have found a cause worth living for. In this paragraph attention is called to the scientist. Note the use of the phrase from everyday life, "through thick and thin." The preacher gives a yardstick of measurement, the giving of oneself to humanity. All three of the following paragraphs end in the same way: "At any rate, he has tasted the powers of the age to come."*

17. The upshot is that one often sees today outside the church men who seem closer of kin to New Testament Christianity than many inside the churches. Sometimes a downright unbelieving scientist who gives himself to his science and for the sake of humanity stands by it, serving it through thick and thin to the end, seems closer to a New Testament Christian than many of us in the churches. At any rate, he has tasted the powers of the age to come.

18. *Note the transition "Or consider the man. . . ." Again, he is con-*

18. Or here is a man who puts his conscience above narrow na-

Analysis of Sermon, "The Power to See It Through" 267

cerned with ships, with which his congregation is familiar. The preacher paints pictures with words. He employs symbolism which the audience is bound to remember. Note the use of "white flag" and "Stars and Stripes." Dr. Fosdick never misses an opportunity to employ the image-provoking word. The prophetic quality of the preacher is evident here. (This sermon was preached in 1935.)

tionalism, who not simply on Sunday, as in the Navy, but every day runs the white flag of the gospel to the top of the mast with the Stars and Stripes under it. He will no longer subjugate his conscience before God to the mad paganism of nationalistic policies that even now, by old familiar steps, are leading mankind to another holocaust. Such a man may be, and often is, very disturbing, but he is closer akin to a New Testament Christian than many in our churches. At least he has tasted the powers of the age to come.

19. The country is emerging from the depression; therefore, the peacher is speaking of a timely topic. In this paragraph Dr. Fosdick speaks of several of the evils of the day: old-law tenements, sharecroppers, a living wage, maldistribution of income, the weakness of the capitalistic system in seeking to create an economy of scarcity. Such illustrations show the background of the preacher; his grasp of facts; his interest in contemporary social problems. Note the use of the word "tinkering"; it colors the entire sentence.

19. Or here is a man who is not beguiled by the present pick-up in business. He knows it is here. Millions of our people are better off than they were, and he, of course, is glad for all improved conditions for anyone. But he knows that not by a thousand miles does that mean that we have solved our economic problem. He is aware that in this, in prosperous days, 1,800,000 people are living in old-law tenements not fit for human occupancy. He knows that in the Southern cotton fields are a million and a half sharecroppers living under a kind of peonage which by comparison makes preferable the lot of many a serf in the medieval age. He knows that in so wealthy a city as Chicago in the heyday of our prosperity an investigation by the organized philanthropies revealed that city

charities were giving to families on their poor list a stipend larger than two-thirds of the unskilled laborers investigated could possibly earn for their families when they were fully employed. He knows that it is conservatively estimated that in 1929, of our American families $\frac{1}{10}$ of 1 percent at the upper end of the economic scale was getting a combined income equal to that of 42 percent at the other end of the scale, a condition in the face of which words like "democracy," "liberty," and "equality" lose their meaning. He knows that whereas we have been plowing under cotton, killing off livestock, reducing wheat acreage, and all the rest, the fact is that an interesting study recently made revealed that if American families maintained a good standard of health diet it would require 41,000,000 more acres under cultivation, not less. A man who keeps hammering on such facts, who will not let them drop, who keeps saying with Jesus, "Inasmuch as ye did it unto one of these brethren, even these least, ye did it unto me," who insists that we must go deeper, think harder, face changes more profound than the things we are tinkering with now, may be disturbing, but once more he is closer to New Testament Christianity than many of us are. He has tasted the powers of the age to come.

20. *This paragraph is an application of what he has been speaking about to the audience. Dr. Fosdick will not let his congregation escape their Christian responsibility. "Fine beginnings" recalls the first part of the sermon. "Comfortable corner" recalls paragraph 14, where Demas is pictured as laying hold of some of the more comfortable aspects of the Christian gospel. Dr. Fosdick is speaking of a condition which he knows exists in his congregation. By going from the greater to the less, the preacher may get some of his hearers to admit that they have acted like Demas. How powerful is the phrase "sell anybody out"!*

20. I suspect that this is the outstanding challenge to us in the churches—our attitude not on theological questions but on practical, ethical, social questions. We find it easy to love this present age. We make fine beginnings, especially at New Year's time, but then some comfortable corner of this present age invites us and we nestle down. So our Christian profession lapses, our faith grows formal, and we do not amount to much in the end as Christians. If I should accuse some of you of being Judas Iscariot, you would be indignant. You would never deliberately sell anybody out. But Demas—ah, my soul, how many of us have been that!

21. *Dr. Fosdick is careful to let his hearers know where he is in the sermon: "Finally." In this point he touches upon faith. His first two points under staying power were concerned with character. Under this third point there are three subdivisions. Note how a text is employed to reinforce the thought. The congregation can remember this. Dr. Fosdick is careful to aim at the memory of his audience. Great truths are carefully packaged. Here is an example of a favorite rhetorical device, a string of four synonyms: "do faint, peter out, go flat, lose our morale." The keyword of the section is "faith." The repetition of "staying power and Demas" link up the thought with the main theme.*

21. Finally, staying power is commonly associated with profound resources of interior strength replenished by great faiths. There is a phrase in the Bible on which a colleague of mine once preached a sermon entitled "An Appalling Alternative" —"I had fainted, unless I had believed." That is true of life. We do faint, peter out, go flat, lose our morale unless our interior resources are replenished by faith in something. We may be sure that Demas, before he left Paul, had lost some of his first convictions about Christ and the God whom Christ revealed.

22. Dr. Fosdick does not preach about the power to see it through but shows how it can be gained. He is practical. Note the power, the energy of such a sentence as "That is off our hands if God has it on his." It is idiomatic. In the following sentence Dr. Fosdick uses five phrases to describe a Godless world. Testimony is a valuable type of material. Dr. Fosdick does not use much quotation. The imagination of the preacher is apparent in the phrase "be haunted by a huge, cosmic apprehension."

23. In this paragraph and the next one the same transitional phrase is used, "Deeper yet, a vital faith in God . . ." The listener cannot escape the thought of the preacher. Dr. Fosdick's style is saturated with Biblical language: "a thousand years are as yesterday when it is past and as a watch in the night." The second sentence is born of experience in dealing with troubled folk. The paragraph then goes into an illustration of contrast and comparison: the immediate versus the long-run view. Note colloquial language—"got Demas." The consciousness of the audience is ex-

22. Suppose that someone should ask you what your faith in the Christian God really does for you. What would you say? For one thing, I should say that when a man believes in God he does not need to worry about the universe any more. That is off our hands if God has it on his. If I imagined the universe as without any God, aimless, purposeless, an accidental dance of atoms, spiritually meaningless, then I would worry about it. As Carlyle said, a cosmos like that is "one huge, dead, immeasurable steam-engine, rolling on, in its dead indifference to grind me from limb to limb." But if a man believes in God, that is off his mind. He can concentrate upon the task in hand, get on with his moral business here on earth with some high hopes about its outcome, and not be haunted by a huge, cosmic apprehension.

23. Deeper yet, a vital faith in God means a faith in an eternal moral purpose in the light of which a thousand years are as yesterday when it is past and as a watch in the night. That gives a man wide horizons, long outlooks, steady hopes, so that when people lose heart over the disappointment of some immediate expectation, such faith still has standing ground and carries on. Of all mad things in history can you think of anything madder, with Nero upon his throne and Paul in

pressed in the "you see." Note the idiomatic "carries on."

his prison, than to have believed that the gospel for which Paul stood would outlast and wear down the empire? That is, of course, what "got" Demas: the tremendous power of Rome on its eternal hills, with its inveterate and triumphant evils, against the seeming weakness of Christ's gospel. Who in a sober and realistic hour could have supposed that Paul would outwear Nero? But that, you see, is exactly what happened. A man who has faith in God always expects that to happen, though it take a thousand years. So, of course, he carries on.

24. This third way of getting staying power forms a climax to the thought. Dr. Fosdick illustrates his uncommon ability to find spiritual power in everyday events. "We never produce power. We always appropriate it." The illustrations are from everyday occurrences. In comparing the presence of the spiritual to the presence of the physical he goes from the known to the unknown. Note the figure of speech "deep wells of staying power."

24. Deeper yet, a vital faith in God gives a man available resources of interior power. We never produce power. We always appropriate it. That is true from the harnessing of Niagara to eating a dinner or taking a walk in the fresh air. We never create power; we assimilate it. So, a man with a real faith in God senses around his spiritual life a spiritual presence as truly as the physical world is around his body, and as truly from that divine companionship, he draws replenished strength. He knows the deep wells of staying power.

25. In this sentence set off as a paragraph, we have a repetition of paragraph 8, and in the next paragraph it is repeated again. This and the next paragraph form a conclusion to this part of the sermon.

25. I celebrate the resources of a Christian faith to see a man through.

26. *Here is the application to man's need of what has been said. The sermon should help man solve his spiritual problems. This paragraph mentions five such problems.*

26. If faith in God means such things, how do men live life through without it? How do they meet the shocks of fate, the ugliness of evil, the shame of man's inhumanity to man, the disheartenment of moral failure, the impact of personal sorrow, and still keep their morale? I celebrate the resource of Christian faith.

27. *Dr. Fosdick ends with an analogy which his cultured audience can appreciate. Living is an art like music. This analogy has the vitality to live on in the memory of his congregation; when they recall the analogy or hear music in the future they will be reminded of the theme of this sermon. Note the powerful phrases "noisy cacophony," "unimportant discontinuities." Dr. Fosdick in this sermon has followed the pattern of the symphony. He keeps to his theme until it marches back once more into the sermon, "glorious like an army with banners." Note the use of the rhetorical device "develops, expands, elevates, and glorifies, fine at the beginning, loveliest of all at the last." This sentence has a noticeable rhythm, a sweep which is characteristic of effective oral composition.*

27. Technically I know little or nothing about music. I venture this comment, however, about the difference between the best of the old music and the ordinary run of the new. The trouble with so much of the new music, as an older man at least sees it, is not its noisy cacophony but something deeper; it never seems to believe in anything enough so that it thinks it worth while to say it over and over again. It picks up a trivial theme and drops it. It never goes through with anything. It lacks sustained convictions. It is fulfilled with unimportant discontinuities. But when one hears a great symphony by Tschaikowsky, let us say, or Beethoven, *there* are convictions so profoundly believed that the music goes through with them to the very end. One says to himself, Surely that theme has been said as beautifully as ever it can be said. Yet that theme returns again and again, elevated and resplendent beyond our dream. A man says to himself, Now, surely, all

the possibilities have been exhausted and lo, at last the theme marches back once more into the music glorious like an army with banners. Whatever may be your judgment about music, great living is like that. Is there anything a man could wish for his friends at New Year's time better than a life like that—great convictions which life develops, expands, elevates, and glorifies, fine at the beginning, loveliest of all at the last? And is there anything that a man could better pray against for himself or his friends than the opposite?—Demas, my fellow-worker; Demas; Demas forsook me.

Appendix

Studies in the Preaching of Harry Emerson Fosdick

Brees, Paul Rexford: A Comparative Study of the Device of Persuasion used by Harry Emerson Fosdick and William Ashley Sunday. Ph.D. Thesis, University of Southern California, 1948.

Drafahl, Elinora M.: An Analysis of the Figures of Speech as Aides to Clearness in the War Sermons of Harry Emerson Fosdick. M.A. Thesis, University of South Dakota, 1948.

Juntsinger, Jerald E.: The sermons of Harry Emerson Fosdick: a Study. S.T.M. Thesis, Templer University School of Theology, 1958.

Kovar, Leonard John: An Analysis of Selected Sermons of Dr. Harry Emerson Fosdick. B.D. Thesis, Andover-Newton Theological School, 1953.

LeVander, Theodor: A Critical Study of Selected Radio Addresses Delivered by Dr. Harry Emerson Fosdick on National Vespers, 1939–40. M.A. Thesis, State University of Iowa, 1940.

Linn, Edmund Holt: *Preaching as Counseling: the Unique Method of Harry Emerson Fosdick*. Valley Forge, Pa., Judson Press, 1966.

Linn, Edmund Holt: A Rhetorical Analysis of the Methods of Proof in Representative Sermons of the Reverend Dr. Harry Emerson Fosdick. M.A. Thesis, University of Iowa, 1949.

Linn, Edmund Holt: The Rhetorical Theory and Practice of Harry Emerson Fosdick. Ph.D. Thesis, University of Iowa, 1952.

Mackey, Jesse Robert: Homiletic Method of Harry Emerson Fosdick. B.D. Thesis, Emory College. Candler School of Theology, 1934.

Miller, George William: A Study of Motivation in the Preaching of Harry Emerson Fosdick. B.D. Thesis, Southern Baptist Theological Seminary, 1955.

Appendix

Pages, Gladys M.: The Comparison of the Oral and Written Style of Harry Emerson Fosdick. M.A. Thesis, University of Wisconsin, 1938.

Watkins, Harold Robert: Human Problems as Presented in the Preaching of Harry Emerson Fosdick. B.D. Thesis, College of the Bible, 1953.

Zenidars, Edward P.: The Persuasive Techniques of Harry Emerson Fosdick. M.A. Thesis, University of Wisconsin, 1938.

Index

A

Abbott, Lyman, 221, 237, 239, 243
Abou Ben Adhem, 113
Abrams, Roy H., 143
Acceptance, appeal for, 206, 217
Action, appeal for, 208
Adler, Selig, 150
Alcoholic, experience with, 13, 52
Alliteration, 125, 258
American Preachers of Today, 100
American Public Address, 115
Amherst College, 236
Analogy, 208, 257, 272
Analytic discrimination, 246
Anderson, Maxwell, 232
Aneid, The, 113
Animated Conversation, 47, 121
Antithesis, 255, 258
Appleton Chapel, Harvard University, 9
Aristotle, 235
Arliss, George, 235
Arnold, Matthew, 237, 244
Arrangement, 203, 233
Association Press, 8, 11
Assonance, 262
Atkins, Gaius Glenn, 101

B

Bach, 87, 99
Baker, Ray Stannard, 19
Barth, Karl, 180
Barthian theology, 162
Beard, Charles A., 169
Beecher, Henry Ward, 44, 108, 114, 124, 128, 156, 169, 211, 221, 236
Beecher, Lyman, 110
Beethoven, 87, 171
Beyond Tragedy, 92
Bible and preaching, 14, 80
Biblical criticism, 244
Biblical language, 270
Blair, Hugh, ix, 245
Books, writing of, 9
Booth, Edwin, 130
Borah, William E., 150, 221
Bowery, The, 139
Bowring, Sir John, 172
Brahms, 87, 99
Brains in the pulpit, 65
Breen, John J., 22
Brees, Paul Rexford, 274
Briand, Aristide, 150
Brigance, W. N., 242
Briggs, Charles A., 138
Briggs, Charles W., 134
Brigham, Albert, 131
Broadway Tabernacle, 242
Brooks, Phillips, ix, 28, 109, 114, 115, 124, 125, 128, 156, 160, 169, 188, 221, 238
Brown, Charles Reynolds, ix
Brownce, Francis, 131, 170
Browne, Border Parker, 137
Browning, Robert, 131, 170

Bryan, William Jennings, 113, 170
Bush, Douglas, 106

C

Cadman, S. Parkes, 101, 105, 221
Calvin, John, 148, 236
Campbell, George, ix, 245
Capitalism, 178
Carder, Eugene C., 103
Carlyle, Thomas, 270
Carnegie, Andrew, 237
Carnegie Hall, 121
Cathedral of St. John, the Divine, 154
Central idea, 187, 192, 257
Chopin, Frederic, 262
Christian Century, The, 246
Chronological development, 203
Cicero, 131, 211
City Temple Church in London, England, 254
Clairvoyance, 34, 51, 56, 122
Clark, John Bates, 19
Clark, Robert D., 128
Clarke, William Newton, 111, 137, 138
Classes in practical theology, 213
Climax, 123, 212, 234
Coffin, Henry Sloane, 5
Coherence, 260
Cole Lectures, 155
Colgate University, 131, 140
Collaboration with congregation, 118, 233
Columbia University, 139
Common ground, 245
Communication of truth, 122
Concerns of the congregation, 29
Concessions and persuasion, 175
Conclusion, 206
Consultation hour, 57
Contrast and comparison, 231, 257
Contribution to rhetorical theory, 224
Conversation, animated, 47, 57
Cooper, Clayton, 8
Cooperative dialogue, 15
Cooperative enterprise, 232
Copernicus, 153
Coptic translation of *The Manhood of the Master*, 10
Counseling, personal, 13, 122, 237

Creasy, Sir Edward Shepherd, 109
Creative process, 188
Creedal conventionality, 65
Crocker, Lionel, 136, 228, 236, 246, 255
Cromwell, Oliver, 76
Cyrano de Bergerac, 169

D

Dale, Robert W., ix
Damascus Road, 53
Dangers of preaching based on counselling, 16, 55
Darrow, Clarence, 169
Darwin, Charles, 131, 136, 148, 165, 177
Debating society at Colgate University, 131, 135
Declamation in learning how to speak, 133
Deductive development of a sermon, 198
Definition, use of, 259
  development of sermon by, 265
Definitions of preaching, 17, 234, 252
Delivery of a sermon, 45, 48, 126, 129, 134, 141, 220, 242
Delta Upsilon fraternity, 132
Demas, 247, 248
Despair, mood of, 121
Developing the sermon, 189
  three ways of
    as a box, 199
    as a river, 200
    as a tree, 199
Dewey, Admiral George, 135
Dewey, John, 150, 165, 166, 169
Dialogue, sermon a, 34, 49, 113
Dickens, Charles, 130, 169, 243
Die Walküre, 171
Dilling, Elizabeth, 161
Dover Beach, 245
Downs, Elinor Fosdick, ix
Drafahl, Elnora M., 179, 274
Drieser, Theodore, 169

E

Echo, use of the, 265
Economy of attention, 264
Eddy, Sherwood, 87
Edinburgh, 148, 238, 254

Edwards, Jonathan, 77, 243
Effect of a sermon, 52
Einstein, Albert, 159, 190
Eliot, George, 130, 169
Eliot, T. S., 97
Elsner, 261
Emerson, Ralph Waldo, 84, 172
Emotional climax, 212
Emphasis, 205
Enemy of the People, An, 90
Enumeration of points, 189, 204, 213
Ettor, 20
Evarts, William M., 239
Evolution; 132, 237, 239
Exman, Eugene, ix
Experience, appeal to, 80, 157
Expository method, 29, 49, 231

F

Fassett, H. Loren, 134
Fatigue, principle of, 213, 217
Fenelon, Francois, ix
Ferguson, Charles W., 156
Figurative language, 124, 173
First Presbyterian Church, New York City, 100, 116
Fiske, John, 239
Fitzgerald, F. Scott, 169
Fort Sumter, 238
Free association of ideas, 43, 188
Freud, Sigmund, 159, 163
Fry, Elizabeth, 169
Function of introduction, 190
Fundamentalist-Modernist controversy, 110
Fuzzy Wuzzy, 133

G

Gandhi, Mahatma, 11, 253
Genung, J. F., 120, 134
Gestures and symbols, 75
Ghosts, 90
Gibbs, Sir Philip, 149
Giddings, Franklin H., 19
Gilbert and Sullivan, 89
Gilkey, Charles W., 228
Giovanitti, 20
Gladstone, William E., 169
Glasgow, 238, 254

God, belief in, 158
God of Grace and God of Glory, 253
Gray, H. D., 133, 134
Grennell, Burt G., 134
Grinnell College, 116
Gulick, Luther, 11, 243

H

Haldane, John Scott, 169
Haldeman, I. M., 174
Hall, Charles Cuthbert, 138
Hamilton, Clayton, 231
Hamilton Theological Seminary, 138
Hamlet, 89
Harding, President Warren G., 160
Harpers' Magazine, 15, 223
Harris, Fred, 243
Harris, Frederick, 8, 11
Harvard University, 9, 248
Harvey, George, 145
Haverford College, 25
Hegelian approach, 166
Hell, 140, 243
Hitler, Adolph, 177
Homiletical neurologist, 56
Homiletical Review, 75
Hope of the World, The, 80
Hough, Lynn Harold, 101
Howlett, James H., 134
Hughes, Charles Evans, 18, 143

I

Ibsen, Henrik, 89
Idea, central, 184
If I Had Only One Sermon to Prepare, 187
Illustration, use of, 172, 266
Imagination, 174
Immortality, 10, 82
Influence of Henry Ward Beecher and Phillips Brooks, 124
Integrity, 176
Intellectualism, 176
Interestingness, 97
Introduction to sermon, 189, 191, 210, 214
Invention
 conversation, 56, 188, 191

Invention (*Continued*)
  free association, 43, 188
  observation, 53, 124, 139, 188
  reading, 119, 188
  thinking, 49, 104, 110, 124
Irving, Sir Henry, 26

J

James, William, 25, 137, 169
Jebusites, 54
Jefferson, Charles E., 110
Jefferson, Thomas, 169
Jesup, Morris K., 26, 141, 142
John, 256
Jones, Edgar DeWitt, 100, 116, 119, 229, 230, 235, 245
Jones, Rufus, 25
Judas Iscariot, 269
Juntsinger, Jerald E., 274

K

Keats, John, 170
Keller, Helen, 159, 169, 172
Kellogg, Frank B., 150
Kellogg-Briand pact, 177
Kemp, Charles F., 225
Kierkegaard, Soren, 162
King, General Charles, 146
Kipling, Rudyard, 133, 170
Knights of labor, 19
Knowledge of audience, 265
Knox, William, 138
Kovar, Leonard John, 274
Kreisler, Fritz, 171

L

La Farge, John, 251
Lane Theological Seminary, 236
Language, use of, 174
Lanier, Sidney, 170
Lawrence, Massachusetts, 19, 21
Lawrenceburg, Indiana, 237
Lawrenceville School, 98
League of Nations, 148, 149, 150, 177
Lear, King, 89
Lecky, William Edward, 131
Lectures, Lyman Beecher, 110
Lee, Ivy, 146
Levander, Theodore, 274

Lewes, George Henry, 230
Lewis Oratorical Contest, 136
Lewis, Sinclair, 164, 169
Liberal Christian faith, 176
Life situation preaching, 225
Lincoln, Abraham, 84, 172, 236, 264
Lindsay, Judge Ben, 161
Line fatigue principle, 217
Linn, Edmund Holt, x, 186, 274
Liverpool, England, 238
Living of These Days, The, 5
Livingston, David, 264
Logical organization, 204
London, England, 238, 254
Lorimer, George C., 6, 140
Lovell, John, 2, 239
Lowell, A. Lawrence, 9
Luke, 255

M

Macbeth, 89, 170
MacIver, Robert M., 169
Mackey, Jesse R., 274
MacVaugh, Gilbert, 167, 210, 229
Madisonensis, 131, 133, 134, 135
Man from Nazareth, The, 114
Manchester, England, 238
Manhood of the Master, The, 10
Mann, Erica, 178
Manuscript in preaching, 126
Mark, 256
Markham, Edwin, 170
Marshman, John, 228
Masten Park High School, 250
Matterhorn, The, 123
Matthew, 256
Marx, Karl, 84, 162
May, Eugene, 80
McCall, Roy, 6, 42
McCartney, Clarence E., 145
McDowell, William F., 221
McGiffert, Arthur Cushman, 138
McGlon, Charles A., 42
McKinley, President William, 23
Meaning of Prayer, The, 10
Memorizing the sermon, 45
Memory in preaching, 98
Metaphor, 125, 172
Miller, George William, 274

Miller, Samuel H., 75, 248
Miracles, 52, 56, 122, 193, 215
Modern Use of the Bible, The, 110, 237, 253
Modernism, 106, 176, 192
Monroe, Alan H., 120
Montclair, N. J., 5, 121, 140
Moody Church, The, 148
Morrison, Charles Clayton, 150
Mortality among sectarian churches, 71
Motivated sequence, the, 166
Motives in preaching, 56, 75, 175, 202
Mott, John R., 8
Moulton, Lord, 92
Mozart, 87, 98
My Account with the Unknown Soldier, 115, 152, 153

N

Napoleon, 21
Narration in the introduction, 210
National Vespers, 155
Nazis, 177
Needs of the congregation, 55, 83, 186
Nelson, John, 57
Nero, 270
Nervous breakdown, 139
Nevins, Allan, 150
New Deal, The, 16
Newton, Charles M., 134
Newton, Joseph Fort, 47, 101, 168, 226, 245, 252
Niebuhr, Reinhold, 86, 88, 105, 109
Nobel Peace Prize, 25
North, Frank Mason, 143
Northern Baptists, The, 106
Number of points in a sermon, 204

O

"O Little Town of Bethlehem," 254
Object in preaching, 17
Observation, 57, 139
Occasions and preaching, 191
On Being a Real Person, 227
Onthank, Dean Karl, 116
Oral Style, 260
Oratory, 135
Orchestra Hall in Chicago, 113
Organic structure, 188, 199

Organization of sermons, 48, 123, 167, 186
  as a box, 199
  as a tree, 199
  as a river, 200
Othello, 89, 90
Outlook Magazine, 19, 20

P

Pacifism, 178, 180
Pages, Gladys M., 274
Painting word pictures, 257
Pantomime, 242
Paragraphs, unit, 198
Parallelism in organization, 195
Park Avenue Baptist Church, 154, 252
Park, William M., 134
Pastoral Psychology, 227
Paul, 255
Pearl Harbor, 178
Peep of Day, The, 129
Personal counseling and preaching, 51, 55, 157, 173, 174
Personal magnetism, 127
Personal problems of parishioners, 161
Personal proof, 117
Personality, appeal to, 140, 176, 235
Persuasion, 81, 166, 173
Phi Beta Kappa, 132
Phidias, 30
Philemon, 255
Phillips, Arthur Edward, 120, 215
Pinkham, Henry W., 149
Poe, Edgar Allen, 233
Polonius, 170
Pragmatist, Fosdick the, 80
Prayer before preaching, 18
Precept upon precept, 129
Prentiss, George L., 139
Preparation of a sermon, 48, 104, 241
  of *The Yale Lectures on Preaching*, 241
Prestige, 117
Preston, John Hyde, 154
Problem solving sermons, 29, 55
Project method in preaching, 14, 17, 37
Protestantism, 63, 101
Psychiatry and preaching, 60

Psychological arrangement of ideas, 121, 141, 201, 228, 233
Public speaking training of Harry Emerson Fosdick, 121, 141, 228, 239
Pulpit tricks, 48
Purpose in preaching, 186
of introduction, 191

Q

Questioning the theme, 189
Questions people ask, 62
Quintilian, 210

R

Radio and preaching, 60, 155
Rate of Phillips Brooks' speaking, 254
Rauschenbush, Walter, 24
Reading as preparation for preaching, 119
Receptivity of the congregation, 218
Refrain in preaching, 108, 168, 193, 258
Reid, Loren, 116
Reign of the Common People, 240
Religion in Life, 86
Renton, Margaret, 146
Repetition, use of, 168, 193, 258
Rethinking the sermon, 50
Rhetoric, 48, 120
Ridgeway, E. J., 19
Riverside Church, 103
Robertson, Frederick William, 114
Rockefeller, John D., 100, 128, 153
Rodin, 20
Roman Catholicism, 58
Romeo and Juliet, 89
Roosevelt, Theodore, 23
Root, Edward Clay, 140
Rough Riders, oration on, 136
Rowland Oratorical Contest, 136
Royalty of the Pulpit, The, 241
Royce, Josiah, 137, 169
Russell, Norman, F. S., 133, 134

S

Sage, Henry W., 229, 241
Saint Paul's Cathedral, 254
Saint-Saens, 87
Salamagundi, The, 133
Sanford, William P., 210
Sanitarium, Harry Emerson Fosdick's stay in, 210
San Juan Hill, oration on, 136
Sanger, Margaret and birth control, 161
Santayana, George and invincible surmise, 82
Sayles, John M., 133
Scarlett, William, 87
Schliermacher, Friedrich, 156
Schweitzer, Albert, 90
Scott, Fred Newton, 230
Second Mile, The, 9
Sectarianism, 59, 70, 144
Sedatives, use of, 126
Sedgwick, Ellery, 10
Sentences
balanced, 266
exclamatory, 258
short, 258
Sermon, definition of, 17, 48, 234, 353
Sermon titles, 193
Shakespeare, 84, 88, 170

T

Taft, President William Howard, 23
Tarbell, Ida, 19
Technique of organization, 186
Tennyson, Alfred, 170, 263
Terrence, 211
Testimony in preaching, 270
Textile strike, 19
Thackeray, William Makepeace, 130, 169
Themes of preaching, 180, 186
Theology of Harry Emerson Fosdick, 156
Thessalonica, 264
Thinking the thought, 126
Thomas, Ralph, 133
Thought value of sermons, 76
Tilton, Theodore, 237
Titles of sermons, 193
Topical preachers, 31, 54, 123
Toscanini, Arturo, 170
Transitions in preaching, 195, 213, 256, 261

Treat, Stuart R., 134
Tschaikowsky, 272

U

Union Theological Seminary, 26, 138, 252
Unity in sermons, 218
Unknown Soldier, My Account with, 115, 151, 152, 153

V

Vacation daily Bible schools, 139
Values in preaching, 175, 176
Van Dusen, Henry, 24, 252
Vergil, 131
Vernacular in preaching, 264
Vespers, national, 155
Vivisection, 138
Voice and body in delivery, 126
Voice, Harry Emerson Fosdick's, 243
Voltaire, Francois, 169

W

Wagner, Richard, 171
Waid, Everett L., 116
Walker, Jimmy, 160
Wants of the congregation, 30, 202, 206
War and Harry Emerson Fosdick, 142
Wastes and Burdens of Society, 240
Watkins, Harold Robert, 215
Webster, Daniel, 169
Wesley, John, 57, 156

Westminster Abbey, 254
Whately, Richard, ix, 120, 245
What's the Matter With Preaching, 15, 104, 112
Whistler, James, 109
White, Andrew D., 9, 137
Whitehead, Alfred North, 169
Whitman, Walt, 131, 178
Wild Duck, The, 90
Wilde, Oscar, 109
Will and persuasion, 171
Wilson, Woodrow, 9, 143, 149, 221
Wise, Stephen S., 156
Words, the study of, 109, 113
Wordsworth, William, 131, 170
Work, Edgar Whitaker, 117
World Court, The, 177
Wren, Sir Christopher, 224
Wright brothers (Orville and Wilbur), 169
Writing the sermon, 45, 189

Y

Yale Lectures on Preaching, Fosdick's, 241
Yale University, 153
Yeager, W. H., 200
Young, O. D., 221

Z

Zenidars, Edward P., 275